BEING GERMAN CANADIAN

STUDIES IN IMMIGRATION AND CULTURE

ISSN 1914-1459

ROYDEN LOEWEN, SERIES EDITOR

17 *Being German Canadian: History, Memory, Generations*, edited by Alexander Freund

16 *Communal Solidarity: Immigration, Settlement, and Social Welfare in Winnipeg's Jewish Community, 1882–1930*, by Arthur Ross

15 *Czech Refugees in Cold War Canada: 1945–1989*, by Jan Raska

14 *Holocaust Survivors in Canada: Exclusion, Inclusion, Transformation, 1947–1955*, by Adara Goldberg

13 *Transnational Radicals: Italian Anarchists in Canada and the U.S., 1915–1940*, by Travis Tomchuk

12 *Invisible Immigrants: The English in Canada since 1945*, by Marilyn Barber and Murray Watson

11 *The Showman and the Ukrainian Cause: Folk Dance, Film, and the Life of Vasile Avramenko*, by Orest T. Martynowych

10 *Young, Well-Educated, and Adaptable: Chilean Exiles in Ontario and Quebec, 1973–2010*, by Francis Peddie

9 *The Search for a Socialist El Dorado: Finnish Immigration to Soviet Karelia from the United States and Canada in the 1930s*, by Alexey Golubev and Irina Takala

8 *Rewriting the Break Event: Mennonites and Migration in Canadian Literature*, by Robert Zacharias

7 *Ethnic Elites and Canadian Identity: Japanese, Ukrainians, and Scots, 1919–1971*, by Aya Fujiwara

6 *Community and Frontier: A Ukrainian Settlement in the Canadian Parkland*, by John C. Lehr

5 *Storied Landscapes: Ethno-Religious Identity and the Canadian Prairies*, by Frances Swyripa

4 *Families, Lovers, and Their Letters: Italian Postwar Migration to Canada*, by Sonia Cancian

3 *Sounds of Ethnicity: Listening to German North America, 1850–1914*, by Barbara Lorenzkowski

2 *Mennonite Women in Canada: A History*, by Marlene Epp

1 *Imagined Homes: Soviet German Immigrants in Two Cities*, by Hans Werner

BEING GERMAN CANADIAN

HISTORY, MEMORY, GENERATIONS

EDITED BY ALEXANDER FREUND

UNIVERSITY OF MANITOBA PRESS

Being German Canadian: History, Memory, Generations

24 23 22 21 20 1 2 3 4 5

University of Manitoba Press
Winnipeg, Manitoba, Canada
Treaty 1 Territory
uofmpress.ca

Cataloguing data available from Library and Archives Canada
Studies in Immigration and Culture, ISSN 1914-1459 ; 17
ISBN 978-0-88755-847-4 (PAPER)
ISBN 978-0-88755-597-8 (PDF)
ISBN 978-0-88755-595-4 (EPUB)
ISBN 978-0-88755-919-8 (BOUND)

Cover image: Library and Archives Canada, PA-124956. Kurt Meden, immigrant to Canada from Germany, searching for work in Vancouver, BC, January 1959. Photo by Villy Svarre.
Cover design by Kirk Warren
Interior design by Karen Armstrong

Printed in Canada

This book has been published with the help of a grant from the Federation for the Humanities and Social Sciences, through the Awards to Scholarly Publications Program, using funds provided by the Social Sciences and Humanities Research Council of Canada.

The University of Manitoba Press acknowledges the financial support for its publication program provided by the Government of Canada through the Canada Book Fund, the Canada Council for the Arts, the Manitoba Department of Sport, Culture, and Heritage, the Manitoba Arts Council, and the Manitoba Book Publishing Tax Credit.

Funded by the Government of Canada | Canada

CONTENTS

ACKNOWLEDGEMENTS

The authors wish to acknowledge that much of the research and writing conducted for this essay collection took place in Canada and thus on traditional territory of Indigenous Peoples. We also acknowledge that generations of European, including German, settlers have benefitted from programs of dispossessing and assimilating Indigenous Peoples. We acknowledge that every new settler accepts a new history and with it a responsibility to learn about colonial history and its ongoing legacy.

Even more so than other kinds of publications, a collection of essays is the work of many. I thank the contributors to this collection for their excellent work, their patience, and their desire to improve their essays with every round of revisions, and their enthusiasm for engaging in a meaningful conversation with each other about the many meanings of being German in Canada.

German Canadian Studies is a small field that benefits from institutional support; I gratefully acknowledge the German-Canadian Studies Foundation's and the Spletzer Family Foundation's long-standing support of German-Canadian Studies at the University of Winnipeg and internationally. Karen Brglez contributed valuable administrative support to this book project (in addition to an excellent chapter). The University of Manitoba Press was the right place to publish this collection, and I am grateful for the support we received from Jill McConkey, Glenn Bergen, David Larsen, and their colleagues. I would also like to thank the anonymous reviewers.

On a more personal note: I began this project in 2016, in the same year that my son, Daniel, was born. Over the past four years, our adventures—together with his two sisters, Isabel and Gabi—taught me many new, sometimes funny or quirky, at other times more serious facets of what it means to be German in Canada. Finally, with my deepest gratitude, I thank my wife Judith for her endless encouragement and love.

Alexander Freund, Winnipeg, February 2021

ACKNOWLEDGEMENTS

[illegible]

INTRODUCTION

Heavy Baggage: Memory and Generation in Ethnic History

ALEXANDER FREUND

Migrants, as the saying goes, arrive with "baggage" in their new homes. Over the past three generations, historians of immigration and ethnicity in North America have studied how such baggage hindered successful assimilation to the normative expectations of the ruling classes and, later, how carefully selected textiles from the immigrants' *Koffer*, *Taschen*, or *Kontainer* (suitcases, bags, or containers) were woven into a colourful yet carefully contained multicultural fabric.[1] Throughout, Canadian immigration historiography has focused on policies and public responses and less so on migrants' lives.[2] More recent immigration researchers have exposed the dominant society's seemingly benign "support" of "newcomers" as paternalistic means of surveillance and social discipline.[3] In many studies, sociological categories—those that can be measured—have dominated definitions of what the immigrants' baggage contained, including language, religion, skills, politics, traditions and folklore, networks, and ethnic institutions. Migration scholars have also shown how migrants have deployed some of their baggage in their new homes. They have used new concepts, such as networks, transnationalism, transculturalism, entanglement, and borderland studies to understand the complexities of migrants' lives beyond the confines of their settlement locales. Nevertheless, migration historians have been struggling to cross the "saltwater curtain" (Thistlethwaite)—that is, to include migrants' primary socialization or their cultural baggage in their

Figure 0.1. "Immigrants crowd the deck of the SS *Beaverbrae*, as the moment comes to disembark at the port of Quebec and commence their new life in Canada" (n.d.; c. 1948–54). Written perhaps by the photographer for the Canadian Pacific Railway or a staff member of the Library and Archives Canada (LAC) at the time, this byline illuminates the "Saltwater Curtain" in commentators' minds: immigrants without a history do not continue lives lived elsewhere but instead begin a "new life." The SS *Beaverbrae*, owned by the CPR and operated for the Canadian Christian Council for the Resettlement of Refugees, transported thousands of German and other European migrants to Canada after the Second World War. Library and Archives Canada (LAC), PA-124423.

analysis.[4] As a result, it has proven difficult to convert "baggage" from a simple signifier of "something from before" to a mature analytical category. This essay collection suggests that historians may more deeply engage with migrants' homeland backgrounds by using the concepts of memory and generation.

Memories of families and home countries are part of migrants' baggage. For refugees such memories may include troubling national histories of extreme violence, family stories of complicity and victimization, and biographies of victims, bystanders, profiteers, perpetrators, and resistance fighters. In the new home country, these complex national, family, and individual memories and histories may shape an entire immigrant generation, even an entire multi-generational ethnic

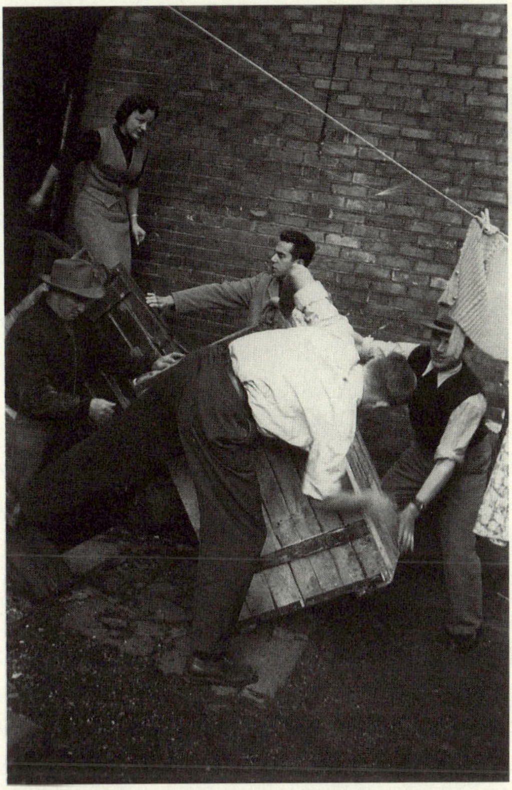

Figure 0.2. Migrants' heavy baggage, carried in boxes as well as hearts and minds: "German Immigrants: Dagmar Wichmar (on steps), paid secretary of Canadian Lutheran World Relief, directs loading of household goods for immigrant Heinrich Lange (right), Kitchener, Ont. (vicinity), 5 July 1952." *Louis Jaques/Weekend Magazine*, LAC, PA-173823.

community. This was particularly true of the twentieth century—the "century of refugees"—that began with the First World War, and this dynamic continues to persist today. In the twentieth century, it was particularly true of several generations of German migrants, who carried heavy baggage of collective memories of two world wars, the Holocaust, two dictatorships, and two revolutions. One revolution turned a failed monarchy into an unstable democracy in 1919, and the other, seventy years later, turned a failed dictatorship into a stable capitalist democracy. More broadly, even if memories from the "old country" were no longer represented in the material form of trunks and trinkets, they nevertheless, even in the form of stories, moulded the next generations' identities and communities.[5]

The authors in this collection show how difficult and painful it has been for several generations of German Canadians to remember and publicly speak about the two world wars. Such silences were prevalent not only among those who experienced the wars, as I show in Chapter 1 in German immigrants' Great War memories, as Robert Teigrob explores in Chapter 2 in Canadians' active forgetting of Mackenzie King's visit to Hitler Germany in 1937, as Patrick Farges explains in Chapter 3 in the German-Jewish refugees' struggles to find a place in the larger Jewish-Canadian society of the 1940s and 1950s, and, in Chapter 4, as Karen Brglez interrogates German-Canadian historian Gottlieb Leibbrandt's silence about his activities during the Second World War. Such silences were also prevalent in the next two generations. In Chapter 7 Sara Frankenberger analyzes how second- and third-generation German Canadians avoid talking about the Holocaust; and, in Chapter 8, Christine Ensslen lays open the silences among third-, fourth-, and even fifth-generation German Canadians about their female ancestors' wartime experiences. All the essays explore how memories about difficult histories shaped several generations' paths toward integration into Canadian society. Several chapters also show that even when the two world wars were not the explicit topic of conversation, they overshadowed intergenerational dialogue, which often broke down when a younger generation believed itself to be more "modern" and thus more potentially successful in their integration. Elliot Worsfold provides a powerful example of such intergenerational conflict in Chapter 5, where, even within seminaries, questions of language illuminated larger conflicts about what it meant to be "Canadian" as a German Canadian. Similarly, Anke Patzelt in Chapter 6 demonstrates how German immigrants who arrived after 1990 closed off any exchange with earlier German immigrants because they viewed earlier generations as antiquated. This included, at least in the later arrivals' perception, the earlier immigrants' views of the history of Nazi Germany. Thus, together, the contributors to this essay collection argue that the concept of memory is a useful category that helps us integrate a deeper analysis of immigrants' baggage—as memories—into our understanding of migrants' lives.

Memory, as the British psychologist Frederic Bartlett argued a century ago, is a misnomer because the term implies a final, finished product that is securely locked in people's brains and can be recalled with the help of the right stimulant. Instead, Bartlett suggested using the term "remembering" in order to signify that individual memories are continually reworked in an individual and social process of remembering. Several authors in this collection make this process visible. In my own chapter, I argue that the act of remembering is shaped not only by experiences and historical context but also by the available forms in which remembering can take place. In my case, an intergenerational oral history project in Winnipeg in the early 1970s shaped the remembering. Ensslen demonstrates a similar dynamic in her discussion of how descendants remember their female pioneer ancestors. Teigrob and Brglez demonstrate the role of historians in such processes of remembering while Farges, Worsfold, Patzelt, and Frankenberger illustrate how remembering is an act of intergenerational negotiation.

Writing in France, Maurice Halbwachs made the same point about social groups' informal, transgenerational knowledge of the past, which he called their "collective memory"; this collective memory as well was continually reworked into usable stories. While research into individual and collective memory has dramatically expanded over the past decades, and both concepts have been fruitfully employed by historians, the basic idea of remembering and contingent memory has remained useful for understanding how individuals and social groups give meanings to their experiences.[6] Together, the authors in this collection show how several generations of German Canadians have struggled to create usable stories and collective memories that help rather than hinder their integration into Canadian society. Such struggles, however, were often unsuccessful; the authors in this volume reference many silenced memories and breakdowns in intergenerational dialogue.

Memory, or better, remembering, is a transgenerational and intergenerational everyday experience. Memory is not simply an heirloom (or a Pandora's box, in the case of German migrants) that is passed down, unchanged, from one generation to the next. Rather, different generations renegotiate family and national memories in countless informal, often private talks around the kitchen table, on the school grounds, and at the water cooler, and in numerous formal, often public commemorative events and presentations. Whether done in a family or in a nation, collective remembering adapts what is remembered, thought, and told to present needs. As Halbwachs showed, the concepts of memory and generation are interconnected. A few years after

Figure 0.3. Immigrant generations: "Group of refugees sponsored to Canada by the Canadian Christian Council for the Resettlement of Refugees, Bremen, Germany, 1954." Foto-Fachgeschäft Rud. Kelch, LAC, PA-165677.

Halbwachs completed his study of collective memory, in 1928 the German Hungarian sociologist Karl Mannheim published an article on the theory of generations. This publication continues to define how scholars think about generation as an analytical concept.

Mannheim argued that generations are not simply defined by the same birth years—they are more than just a biological or demographic coincidence. Rather, generations, or socio-historical cohorts, are shaped by the specific socio-economic context and historical events in which they come of age; for example, the generation that came of age in Canada during the Great Depression was uniquely marked by that event. This early formation of a collective mentality characterizes how this cohort thinks and acts in later life, and thus, in turn, how it influences society and history. Within each generation, different groups can emerge with diverse and even opposing agendas (men and women, the rich and the poor, country folk and urbanites), but all focus on the major events and processes that mould them in their youth. For Mannheim, generation was a potentiality: only some members became conscious of the possibilities laid out by history, and only some acted upon these possibilities. Similar to the concept of collective memory, the concept

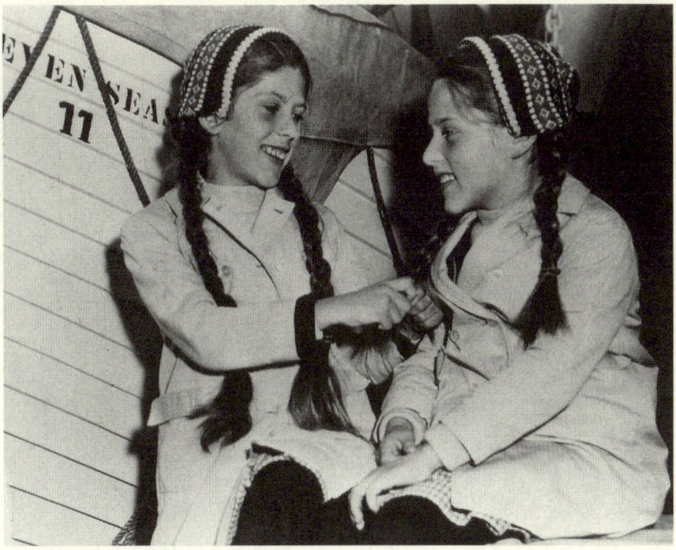

Figure 0.4. What memories were woven into the girls' pigtails and headdresses? How did they remember their childhood in postwar Germany? Traute (left) and Ingelore Dehn arriving from Germany aboard SS *Seven Seas*, Montreal, October 1959. LAC, C-45084.

of generation allows us to understand historical events and processes by linking them to the formative experiences of the acting cohorts. Indeed, Mannheim argued that generation was a dynamic phenomenon because it was based on social remembering and forgetting. Without the constant flow of generations and the need to pass on knowledge, but also the necessity to forget some experiences to make room for the next generation's ideas and actions, history would not be dynamic. Writing after the First World War, Mannheim diagnosed an acceleration of this phenomenon as a result of the acceleration of historical time.[7]

When it comes to the study of generations, Canadian immigration and ethnic historians have focused on the so-called first generation, the pioneers who, presumably, made the greatest sacrifices, often for the sake of their children for whom they wished a better life in Canada. This pioneer generation, however, is rarely studied from a generational perspective that asks what historical events shaped that specific generation of immigrants in their homeland. More so, this generation is rarely studied from an *inter*generational perspective that would ask about the immigrant generation's relationships with preceding and succeeding

Figure 0.5. Remembering immigrants as "pioneers": German immigrants from East Prussia, who arrived in Canada on 15 March 1928, on a farm in Durban, Manitoba. LAC, C-077875.

generations. In this collection, Chapters 1 and 8 directly tackle this phenomenon by investigating how later generations actively constructed memories and histories of German-Canadian pioneers—both in urban settings (Chapter 1 in Winnipeg) and rural settings (Chapter 8 in Saskatchewan), and in different ways (through oral history projects, as discussed by me, and through biographies, as discussed by Ensslen).

Also, rarely studied are the succeeding generations. They are usually seen as members of an ethnic group, hyphenated, multiethnic, or hybrid Canadians; they have their own "problems," but these seem remote, if not completely detached, from those of their parents and grandparents. While some sociologists have praised the loss of the parents' culture as an indication of successful integration, ethnic historians (like other ethnic gatekeepers) have bemoaned it as the disintegration of community. More recently, cultural scholars have celebrated second and third generations' creative pastiches of hybrid cultural identities. Yet, little connection has been made between different generations' experiences. Few researchers have explored how different generations communicate with each other or what they talk about. What do immigrants tell their

Figure 0.6. Would they ever talk about the war? Hans Petersen, who came to Canada from Germany, constructs a fishing boat, Kitimat, BC, 1960. LAC, PA-186358.

children or grandchildren about "the old country," how do they do it, and in what circumstances? This lack of generational and intergenerational perspectives in immigration historiography is particularly true when it comes to the study of how ethnic groups negotiate memories of and from their homeland.[8] In this regard, Chapters 1, 7, and 8 provide new insights into how later generations were shaped by their ancestors' experiences, memories, and stories.

As we know from the survivors of the Shoah, most of whom became forced migrants, the next generations were affected by the first generation's traumatic memories of extreme violence, deportation, and survival to such a degree that at times these events came to overshadow the next generations' own experiences and memories—a phenomenon the literary scholar Marianne Hirsch has called "postmemory."[9] Even if ancestors' experiences and memories did not weigh as heavily on the next generations as they did on those dealing with postmemory, family narratives and individual identities were profoundly shaped by national and family histories, myths, legends, and silences. We know from social psychologists working with families of Germans who were adults during the Nazi years that their children and grandchildren often constructed—and confabulated—family stories that had less to do with history and more with their own present pressing needs.[10] This was, of course, just as true of those Germans and their descendants who left Germany after 1945. And it was true of German-speaking immigrants in Canada, albeit with different dynamics.[11] In the past, German-Canadian historians have shied away from directly asking German immigrants and their children: how did you talk about the Holocaust? Sara Frankenberger (Chapter 7) and Roger Frie (Afterword) tackle this question head-on and teach us what can be gained from courageous inquiry. Thus, in twentieth-century German-Canadian history—which was so profoundly shaped by the two world wars, both in Europe and on the Canadian homefront—memory and generation have emerged as central categories of analysis that help us parse the multilayered experiences and narratives of a historically complex and culturally diverse group of German Canadians.

In the case of migrants and memory, the concept of generation functions on two separate yet connected levels: one shaped by the homeland experience and the other by the experience in the receiving society. This is quite obvious and pertinent in the case of Germans in Germany and in Canada. In Germany, a substantial literature has emerged about the legacy of the Second World War and the Holocaust. From the 1980s onward, academics began to distinguish three different generations: the eyewitnesses, who had lived through the Third Reich as adults and constitute the first generation; their children, born during or after the war, who made up the second generation; and their children (the first generation's grandchildren), born in the 1960s and 1970s, who are conceived of as the third generation. With German unification in 1990, this picture has become more complex with the addition of three generations of East Germans with distinct experiences and memories. Furthermore, since the 1990s, new generations have emerged that are increasingly multicultural.[12]

All of these generations, but particularly members of the first and second West-German generations, have migrated across the Atlantic.

From a Canadian immigration perspective, Germans arriving in Canada in the 1950s are considered the first generation (the immigrants), their children are defined as the second generation (no longer immigrants but "ethnic Canadians"), their grandchildren the third, and so on. This is further complicated by an in-between generation: immigrants who arrived in Canada as children are often referred to as the 1.5 generation. Also, the postwar immigrants encountered previous generations of German immigrants (who had arrived before 1945) and their descendants, and later, would encounter more recent arrivals (who arrived after 1960). The major waves of German immigration to Canada in the twentieth century occurred in the decade before the First World War, in the second half of the 1920s, from the late 1940s to the early 1960s, and finally in the 2000s. There were also smaller refugee migrations in the 1930s. This complex pattern of immigration from different historical Germanies—Imperial Germany, Weimar Republic, Nazi Germany, postwar Germany, West Germany, and unified Germany—further complicates the analysis of generation.

For example, a German immigrant family arriving in 1953 may have included parents born in 1913 and children born in the late 1930s and 1940s, thus including first and second generations (from the German perspective) and immigrant and 1.5 generation from a Canadian perspective. Depending on whether they were from West Germany, had fled from East Prussia in 1945 or from East Germany in 1952, or had been expelled from a German enclave in Czechoslovakia or Poland in 1945, these immigrants' socialization and wartime experiences would have differed significantly (not to speak, of course, of linguistic, religious, cultural, ideological, class, or gender differences). Whatever their experiences and actions during the Nazi period may have been, and whether they wished it so or not, their "national" history of war and genocide pushed them into the same frame of identification. German immigrants needed to figure out how to integrate their homeland's extremely violent history into their individual and family memories. Each generation approached this task from a different point of generational experience.

The authors in this collection tackle the intricacies of multiple interacting generations in several ways. In one respect or another, they all look at the ways in which memories were shared and negotiated across generations. In my chapter on German-Canadian memories

Figure 0.7. German generations: Working together—remembering together? Edward Henseler, former agronomist from Cologne, Germany, and his son, Ulrich, St-Thomas de Caxton, Quebec, c. 1962. LAC, PA-186362.

of the Great War (Chapter 1), I ask how the relationship between the pre–First World War immigrants who were interviewed and the post–Second World War immigrant who interviewed them shaped interview dynamics and resulted in silences regarding the Great War. Teigrob probes how Canadian generations after the Second World War attempted to forget their prime minister's visit to Nazi Germany (Chapter 2). Similarly, Brglez confronts us with the fact that the *völkisch* ideology of some post–Second World War immigrant scholars infused the language of later generations of German-Canadian academics (Chapter 4). Moreover, unspoken and concealed knowledge and memory of the Nazi period and especially of the Holocaust has led to intense intergenerational conflicts among German Canadians, as is illuminated by Patzelt (Chapter 6), Frankenberger (Chapter 7), and Frie (Afterword). The experiences of the Second World War also shaped the intergenerational dynamics of German-Jewish refugees, as is demonstrated by Farges (Chapter 3), and of clergy in the Lutheran Church, as is shown by Worsfold (Chapter 5). In other cases, as Ensslen reveals in Chapter 8, the difficult legacies of the two world wars led later generations to transfigure and idealize their ancestors into heroic pioneers.

This phenomenon—a multitude of different generations living in the same place at the same time—is best described by the term *Ungleichzeitigkeit des Gleichzeitigen.* The phrase, first formulated by German art historian Wilhelm Pinder in 1926, is translated variously as non-contemporaneity of the contemporaneous or the simultaneity of the non-simultaneous.[13] *Ungleichzeitigkeit des Gleichzeitigen* was a central idea for Mannheim. He explained that while different generations lived in the same chronological time, they experienced this time differently and thus they lived in different experienced times—or they experienced the same historical time differently. They accessed the different possibilities of thinking and acting in the world that were available to them at any given moment in distinct ways. It was these different approaches to the same historical possibilities that constituted their generation. Historians must therefore think in a "polyphonous" (Mannheim) way in order to hear the voices of each generation expressed at any given moment in time.[14] And so it is with German Canadians: different generations—shaped not only by birth year but also by shared historical events and socio-economic contexts, differentiated by time of immigration but connected through diaspora—lived with each other but experienced time in different ways.[15] Generation and memory help us grasp this complexity of "polyphonous" history.

The German-Canadian *Ungleichzeitigkeit des Gleichzeitigen* is further complicated by the diverse geographic origins of German migrants. Until the First World War, only about 10 percent came from Germany proper—the German Empire forged by Bismarck in 1871—whereas the rest of German immigrants came from German ethno-religious enclaves of Catholics, Lutherans, and other Protestants in Central and Eastern Europe and the Austro-Hungarian Empire as well as from the United States. During the interwar years, the percentage of migrants from Germany proper—then the Weimar Republic—increased. The emigration after the Second World War consisted predominantly of West Germans, but also included East Germans as well as refugees and expellees from the former German territories in Central and Eastern Europe and from German ethnic enclaves in Poland, Czechoslovakia, Hungary, Bulgaria, Romania, and Yugoslavia.[16] Thus, the 3.2 million Canadians who claimed full or partial German ethnic origin in 2011 did not constitute a homogenous ethnic group, let alone a "community."[17] Some individuals could trace their immigrant ancestors back to the eighteenth century, when Germans arrived as merchants, mercenaries, or missionaries. Others could follow them back to the various agricultural settler groups that arrived in the nineteenth century. Yet others' grandparents or parents had arrived as manual and industrial workers in the twentieth century. The latest newcomers arrived after the end of the Cold War, in a digital media age, when reality-TV shows were made about them because German television audiences were fascinated by the idea that Germany did not only receive immigrants but that Germans continued to emigrate.[18] The generational perspective presented by the 2011 census is particularly interesting for historians of German immigrants: approximately 346,000 belonged to the first generation, 612,000 to the second generation, and 2.25 million to the third or later generations. While only about 13 percent of the individuals in this heterogeneous group spoke German as their main language at home (most likely the first generation), they were somewhat united in their understanding that they saw themselves as German or, even if they wished not to be recognized as German, knew that others viewed them as "Germans." And they were united in their understanding—vague as it may be after four generations—that since 1914, and especially since 1945, this label could at times be a heavy baggage to carry.

This collection of essays provides a glimpse into how multiple generations of German immigrants and their descendants have carried this heavy baggage—or tried to dispose of it, or pass it on to the next generation, or renegotiate it with preceding generations—over the twentieth century. In these different approaches to making sense of what it meant to be (seen as) German, individual memories clashed with family myths and national legends; history often played a supporting role at best in these negotiations and narrations. In the chapters of this book, however, history serves as an approach to construct plausible narratives about German-Canadian generations' memories of the twentieth century. As such, we hope and believe that this collection can serve as an inspiration for further studies into the significance of generation and memory among Canada's immigrant and ethnic groups.

The authors in this collection draw on a wide range of theoretical, methodological, and empirical literature to contextualize their case studies. One discipline they have drawn upon is German-Canadian Studies, which has seen an increasing number of publications of high academic excellence emerge over the past two decades. Since the publication of *Beyond the Nation?*, which I edited in 2012, wherein authors tackled questions of transnationalism and transculturalism in German-Canadian Studies, several important studies have been published in German-Canadian history. Many of them share a comparative approach. Barbara Lorenzkowski's study *Sounds of Ethnicity* (2010) explored the cultural worlds of Germans in Berlin, Ontario, and Buffalo, New York, between 1850 and 1914. Pascal Maeder's book *Forging a New Heimat* (2011) compared the politics and experiences of expellees—ethnic Germans driven out of their homes in Central and Eastern Europe at the end of the Second World War—in West Germany and Canada. Patrick Farges's study *Bindestrich-Kanadier?* (2015) traced the fates of German refugees who fled to Canada in the 1930s—Social Democrats from the Sudetenland and Jews from Germany. Finally, in *Escape Hatch* (2017) the doyen of German-Canadian history, Gerhard P. Bassler, explored yet another aspect of German experiences in Newfoundland. Bassler scrutinized the economic relations between West Germany and Newfoundland from 1950 to 1970. Many other studies have yet to be published, including several excellent dissertations and master's theses.[19]

German-Canadian history provides a rich field for studies of all kinds of phenomena in a vibrant multicultural society with a long and troubled history of colonization and decolonization, inclusion and exclusion, discrimination and racism, class strife, and gender conflict. A nearly global German diaspora lends itself to comparative and transnational approaches. The multiple ethnic, religious, linguistic, and geographic origins of "German" migrants themselves stimulate questions about concepts such as ethnicity, language, tradition, and identity that are often seen as primal and essential rather than as contingent and in flux. And Germany's troubled and troubling history in the twentieth century provides ample material for deeper studies of memory and generation. It is in this context that the authors in this book seek to contribute to Canadian immigration and ethnic historiography.

The Chapters

The research presented in this collection tackles the problem of memory and generation in immigration and ethnic history, viewed through the prism of German experiences in twentieth-century Canada. Together, the authors ask how immigrants and their descendants grappled with national histories and family memories of war, genocide, deportation, expulsion, flight, and other forms of violence in, what German historian Christian Gerlach has called, "extremely violent societies."[20] They draw on diverse concepts of memory and generation that have been elaborated in German post-Holocaust historiography and in Canadian immigration and ethnic historiography, thus entangling diverse fields commonly separated by the "saltwater curtain." Such entangled history provides a first step toward integrating experiences, memories, and narratives from the societies that immigrants depart with those that they arrive in.

In Chapter 1, I turn to a central event in Canadian identity and history—the First World War. I ask how German Canadians remembered the war and demonstrate that answers are not easy to come by. I argue that Canadians of German descent have stowed away memories of state repression and social hostility into small parcels of narrative that are barely visible in their life stories. In an oral history project in 1971–72, German pre-1914 immigrants in Winnipeg told historian Art Grenke about their lives from the 1870s to the 1920s. Yet, despite multiple opportunities to tell Grenke of their experiences during the Great War, interviewees were mostly silent on the subject. This silence, however, was not simply a lack of words or voices, nor was it simply a function of forgetting after the passing of two generations. Rather, an iconic story about vandalism surfaced to uphold the German community's perception of their harassment as an absurd experience. In the intergenerational dialogue between Grenke, a post-1945 immigrant working on his doctoral dissertation, and immigrant pioneers—who were in their seventies, eighties, and nineties at the time of the interviews—silences about the Great War were overshadowed by the resounding silences that demarcated the troubling attempts at remembering and forgetting the Nazi regime, the Second World War, and the

Holocaust. German-Canadian histories and memories of these latter events indeed make up the bulk of German-Canadian scholarship on memory and generation presented in this book.

The Second World War cast a long shadow over the experiences and memories of several generations of German Canadians in the twentieth century. As Robert Teigrob reminds us in Chapter 2, Canadians were well informed about the rise of fascism and Nazism in Europe in the 1930s. However, their response was troubling. This was manifested not only through various homegrown Nazi and fascist movements, but also in the Canadian prime minister's adoration of Adolf Hitler. William Lyon Mackenzie King, a flawed man still admired today as Canada's greatest leader, visited Hitler in 1937. The visit came a year after the Berlin Summer Olympics and a year before *Kristallnacht*, the first major pogrom in the Nazi state. It was, according to Teigrob, "the only such visit by a head of state from the Western democracies." After the war, two generations of Canadians tried to ignore this visit or explain it away as diplomatic ingenuity. Recent admonishments by historians, however, have failed to explain why "in the Canada of 1937 King's mission was remarkably ... *uncontroversial.*" Teigrob argues that King's visit was not simply a result of his quirkiness, but rather representative of Canadian attitudes at the time. Thus, King spoke as a member of a generation to whom his visit to Hitler made sense. Still, later generations, who came of age with the full knowledge of Nazi atrocities, could no longer fathom this action and have tried to suppress its collective memory by explaining it away as a quirk of history. As Teigrob concludes, it has taken an enormous amount of public forgetting to continue to hail King as a model leader in a multicultural society that prides itself on welcoming refugees.

That King's visit to Nazi Germany was, at the very least, a misguided attempt at pacification became clearer to Canadians over the course of 1938: as the Nazis annexed Austria in March; commandeered the Sudetenland, the western region of Czechoslovakia, in October; and carried out *Kristallnacht* in November. As Teigrob reminds us, the memory of the Great War's horror induced the West to make huge concessions to avoid another war. Instead, appeasement emboldened Hitler. After *Kristallnacht*, Mackenzie King wrote in his diary about the plight of German Jews: "Something will have to be done by our country."[21] But, as Teigrob tells us in his chapter, King, aware of the homegrown anti-Semitism, did almost nothing for the 350,000 German-speaking Jews fleeing Nazi Germany and Austria during the 1930s, accepting no more than 6,000 refugees from Germany.

In Chapter 3, Patrick Farges, who has studied the experiences of German Jewish exiles in Canada and Israel, compares and contrasts Jewish German refugees' identity formation in Canada and Israel by focusing on the term Yekkes. The predominantly bourgeois Jewish refugees from Germany were ridiculed for their formal clothes and manners; their jackets (*yekkes* in Yiddish) made them the target of mockery by other Jews, who viewed them as being out of place in their new surroundings. Farges traces the development of the term Yekke as a descriptive ethnic identity marker in two different cultural and social environments. While Yekkes faced anti-Semitism and anti-German hostility in Canada, they experienced antagonism in Mandatory Palestine (later Israel) for their "Germanness." Yekkes, as Farges writes, were "heirs of an impossible cultural heritage for which there was little understanding after Auschwitz." Yekkes in Canada tried to blend in by trying to hide their German and Jewish identity markers. Further layers of silence were added after the war, when pre-war refugee stories could not be told in the shadow of the Shoah. Integration into Israeli society was, in some regards, even more difficult for the 90,000 Yekkes who had arrived in the Middle Eastern country in the 1930s. Interviewees in Israel were more likely than those in Canada to speak German. But they were also more assertive and politically engaged and eventually gained control over the discourse about Yekkes. Thus, over several generations, memories of Jewish-German culture changed and "Yekkishkeit" became a positive marker of ethnic identity—powerful enough to unite a heterogeneous group, first in Israel and then transnationally. This was not an easy process. Again, as in other cases, memory and culture—at least in families—was often transmitted along with silences. At the same time, a vibrant, transnational Yekke historiography has emerged, carried on increasingly by Yekkes' children and grandchildren. This historiography shines light, however, on a glaring gap in German-Canadian historiography regarding the experiences of Jews in German-Canadian history.

Indeed, German-Canadian historiography has been a troubled field of research. This became most obvious in the debate among German-Canadian historian Gerhard Bassler, the German migration historian Dirk Hoerder, and the former Chair in German-Canadian Studies Angelika Sauer who, in the 1990s, discussed the merits and politics of German-Canadian historiography and the label "German Canadian." Bassler argued that Germans had never received their fair due as "co-founders" of Canada because, ever since the First World War, Canadian historians had viewed "the nation's German heritage as an embarrassment" and "[systematically excluded] German Canadians from the historical image presented to the general public."[22] Similar opinions and worries about German cultural decline in Canada and their "silencing" by the dominant Anglo-Canadian society had been expressed by a generation of German Canadians since the 1970s, a sentiment Sauer described as a "culture of complaint."[23] Sauer maintained that German-speaking immigrants were absent from Canadian history because German-Canadian studies had failed to produce academically sound studies, and not because two world wars had eternally branded them as pariahs. German-Canadian historiography, she asserted, needed to "abandon the temptation to portray German Canadians as a persecuted minority through a persistent invocation of the wars."[24] On his part, Hoerder argued that "the German-speaking peoples" that arrived in Canada from around the world were too diverse to be grouped under one ethnic rubric. German-Canadian historians, he wrote, had inflated the size of their group by exaggerating statistics and imposed ethnic homogeneity by conflating cultures in order to claim special status and thus satisfy group politics.[25]

Indeed, the label German Canadian is not inherent but constructed and politically motivated and, in the second half of the twentieth century, the usage of this label was motivated by several factors. One of these factors was, as Sauer pointed out, the introduction of multiculturalism in Canada: "Predictably, individual groupings soon began vying for the status of largest, most important ethnic group with the longest history."[26] The federal and provincial governments provided funding to ethnic groups to research their history and without a recognizable group there would be no funding. The prospect that the bigger the group was the greater the funding would be was perhaps also present in some of these academic manoeuvres. While such numbers games may have lacked academic integrity or distorted historical accuracy, they nevertheless produced results. This was most evident in the formation of German-Canadian institutions such as the German-Canadian

Figure 0.8. Scholars continue to navigate the stormy waters of interpreting German migrants' lives in Canada: German children aboard the SS *Seven Seas*, c. 1958. LAC, PA-124957.

Historical Association (founded in 1973), the *German-Canadian Yearbook* (published from 1973 to 2004), and the Chair in German-Canadian Studies at the University of Winnipeg (established in 1989).

The notion of a unified "German" group, however, had deeper and darker roots than official multiculturalism. These roots are only now coming to light. In a way, Bassler, Hoerder, and Sauer touched upon these roots by referring to the two world wars as presumed sources of ongoing discrimination. But they talked about the experience of war *in Canada*. Yet, the subtext to this political discussion about "German Canadians" was the long shadow cast by the Holocaust originating *in Germany*. As Sauer wrote: "It could be argued that at the center of German-Canadian identity today lies the perception of victimization, stigmatization and discrimination. This is the meaning given to the group's history by its members and used by them as an explanation of the group's invisibility in Canadian society. The culture of complaint—this sense of grievance and victimhood—cannot be ignored, yet its origins have to be examined: do they lie in the Canadian reality of two postwar periods, or do they rather lie in German culture of the 1950s?"[27] She left the question unanswered, but urged that "it is time . . . to shed the image of German Canadians as permanent victims."[28] Two chapters in this collection begin to provide some answers. They point to memories of the Holocaust and a troubled process of *Vergangenheitsbewältigung*—a coping or dealing with a troubling national past—among German Canadians in general and German-Canadian historians in particular.[29]

In Chapter 4, Karen Brglez initiates an important conversation about some of the more disturbing roots of German-Canadian historiography by tracing the intellectual biography of one of its main advocates in the 1970s and 1980s—Gottlieb Leibbrandt (1908–1989). Leibbrandt, originally from the Ukraine, had studied in Germany and Austria, where he joined the Nazi party. By 1937, he worked for Goebbels's propaganda ministry, publishing anti-Semitic and anti-Bolshevik texts. In 1938 he volunteered for the Wehrmacht, and in 1941 he participated in the attack on the Soviet Union, interrogating captured Red Army soldiers. According to Brglez, "Gottlieb [Leibbrandt] was part of the Nazis' attempt to use Russian-German émigrés as eastern 'experts' in their war on the Soviet Union." After the war, he became active in Russian-German expellee organizations and wrote "narratives of German victimization" in their publications. In 1952, he migrated to Galt, Ontario, where he ran an import business and was active in a number of German-Canadian organizations. He taught about the Soviet Union at the University of Waterloo. He also wrote about German-Canadian history and co-founded German-Canadian historical institutions. From the early 1970s, he became one of the founders of German-Canadian historiography, without ever letting on, however, that in his earlier life he had advocated German racial superiority. While Brglez does not say so, to me, her research helps us understand why terms such as *Deutschtum* and *Volkstum*, which the Nazis had aggressively redefined as racial (instead of cultural or linguistic) categories, continued to be used in segments of German-Canadian historiography—long after this language had been abandoned by German academia.

As Sauer noted, this problematic German-Canadian *Vergangenheitsbewältigung* is not specific to historiography. Did the origins of German Canadians' "sense of grievance and victimhood" lie in German culture of the 1950s rather than immigrant experiences in postwar Canada? In several articles, I have asked how German post-1945 immigrants and their descendants have dealt with the Nazi past.[30] In Chapter 7, Sara Frankenberger takes a fresh look at this question by focusing on the second and third generations. She comes back, once again, to the overarching question of silence. Rather than asking how the first generation spoke (or did not speak) about the Second World War and the Holocaust, Frankenberger reconstructs through interviews what family stories the next two generations remembered and how they narrated them. Coping with this legacy, she writes, was difficult as more often than not the next generations avoided the topic or remained silent. Remarkably, silences were transmitted even when the German language was not passed down to the next generations. These silences became obvious when Frankenberger pointedly asked her interlocutors about their parents or grandparents being implicated as perpetrators of, or bystanders to, Nazi atrocities. Nonetheless, such intergenerational silences resulted in continued destructive feelings of shame and guilt, which led to insecurity about German heritage. Often, this insecurity led Frankenberger's interviewees to make historically inaccurate arguments that relieved Germans of responsibility and relativized the Holocaust. One interviewee implied that Germans could not be held responsible for concentration camps in Poland while another accepted her father's argument that compared the Holocaust and Japanese-Canadian internment. Yet others replicated the first generation's arguments that they knew nothing, and that if they had known, they could not have spoken up for fear of their own lives. Members of the third generation claimed that they were too far removed in space and time to meaningfully talk with their family about the Holocaust. As Frankenberger writes, there is still much we need to learn about the specifics of German-Canadian *Vergangenheitsbewältigung.* Did West German immigrants, who had experienced the war as aerial bombings of cities and evacuation to the countryside, relate different stories to their children and grandchildren than the refugees and expellees, whose

Figure 0.9. Absent fathers: In the 1950s, Canadian immigration authorities encouraged fathers to migrate ahead of their families; they also admitted a small number of war widows with children. Pictured here, women and children sailed to Canada aboard SS *Arosa Kulm* under the auspices of the Canadian Christian Council for the Resettlement of Refugees, Bremen, West Germany, 1954. LAC, PA-165111.

dominant memory was that of flight from the Red Army or violent expulsion and permanent loss of their homeland? How were their responses shaped by experiences in Canada? We know that only a small group of German Canadians embraced the views of German-Canadian Holocaust denier Ernst Zündel from the 1970s to the 1990s, but we also know that the much more common twisting of history, through willful ignorance, has been damaging to individuals, families, and society for three quarters of a century.

Intergenerational conflict also shaped the German-Canadian experiences outside of the shadow of the Holocaust. In Chapter 5, Elliot Worsfold uses Mannheim's concept of generation to parse out the power struggles within the Lutheran church in Ontario, which pitted established pastors against students during the 1960s. Pastors, who were often immigrants or children of immigrants, sided with the recent arrivals in their goal to keep churches German-speaking. Students, on the other hand, usually came from established German-Canadian families who had arrived several generations before. They did not speak German and advocated for the introduction of English in the communities, in order to speed up, as they argued, integration. Worsfold's case study illuminates a summer of generational conflict within Ontario's Lutheran church that played out during broader generational conflicts in Western society in the heady sixties. Indeed, the seminary students were inspired by the Beatles' concerts rather than their pastors' "seventeenth century" practices in designing their own sermons. The older pastors countered that their antagonizing students were the immature products of a "fatherless society." In this struggle, as Worsfold shows, the young students attempted to position themselves as gatekeepers. They became part of a larger cohort of Anglo-Canadian gatekeepers intent on assimilating postwar newcomers.

Worsfold's chapter demonstrates the usefulness of Mannheim's concept of generation for the study of immigrant and ethnic communities. It also opens up a number of questions not yet addressed in German-Canadian historiography. While some attention has been paid to the immigrants that arrived from the late 1940s to the early 1960s, we know little about the effects of religion and secularization, de-industrialization, and modernization on this group. These immigrants quickly moved out from inner-city neighbourhoods to new suburbs in the 1960s—which created new problems for churches, as Worsfold depicts. Further, the young seminary students were able to connect with the younger immigrants because both groups felt more uncomfortable about their German background—the immigrants because they were called "Nazis" by Canadians, and the seminary students because they did not speak any German. Although the latter is only a minor point in Worsfold's study, it makes one wonder whether—in the context of anti–Vietnam War protests, historical research revealing the Evangelical church's support of the Nazi state from 1933 onward, and the U.S. civil rights' leaders references to organizers of the *Bekennende Kirche* (Confessing Church movement) such as Dietrich Bonhoeffer and Karl Barth—the Nazi past was not indeed one of the unmentioned subtexts to this intergenerational (and to some degree inter-ethnic) conflict. Certainly, a good part of the struggle was about the right extent of authority—what kind of authority was still democratic and what kind was already authoritarian?

A different type of intergenerational relationship is at the centre of Anke Patzelt's chapter (Chapter 6) on recent German immigrants in Ottawa. Using an amended version of Mannheim's concept of generation, Patzelt argues that different immigrant generations constructed their sense of self—discursively—by comparing themselves to earlier generations. In this concept of generation, proposed by Portuguese sociologists Sofia Aboim and Pedro Vasconcelos, generations establish a collective sense of self through discourse. Based on interviews with Germans who immigrated to Ottawa in the 1990s and 2000s, Patzelt shows how her interviewees used stereotypes of postwar immigrants as old-fashioned and nationalistic to cast themselves as "modern migrants" who may leave Canada at any moment to move elsewhere. This, however, was not a unique phenomenon. Previous generations had also imagined themselves as modern by juxtaposing themselves to earlier generations that were imagined as "traditional." Similar to some of Farges's interlocutors, who were described as "accidental" immigrants because they had been deported to Canada as enemy aliens and, after the Canadian government figured out that they were actually refugees from Nazi Germany, they were permitted to stay, some of Patzelt's interlocutors depicted themselves as accidental immigrants to Canada, explaining that they could just as well have settled anywhere else. Furthermore, Patzelt's interviewees described themselves as well-off *Kontainerdeutsche* and everyone who had come before them as *Kofferdeutsche*. As I have found in my own discussions with postwar German immigrants, they commonly describe themselves as *Kofferdeutsche* and those who came in the 1960s (not the 1990s) as *Kontainerdeutsche*. Consequently, there is a referential shift in such identifications of self and other that is more useful to craft a specific immigrant identity than to describe a reality. Patzelt's interviewees' explanation that they came to Canada "by accident" and thus for no good reason illuminates another shift in historical context. The German psychologist Folkert Lüthke found in his interviews with German postwar immigrants in Australia in the 1980s that they were reluctant to tell people that they had really no good reason to emigrate. Instead they came up with "good" "public" reasons that would be easily accepted by family, friends, and colleagues. The same was true of the German postwar immigrants I have interviewed.[31] But Patzelt's interviewees were not at all reluctant to tell her that they really had no particular reason to emigrate or to settle in Canada. Indeed, they were still unconvinced about their final destination and simply claimed that they had arrived there "by accident." Patzelt's interviewees, who had grown up with German *Vergangenheitsbewältigung*, seemed to be similarly unfazed by what others might think of them as Germans. In their view, "Germany's history was no longer a dominant issue." Still, even these immigrants—members of the so-called second and third generations in the context of German *Vergangenheitsbewältigung*—could not evade their historical memory. Nationalism, anathema to many younger Germans, was viewed with as much scepticism when it appeared in its Canadian incarnation. If anything, they believed they needed to inform Canadians about the Nazi period. Yet, many felt as attached to Germany as many members of previous generations, if not more so. Earlier generations left Germany because, in light of Nazi destruction, they saw no future in Germany or because they no longer wished to be associated with the country. Patzelt's interviewees, however, simply had not wished to leave Germany (or so they said) while Canada was their coincidental place of living.

Not all German-Canadian intergenerational relations were burdened by traces of the recent past. In Chapter 8, Christine Ensslen examines how Canadians of German background narrated their German pioneer ancestors' lives. Using a case study that compiled forty independently written biographies, Ensslen demonstrates—through comparison and contrast—the remarkable similarities of writing German-Canadian pioneer lives at the beginning of the twenty-first century. Throughout, the biographers (almost all of them women) crafted stories of their ancestors (all female pioneers) as heroes of their own lives and of Canadian history. Perhaps nothing else can be expected in a memorial project that sets out to celebrate idolized Canadian prairie pioneers. As such, the forty-two German stories were probably not much different from the other 371 biographies of Saskatchewan pioneers from other ethnic backgrounds published in the same 2009 book by the Saskatchewan Genealogical Society. Yet, in the presence of so much silence in twentieth-century German-Canadian history and historiography, it is refreshing to see the creativity with which descendants filled in the gaps that had been left open by missing memories, memorabilia, and mementos. This production of history reminds us of Michel-Rolph Trouillot's point that "professional" historians are seldom the first and often the last to tell a story about the past. Thus, history is not just what academic historians write. Indeed, university historians have often tended to simply adopt, quite uncritically, voices of previous recorders, who in turn have assumed significant power in shaping "official" histories.[32] Here then, too, we see historians—"memory makers," as Ensslen calls them—at work. In this case, memory, myth, and history were interwoven in stories about Catherine the Great's invitation to Germans (she had actually invited settlers from throughout Europe), the sacrifices of pioneer life, or the "Germanness" of Russian food like *holuptsi* (cabbage rolls).

This final chapter returns us to memories of the First World War discussed in Chapter 1 as well as to memories of the Second World War discussed in most of the other chapters. Unlike in Winnipeg, in rural Saskatchewan descendants investigated and imagined how their grandmothers and great-grandmothers had experienced prairie life, including the imposition of language restrictions in 1918, bans on "enemy aliens," but also conscription and sons going off to war. Writing in 2008, descendants still remembered the sadness their ancestors felt hearing news of their relatives' deaths in Europe. They also remembered news of the Russian Revolution, in which many family members of settlers perished—a memory completely absent from Winnipeg's German community, even though many of these immigrants had also come from German settlements in Russia. And yet, there were also silences, as Ensslen writes: "None of the accounts included memories of how these individuals were treated as Germans in the prairies during the wars," when "general hostility toward German Canadians mounted." Descendants were aware of these silences, but did not ascribe them to experiences in Canada but rather in Europe. The underlying motivation, however, was the same: they wanted to be left in peace, forget, and no longer talk about hard times, not even to their children or grandchildren. Nonetheless, their descendants were not deterred and took advantage of this "opportunity to publicly memorialize their ancestors." Yet, perhaps without realizing it, they could only do so within a narrow framework of celebrating Canadian pioneer life.

Finally, in his Afterword Roger Frie returns to some of the central questions of this book: "To what extent has this history [of National Socialism and the genocide of Jewish communities throughout Europe] been remembered and acknowledged by German immigrants and their descendants in Canada?" German-Canadian historians have only begun to scratch the surface of this difficult research, but this book hopes to contribute new approaches and insights. From an autobiographical perspective, wherein he grew up as a child of German immigrants in Canada, Frie tells us that many German-Canadian families have evaded answering this question through processes of neglect, dissociation, or even outright denial. This "lack of concerted intergenerational dialogue about the history of National Socialism had serious consequences." The parents' silences placed a heavy burden on their children, who had to figure out—without knowing their own history—why neighbourhood kids called them names and children at school refused to play with them. Frie argues that no matter what generation, "the obligation to know and remember the massive crimes of the Shoah has not correspondingly lessened with time. Historical injustices don't simply fade away." In one sense, this book is a step toward fulfilling this, as Frie calls it, "ethical obligation."

Together, the chapters demonstrate that German-Canadian historiography continues to be a vibrant field that can stimulate discussion in related fields in immigration and ethnic history. Yet, much basic historiography remains to be done. The authors point to further research lacunae in their individual chapters, but here, a few glaring gaps—focused on the twentieth century—should be mentioned. Despite this collection's focus being the two world wars, we still know little about the actual experiences of German Canadians in various locales throughout Canada during the two wartime and postwar periods. Nor do we have concrete case studies that investigate the effects of the wars on the various German groups, communities, and organizations in Canada. Research on the interwar period is just as underdeveloped. We know from past case studies about the experiences of Nazi sympathizers, civilian internees and prisoners-of-war, and the Jewish and Sudeten German refugees. At the same time, we know that a small German-Canadian political left existed, but have no in-depth studies about leftist (in the broadest sense) German immigrants in Canada. We have a general idea of the experiences of German immigrants who arrived between 1947 and the late 1950s, but we have few detailed examinations. We know virtually nothing about these postwar immigrants' later experiences from the 1960s onward. In particular, we know almost nothing about intergenerational relations and conflict. Nor do we know how individual and collective memories of war, depression, genocide, and forced displacement played out in a multi-generational ethnic community over time. The smaller successive waves of German immigrants from the 1960s onward have also not been studied to any greater extent. German temporary migrants—itinerant workers in the

Figure 0.10. Some immigrants, "pioneers" of the working-class, have been largely forgotten: Members of the Vancouver Branch, Deutsche Arbeiter und Farmer Verband, at picnic, c. 1928. LAC, PA-148638.

first half of the twentieth century, exchange students, West German soldiers stationed at NATO bases in Canada, and career migrants—have also slipped under the radar of German-Canadian research. Further, inter-ethnic relations, class relations, and gender relations have been absent from German-Canadian historiography as any attempt to investigate German immigrants as members of the colonizing settler society that benefitted from the ruthless exploitation of Indigenous peoples. Indeed, this last aspect—German immigrants as colonizers and settlers—requires close attention. As Frie reminds us in his Afterword, German Canadians are Germans with an ethical obligation to remember the Holocaust—and they are Canadians with an ethical obligation to acknowledge Canada's historical crimes against Indigenous peoples.

Such vast omissions are not unique to German-Canadian historiography. The community of Canadian historians is small, that of immigration and ethnic historians even smaller, and within that group, there are only a handful of researchers focusing on German immigrants and their descendants. But this dearth of researchers does not alone explain the scarcity of research. German Canadianists have also failed to integrate their specific case studies into larger historical questions and contexts; instead, they remain within a German-Canadian bubble that is too small to sustain dialogue. The fact that Germans have historically constituted one of the earliest and largest immigrant groups in Canada is not a cause for celebration nor is it justification to demand greater recognition. Rather, it is an opportunity to push for significantly increasing and improving the research that has been produced in the past half century. The sheer size of this immigrant and ethnic group, its great heterogeneity, and the particularly heavy burdens of history and memory on its members make it possible to explore core questions about Canadian, migration, and ethnic history. The complex diversity of "German Canadians" and the deeply troubling history of Germany in the twentieth century shout out for more studies that relate to current social and political issues. For example, as Worsfold points out in his chapter, immigration historians have investigated the role of gatekeepers from the dominant society and from within ethnic groups, and have focused on the role of gatekeepers in shaping networks, settlement patterns, employment opportunities, and the maintenance of culture. But to what degree did such ethnic gatekeepers also attempt to control the group's memory and historical narratives, particularly when the homeland's history was seen as damaging to the group's reputation and image? In another example, a large number of post-1945 German immigrants were children during the war; today, we study war-affected children's integration into Canadian society. Are there any lessons to be drawn from a population that has lived through the aftermath of such an experience for over seventy years? Similarly, some of the post-1945 immigrants were members of the Hitler Youth and were drawn into the bloody street fighting at the end of the "total war" proclaimed by Goebbels. At present, we examine the integration of child soldiers into Canadian society. Are there any lessons to be learned from the German immigrants? Finally, while German society has been grappling with its dark history for over half a century, Canadian society is only beginning to come to terms with its devastating colonial past. Can German Canadians, including German-Canadian historians, act as intermediaries, sharing the lessons from German *Vergangenheitsbewältigung*?

Throughout the twentieth century and into the twenty-first century, Canada has received (if not always welcomed) immigrants and refugees who brought with them the heavy baggage of troubling memories. In a recent oral history project I conducted with refugees who, over the

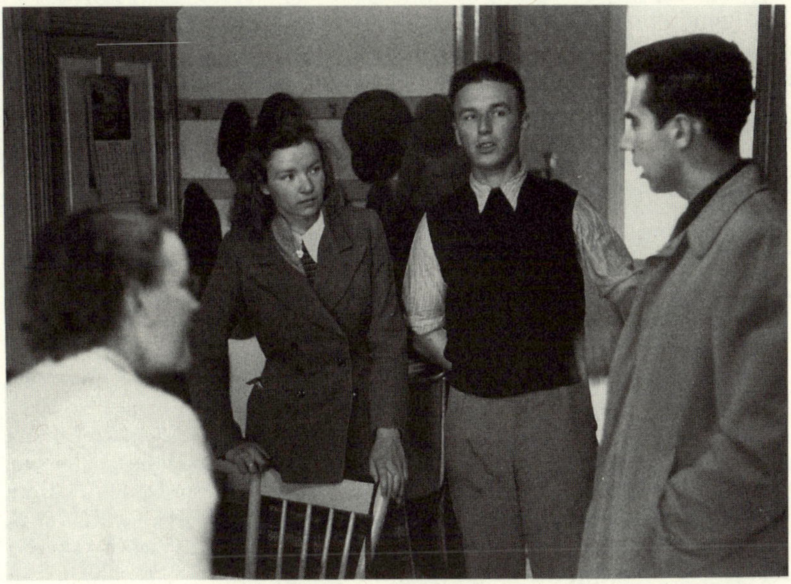

Figure 0.11. Ready to work. Ready to remember? German immigrants are greeted by a new employer and a relief worker, Kitchener, Ontario, 5 July 1952. LAC, PA-173819.

past forty years, had come to Winnipeg from El Salvador, Guatemala, Colombia, Burma (Myanmar), and Afghanistan, the legacy of intergenerational silence and the salience of intergenerational dialogue became clear. Many second-generation family members had never heard their parents speak about their experiences in their homelands. They did not know that their parents had fought in a civil war or against foreign occupation. They did not know that their parents had to flee at a moment's notice. They did not know how their parents had survived in refugee camps or in hiding. They did not know why they had come to Canada. Because of this project, oral history built a bridge across generations. Oral history also served as an archival practice that ensured—even if younger generations were not yet ready to hear their parents' or grandparents' stories—that these stories would still be available and accessible at a later time. Memory and generation allowed project participants to cross the "saltwater curtain" (in whatever form), to understand how homeland experiences and memories continued to shape the lives of immigrants, their children, and their grandchildren.[33] This book hopes to initiate a greater conversation about the value of looking for intergenerational continuities and discontinuities in remembering the history of immigrant families and homelands among scholars studying immigration and ethnic groups.

Notes

1 Roberto Perin, "Clio as an Ethnic: The Third Force in Canadian Historiography," *Canadian Historical Review* 64, no. 4 (1983): 441–67; Franca Iacovetta, "Manly Militants, Cohesive Communities, and Defiant Domestics: Writing about Immigrants in Canadian Historical Scholarship," *Labour/Le Travail* 36 (1995): 217–52; Franca Iacovetta, *The Writing of English Canadian Immigrant History* (Ottawa: Canadian Historical Association, 1997); Marlene Epp and Franca Iacovetta, Introduction, in *Sisters or Strangers?: Immigrant, Ethnic, and Racialized Women in Canadian History*, 2nd ed., eds. Marlene Epp and Franca Iacovetta (Toronto: University of Toronto Press, 2016). For the United States, see David A. Gerber, "Immigration Historiography at the Crossroads," *Reviews in American History* 39, no. 1 (March 17, 2011): 74–86; and Ronald H. Bayor, ed., *The Oxford Handbook of American Immigration and Ethnicity* (Oxford: Oxford University Press, 2013).

2 Most recently, see Christopher G. Anderson, *Canadian Liberalism and the Politics of Border Control, 1867–1967* (Toronto: University of Toronto Press, 2013); earlier work includes Ninette Kelley and Michael J. Trebilcock, *The Making of the Mosaic: A History of Canadian Immigration Policy*, 2nd ed. (Toronto: University of Toronto Press, 2010); Valerie Knowles, *Strangers at Our Gates: Canadian Immigration and Immigration Policy, 1540–2006* (Toronto: Dundurn, 2007); and Donald H. Avery, *Reluctant Host: Canada's Response to Immigrant Workers, 1896–1994* (Toronto: McClelland and Stewart, 1995).

3 Franca Iacovetta, *Gatekeepers: Reshaping Immigrant Lives in Cold War Canada* (Toronto: Between the Lines, 2006); and Epp and Iacovetta, *Sisters or Strangers?*

4 Frank Thistlethwaite, "Migration from Europe Overseas in the Nineteenth and Twentieth Centuries," *XIe Congrès International des Sciences Historiques Stockholm: Rapports, vol. 5* (Göteborg, 1960), repr. with a new "Postscript" in *A Century of European Migrations: 1830–1930*, ed. Rudolph J. Vecoli and Suzanne M. Sinke (Urbana-Champaign: University of Illinois Press, 1992), 17–49, 50–7; Benjamin Bryce and Alexander Freund, eds., *Entangling Migration History: Borderlands and Transnationalism in the United States and Canada* (Gainesville, FL: University Press of Florida, 2015); and Dirk Hoerder and Nora Faires, eds., *Migrants and Migration in Modern North America: Cross-Border Lives, Labor Markets, and Politics* (Durham, NC: Duke University Press, 2011).

5 Laurie K. Bertram, "New Icelandic Ethnoscapes: Material, Visual, and Oral Terrains of Cultural Expression in Icelandic-Canadian History, 1875–Present," PhD diss., University of Toronto, 2010, Chapter 4.

6 Frederic C. Bartlett, *Remembering: A Study in Experimental and Social Psychology*, 2nd ed. (1932; repr., Cambridge: Cambridge University Press, 1995); Maurice Halbwachs, *On Collective Memory* (1925; repr., Chicago: University of Chicago Press, 1992). Two excellent introductions to the history of memory and the study of memory in history are Alison Winter, *Memory: Fragments of a Modern History* (Chicago: University

of Chicago Press, 2012); and Geoffrey Cubitt, *History and Memory* (Manchester: Manchester University Press, 2007).

7 Karl Mannheim, "Das Problem der Generationen," *Kölner Vierteljahrshefte für Soziologie* 7 (1928): 157–85, 309–30. English translation in Karl Mannheim, *Essays on the Sociology of Knowledge: Collected Works, Volume 5*, ed. Paul Kecskemeti (1952; republ., New York: Routledge, 1972), 276–322.

8 For an excellent exception, see Hans Werner, *The Constructed Mennonite: History, Memory, and the Second World War* (Winnipeg: University of Manitoba Press, 2013).

9 Marianne Hirsch, *Family Frames: Photography, Narrative, and Postmemory* (Cambridge, MA: Harvard University Press, 1997); and Marianne Hirsch, *The Generation of Postmemory: Writing and Visual Culture After the Holocaust* (New York: Columbia University Press, 2012).

10 Gabriele Rosenthal, ed., *The Holocaust in Three Generations: Families of Victims and Perpetrators of the Nazi Regime* (New York: Continuum, 1998); Dan Bar-On, *Legacy of Silence: Encounters with Children of the Third Reich* (Cambridge, MA: Harvard University Press, 1989); Dan Bar-On, *Fear and Hope: Three Generations of the Holocaust* (Cambridge, MA: Harvard University Press, 1998); and Harald Welzer et al., *"Opa war kein Nazi": Nationalsozialismus und Holocaust im Familiengedächtnis* (Frankfurt / M: Fischer, 2002).

11 Roger Frie, *Not in My Family: German Memory and Responsibility After the Holocaust* (Oxford: Oxford University Press, 2017); and Alexander Freund, "A Canadian Family Talks About Oma's Life in Nazi Germany: Three-Generational Interviews and Communicative Memory," *Oral History Forum d'histoire orale* 29 (2009), Special Issue "Remembering Family, Analyzing Home: Oral History and the Family," 1–26. Abridged in *The Canadian Oral History Reader*, eds. Kristina Llewellyn, Alexander Freund, and Nolan Reilly (Montreal: McGill Queen's University Press, 2015), 159–79.

12 A recent synthesis appears in Caroline Sharples, *Postwar Germany and the Holocaust* (London: Bloomsbury Academic, 2015); and Viola B. Georgi, *Entliehene Erinnerung: Geschichtsbilder junger Migranten in Deutschland* (Hamburg: Hamburger Edition, 2003) shows how immigrant children in Germany approach the topic of the Holocaust.

13 Wilhelm Pinder, *Das Problem der Generation in der Kunstgeschichte Europas* (Berlin: 1926), cited by Mannheim, "The Problem of Generations," 282–83.

14 Mannheim, "The Problem of Generations," 283.

15 Alexander Freund, "A German Post-1945 Diaspora? German Migrants' Encounters with the Nazi Past," in *German Diasporic Experiences: Identity, Migration, and Loss*, eds. Mathias Schulze et al. (Waterloo, ON: Wilfrid Laurier University Press, 2008), 467–78.

16 Heinz Lehmann, *The German Canadians, 1750–1937: Immigration, Settlement and Culture*, ed. Gerhard Bassler (St. John's, NL: Jesperson Press, 1986); Gerhard P. Bassler, *The German Canadian Mosaic Today and Yesterday: Identities, Roots, and Heritage* (Ottawa: German-Canadian Congress, 1991); Alexander Freund, *Aufbruche nach dem Zusammenbruch: Die deutsche Nordamerika-Auswanderung nach dem Zweiten Weltkrieg* (Göttingen: V&R Unipress, 2004); and Jonathan Wagner, *A History of Migration from Germany to Canada, 1850–1939* (Vancouver: UBC Press, 2006).

17 Statistics Canada, "Ethnic Origin (264), Single and Multiple Ethnic Origin Responses (3), Generation Status (4), Age Groups (10) and Sex (3) for the

Population in Private Households of Canada, Provinces, Territories, Census Metropolitan Areas and Census Agglomerations, 2011 National Household Survey," NHS data table 99–010–X2011028, http://www12.statcan.gc.ca/nhs-enm/2011/dp-pd/dt-td/Lp-eng. (accessed 15 May 2017).

18 Alexander Freund, "German Emigration Fever Redux," *German-Canadian Studies Newsletter* 14, 1 (March 2009): 1–2, https://www.uwinnipeg.ca/german-canadian/docs/newsletters/newsletter-14.1.pdf (accessed 30 June 2017).

19 Alexander Freund, ed., *Beyond the Nation?: Immigrants' Local Lives in Transnational Cultures* (Toronto: University of Toronto Press, 2012); Barbara Lorenzkowski, *Sounds of Ethnicity: Listening to German North America, 1850–1914* (Winnipeg: University of Manitoba Press, 2010); Pascal Maeder, *Forging a New Heimat: Expellees in Post-War West Germany and Canada* (Göttingen: V&R Unipress, 2011); Patrick Farges, *Bindestrich-Kanadier?: Sudetendeutsche Sozialdemokraten und deutsche Juden als Exilanten in Kanada* (Bremen: Edition Lumière, 2015); Gerhard P. Bassler, *Escape Hatch: Newfoundland's Quest for German Industry and Immigration, 1950–1970* (St. John's, NL: Flanker Press, 2017); Christian Lieb, "Moving West: German-Speaking Immigration to British Columbia, 1945–1961" (PhD diss., University of Victoria, 2008); Hugh Avi Gordon, "Cheers and Tears: Relations Between Canadian Soldiers and German Civilians, 1944–46" (PhD diss., University of Victoria, 2010); Benjamin Bryce, "Making Ethnic Space: Education, Religion, and the German Language in Argentina and Canada, 1880–1930" (PhD diss., York University, 2013); Curtis B. Robinson, "Ethnic Elites, Propaganda, Recruiting and Intelligence in German-Canadian Ontario, 1914–1918" (PhD diss., Memorial University, 2019); Grant W. Grams, *Coming Home to the Third Reich: Return Migration of German Nationals from the United States and Canada, 1933–1941* (Jefferson, NC: McFarland, forthcoming); Maike Storks, "German Migrants in Montreal: Uses and Meanings of an Ethnic Category" (Master's thesis, Concordia University, 2011); Elizabeth Schulze, "Prisoners of War: A German-Canadian Post-war Memory Project" (Master's thesis, Simon Fraser University, 2012); Crystal Leochko, "Acknowledgement or Avoidance?: German-Canadian Immigrant Women's Memories of National Socialism" (Master's thesis, University of Manitoba, 2009); and Karen Brglez, "Canada at the End of the Cold War: The Influence of a Transatlantic 'Middle Power' on German Unification" (Master's thesis, University of Manitoba, 2014).

20 Christian Gerlach, *Extremely Violent Societies: Mass Violence in the Twentieth-Century World* (Cambridge: Cambridge University Press, 2010).

21 Quoted in Teigrob, Chapter 2 in this volume.

22 Gerhard P. Bassler, "Silent or Silenced Co-Founders of Canada?: Reflections on the History of German Canadians," *Canadian Ethnic Studies* 22, no. 1 (1990): 38–46.

23 Rudolf A. Helling and Bernd Hamm, *A Socio-Economic History of German-Canadians: They, Too, Founded Canada: A Research Report* (Wiesbaden: F. Steiner, 1984); Angelika E. Sauer, "The 'Ideal German Canadian': Politics, Academics and the Historiographical Construction of German-Canadian Identity," in *A Chorus of Different Voices: German-Canadian Identities*, eds. Angelika E. Sauer and Matthias Zimmer (New York: Peter Lang, 1998), 227–44.

24 Sauer, "The 'Ideal German Canadian,'" 237.

25 Dirk Hoerder, "German-Speaking Immigrants: Co-Founders or Mosaic?" *Zeitschrift für Kanada-Studien* 14, no. 2 (1994): 51–65.

26 Sauer, "The 'Ideal German Canadian,'" 231.

27 Ibid., 236–37.

28 Ibid., 237.

29 At times, *Vergangenheitsbewältigung* is put in quotation marks to signify that "overcoming the past," as the term implies, is impossible and also the opposite of the objectives of *Vergangenheitsbewältigung*.

30 Alexander Freund, "Toward an Ethics of Silence? Negotiating Off-the-record Events and Identity in Oral History," in *Oral History Off the Record: Toward an Ethnography of Practice,* ed. Anna Sheftel and Stacey Zembrzycki (New York: Palgrave, 2013), 223–38; Freund, "A Canadian Family Talks About Oma's Life in Nazi Germany"; Freund, "A German Post-1945 Diaspora?"; Alexander Freund, "Troubling Memories in Nation-Building: World War II Memories and Germans' Interethnic Encounters in Canada after 1945," *Histoire sociale/Social History* 39, no. 77 (2006): 129–55; Alexander Freund, "'How Come They're Nice to Me?' Deutsche und Juden nach dem Holocaust in Nordamerika," in *Migration und Erinnerung: Reflexionen über Wanderungserfahrungen in Europa und Nordamerika,* ed. Christiane Harzig (Göttingen: V&R unipress 2006), 143–56; Alexander Freund, "'Where were you während des Kriegs?' Kriegserzählungen deutscher Migranten in Nordamerika seit 1945," in *Zeichen des Krieges in Literatur, Film und den Medien, Vol. 1: Nordamerika und Europa*, ed. Christer Petersen (Kiel: Verlag Ludwig, 2004), 31–67; and Alexander Freund, "German Immigrants and the Nazi Past: How Memory Has Shaped Intercultural Relations," *Inroads: A Journal of Public Opinion* 15 (Summer/Fall 2004): 106–17.

31 Folkert Lüthke, *Psychologie der Auswanderung* (Weinheim: Deutscher Studienverlag, 1989); Freund, *Aufbrüche nach dem Zusammenbruch,* 268–69.

32 Michel-Rolph Trouillot, *Silencing the Past: Power and the Production of History* (Boston, MA: Beacon Press, 1995).

33 Alexander Freund, "Transnationalizing Home in Winnipeg: Refugees' Stories of the Places Between the 'Here-and-There,' in "Transforming Citizenship: Ethnicity, Transnationalism, and Belonging in Canada," special issue, *Canadian Ethnic Studies* 47, no. 1 (2015): 61–86. See also the large oral history project with refugees in Montreal conducted by the Centre for Oral and Digital Storytelling at Concordia University. See Steven High, *Oral History at the Crossroads: Sharing Life Stories of Survival and Displacement* (Vancouver: UBC Press, 2014); and Steven High, Edward Little, and Thi Ry Duong, eds. *Remembering Mass Violence: Oral History, New Media, and Performance* (Toronto: University of Toronto Press, 2014).

CHAPTER 1

A Flying Piano and Then—Silence: German-Canadian Memories of the Great War

ALEXANDER FREUND

> *The club on Mountain Avenue was broken into at one time and they threw the piano out the window [laughs]. I remember that.*
>
> —Mr. A. Kimmel, c. 1971

The Great War has often been viewed as a mythical coming of age of the Canadian nation state.[1] Although Canada was forced into the war by Great Britain and its troops fought under British command, the bloody battles of Ypres, Vimy Ridge, and Passchendaele nevertheless were constructed as rallying points for national identity politics. Public memories of the Great War have changed over time, however, and have differed across social divides.[2] Over the past decades, the narrative of Canada's making in the trenches of Flanders and Artois has become more inclusive, acknowledging women's and Indigenous people's contributions. But this democratization of history has not questioned the underlying myth.[3] Studies of the Canadian home front have done more to illuminate the diversity of local responses, the resistance to the war and conscription in Quebec and on the Prairies, and the religious and political pacifism of various groups within the nation.[4] Recent studies have focused more pointedly on the history of mythmaking and have highlighted the complexity of Canada's collective memories of the Great War.[5] Grating against the story of national unity forged through militaristic heroism are the experiences of those who were publicly excluded from the nation for the sake of unity—"enemy aliens."

Immigrants broadly associated with the Central powers (Germany, Austria–Hungary, the Ottoman Empire, and Bulgaria) were branded potential spies and saboteurs; they were considered no longer trustworthy even if they had long become naturalized Canadians.[6] The experiences, memories, and narratives of German Canadians are critical in understanding the lasting and complex legacy of the Great War in Canadian collective memory. Rather than simply expanding Canada's history of the Great War by including yet another group's experiences, this chapter studies German-Canadian memories of the conflict in order to explore the fragility and the costs of maintaining a dominant national narrative of a unified nation.

If the Great War was remembered as "the crucible in which the nation was forged," how did German Canadians remember the First World War?[7] Answers are not easy to come by. One reason is that we know little about how German Canadians *experienced* the war. German-Canadian historian Gerhard Bassler argued in 1991 that "the First World War was the main watershed" for the community. Throughout the conflict, German Canadians were demonized, with fatal effects on German-Canadian social and cultural life.[8] In Manitoba, according to Art Grenke, who in the early 1970s studied Winnipeg's German community during the war years, churches and clubs remained open, even though they shifted their activities from celebrations to helping those who were unemployed and interned. Germans in the countryside suffered less discrimination than did those in the cities.[9] Nevertheless, Germans across the nation experienced both state repression and Anglo-Canadian hostility. Toward the end of the war, the German language became increasingly censored and suppressed in education and journalism and all enemy aliens had to register, report regularly to authorities, and surrender their weapons. Those who had become naturalized after 1902 were also disenfranchised. Some German Canadians were interned.[10] According to Peter Moogk, "all these provisions seem reasonable and justifiable, but their application was increasingly harsh, punitive, and unselective."[11] Agreeing with Bassler, Grenke argued that by the end of the war the German community had been shattered.[12]

How did members of Winnipeg's German community remember this "watershed" time, this "shattering" of their community? One answer, the one pursued here, lies in an obscure collection of oral history interviews conducted around 1971–72 with German-speaking, pre-1914 immigrants in Winnipeg. The interviewer was Arthur (Art) Grenke, who in the early 1970s was writing his doctoral dissertation at the University of Manitoba about Winnipeg's 1872 to 1919 German community. Grenke came from West Germany to Canada sometime in the 1950s or 1960s and ended up interviewing pioneers for the Manitoba Museum. The project constituted an intergenerational dialogue among German immigrants about the Great War. This exchange, as I argue in this chapter, was shaped by silence and it generated silence. Silence emerged, in part, through the dynamics of the oral history project itself, as I show in the first half of this chapter. Grenke did not pursue the First World War in any systematic fashion, and his interviewees, even when prompted, offered only sparse memory fragments. Indeed, only one "story" was shared by several interviewees. At some point during or after the war—so the story was told—an unknown group of men went to one of the city's three German clubs and threw a piano out of the window. As I demonstrate in the second half of this chapter, the story of the flying piano, however, was a story of silence and avoidance of conflict rather than of engagement. Indeed, it is difficult to call it a story; it is more of a story fragment. In several interviews, the piano story was accompanied or surrounded by other, often more personal and developed stories. Yet, these often idiosyncratic stories were as well stories of silence. As Christine Ensslen shows in Chapter 8, community silences about the war also infused memories of later generations of German Canadians in Saskatchewan.

All of these silences in the German-Canadian community's collective memory of the Great War help us understand that even two generations after the war, German-speaking immigrants found it difficult to adopt and adapt the national narrative of the Great War as a national turning point. Furthermore, they failed to develop their own counter-narrative that would provide meaning to their wartime experiences (despite Québécois and ethnic counter-narratives to Anglo-Canadian identity flourishing in the wake of the Quiet Revolution and the official introduction of multiculturalism in the 1960s). Rather than being simply a result of forgetting, the silences indicate that German Canadians found it difficult, if not impossible, to feel that they belonged, whether to a concrete local community or an imagined nation.

Intergenerational Silences in Oral History

Grenke's collection of interviews with members of Winnipeg's pioneer German community was filled with silences about the First World War. Some of these silences can be explained by the way in which the oral history project was carried out and by the broader social context wherein the research was undertaken. By the early 1970s, when Grenke conducted his interviews, Canadian society's need for remembering the Great War had changed. Canada was slowly transforming from an Anglo-Protestant to a more inclusive, "multicultural," and "peacekeeping" society that celebrated diversity and prided itself on welcoming immigrants and refugees. In the flurry of activities and publications at the fiftieth anniversary of the war in the mid-1960s, politicians, historians, veterans, and other commentators declared Vimy Ridge to constitute "the birth of the nation," but the Great War receded into the background shortly thereafter.[13] At the time of the interviews, Canadians were less concerned with remembering the Great War and more involved in a frantic search for a new "Canadian" identity—carefully balanced between Great Britain and the United States. Those years were a time of reflection on the nation's history. In 1967, Canada celebrated 100 years of confederation. In 1971, Manitoba celebrated its 100th anniversary as a province. Two years later, it was Winnipeg's turn to celebrate its 100th birthday. Historians all over Manitoba scoured the archives to reconstruct the previous century in order to understand how and why things had changed. This was also a time when the discipline of history was in turmoil. Increasingly, historians wanted to research the lives of "common people" and write history "from the bottom up."[14] In North America, "ethnic" historians began to write their groups' histories, slowly replacing earlier hagiographic and assimilationist approaches with a more stringent, social scientific approach that celebrated ethnic diversity and cultural maintenance. As they expanded their scope and found insufficient documents in the archives, some historians, archivists, and museum curators adopted oral history as a new method of generating material where there was none.[15] At the Manitoba Museum, one such project involved the collection of oral histories with local notables and pioneers.

One of the interviewers working for the Manitoba Museum around 1971–1972 was Arthur Grenke. In his dissertation, he used quantitative and qualitative methods to study the early German settlement in Winnipeg. Of the sixty-five interviews he conducted with Germans, Austrians, Russian Germans, and German Americans who had immigrated before 1914, forty are accessible. The interviews focused on immigration, settlement patterns, homesteading, church, and religious and cultural traditions at such events as weddings, funerals, and Christmas and New Year's Eve celebrations.[16] The First World War was mentioned in merely twenty-two of the forty interviews, seldom more than once, and almost always in response to a question by Grenke. Few interviewees offered elaborate wartime stories. Great War memories came in fragments and focused almost exclusively on experiences within the local German-Canadian community. Neither Grenke nor his interlocutors talked about the national German-Canadian experience and no one mentioned perhaps the most notorious example of anti-German sentiment, the renaming of Berlin to Kitchener, Ontario, in 1916.

This limited focus is, in part, a result of Grenke's own interest in local experiences and the propensity in oral narration to draw upon experience rather than memorized facts. This is particularly true of stories that rely solely on local, personal experience and hearsay, rather than historical literacy. If any of the interviewees had read histories of the war that were published in the 1960s or had followed any of the media coverage of the fiftieth anniversary of the First World War, they did not disclose such knowledge in the recordings.[17] The idea that the war was somehow central to Canadian identity and history was completely absent from Grenke's interviews. But then again, perhaps silence was German Canadians' only possible response to what Canadian historians have called a "nationalistic story."[18] Yet, while it is plausible that German Canadians would not recall Vimy Ridge as Canada's "birthplace," it is less clear why they seemed to remember almost nothing of their own home front experiences.

Some of the German-Canadian silences about the war were generated by Grenke's interview questions. In the recordings, church, tradition, language, and employment were substantially more important to both interviewer and interviewees than the ostensibly political experience of the First World War. In part, this may be the result of historiographical conventions *en vogue* at the time. In the early 1970s, social history was understood as history with the politics left out. Thus, Grenke asked systematically and extensively about foodways, settlement patterns, religion and church, and cultural practices and traditions. But he inquired little (and not systematically or even consistently) about political activities, ideology, or political events, including the two world wars that all of his interviewees lived through. Even a social historian may have been interested in finding out how domestic changes brought on by the war affected settlement, employment, and culture; Grenke, however, asked only some of his interviewees about the war, and then only few questions. The First World War most frequently came up in discussions about German language instruction at school, church, and German clubs. When two of his interviewees told him that they had served in the Canadian army in 1917–1918—an unusual experience for a German Canadian—he did not follow up.[19]

In the few instances when Grenke tried to pursue wartime experiences in greater detail, he encountered other problems. His interviewees were elderly and often had difficulty hearing or remembering. The recording conditions were noisy: children were playing in the background, other participants held conversations in the same room, and televisions and radios were blaring. Male narrators' pronunciation was often slurred, which was made worse by their deeper voices that were difficult to understand in a noisy environment. Several interviewees did not seem to be interested in being interviewed—oral history with "ordinary folk" was still uncommon at the time. Some participants were confused about the purpose of Grenke's project and wondered whether he worked for a newspaper or the government. Nevertheless, I argue that the silence about the Great War was not simply a result of forgetting: the narrators told many elaborate stories about other topics and gave detailed descriptions of traditions, parishes, pastors, and neighbourhoods.

Since, in the early 1970s, Canadians in general thought little about the First World War, Grenke's project was, in many ways, not conducive to capturing wartime-related stories. Yet, Grenke provided ample opportunities for his interviewees to tell "their" stories, stories that were important to them, whether he asked for them or not. We know from other oral history projects that narrators often tell stories that are urgent for them to share in spite of their interviewer's agenda. Grenke used semi-structured interviews that present open questions (e.g., tell me about the German Club) rather than closed prompts that require one-word responses (e.g., what year did you join the German Club?).

This interview format invites participants to reminisce and narrate and to go off on "tangents," in other words tell anecdotes and tales important to them rather than their interviewers. Grenke was a patient listener who remained silent when interviewees collected their thoughts. He asked his interlocutors about personal experiences and observations of the German community. Thus, interviewees had sufficient opportunities to reminisce and "vent." While a few narrators used such opportunities, these lonely voices did not constitute—and indeed illuminated the lack of—a collective German-Canadian memory of the Great War.

There were other factors that may not have been conducive to capturing wartime stories. Most of the interviewees were from Eastern Europe and perhaps that is why the political memory of the First World War was not as poignant. For many participants, it was possible to switch identities from German to Russian during wartime. Some identified themselves in public as Russians rather than Germans in order to avoid harassment or unemployment. Others lost their jobs but quickly found new employment. A few remembered that either during or after the war German-language teaching became prohibited, but for most interviewees, the maintenance of German language appeared not to be important. Those who remembered other Germans being interned generally agreed that they had foolishly talked too much. Only two interviewees had served in the Canadian army, none were interned, and none had relatives who served in the Canadian army or were interned. Further, Grenke had recruited most subjects through local churches, which were largely unaffected by the war. While some interviewees had been members of one of the German clubs (which were more negatively influenced by the war), these were not their main sites of social life and cultural identification. Participants' wartime experiences were not poignant and thus not memorable—at least that is what the recordings suggest.

For historians using these interviews forty-five years after they were recorded, further silences were introduced by the lack of contextual information about the interviews, at times poor audio quality, and multiple transfers from original reel-to-reel tapes to sixty- or ninety-minute cassette tapes, and eventually to digital audio files. The lack of contextual information is the most problematic. None of the recordings—digitized copies made accessible by the Manitoba Museum—have an introduction that states the interviewer's and interviewee's name or date and place of interview.[20] Many recordings begin in mid-sentence and often end in mid-sentence. Did Grenke run out of tape or was the rest of the interview lost somewhere in the transfer from Grenke to the museum or during the museum's process of archiving, copying, or digitizing? The museum has no further information and there is no clue in the other recordings. We know the interviewees' names solely from the digital copy file names (e.g., "Mr. Henry Kendel"), but not all participant names are recorded (e.g., Henry Kendel's wife is not mentioned as an interviewee, even though she participated in the interview). At least one audio file seems to be mislabelled, and there appear to be more than one interview (or parts of an interview) split over several audio files.

It is not unusual for oral history collections, even those housed at public archives, to lack basic contextual information. Fortunately, Grenke's publications provide crucial information. Therefore, these aural fragments provide insight into past experiences and memories and show that German Canadians' silences about the war were not simply the result of improper historical method and technology. The recordings, despite their shortcomings, illuminate how the processes of silence and evasion function in the narrators' story fragments about the war.

The Flying Piano—An Iconic Story of Collective Memory

Grenke's oral history collection helps us understand how Germans in Winnipeg in the 1970s, over half a century after the conflict, remembered the Great War. In 1914, Winnipeg, with a population of about 150,000, was Canada's third-largest city, and it was the Dominion's most ethnically diverse centre.[21] Among the immigrants, "there were some ten thousand people of German origin."[22] Many of these Germans, including the interviewees, were still struggling to establish themselves and their families when the First World War began.

Nevertheless, dominant narratives of war, annually recited in major news outlets and at government-sponsored ceremonies at publicly and privately funded war memorials, do not simply make a nation's collective memory. Across the political ruptures of wars, people continue to live their everyday lives. The experiences of personal loss and devastation during war in the battlefields and on the home front sit next to the disruptive everyday experiences. Such occurrences include sickness, unemployment, and other losses (often as a result of poverty and inadequate access to hygiene and medical care) as well as religious rituals, cultural traditions, and personal celebrations that provide a sense of continuity and communal cohesion. The Great War, Jim Blanchard wrote in his history of Winnipeg, "is remembered in fragments": monuments on streets, plaques in churches, and private memorials to lost relatives, friends, and colleagues.[23] But remembered and lived experiences do not always correspond. For those Winnipeggers who actually lived through the war, however, "the situation was very different. War was a daily reality, colouring everything, changing everything, derailing the bouncy confidence that had been the ethos of the place until then. Winnipeggers learned resignation and grim determination from the war, and many were worn down by grief and worry."[24] While German Canadians lived in Winnipeg during the war, few lived "through" the battlefield experience that left deep scars on the bodies and minds of soldiers and their families.

What were German-speaking immigrants' everyday worries in the wake of the war? Few German immigrants were allowed to join the Canadian army. The harsh realities of death, mutilation, and shell shock did not enter Winnipeg's German-Canadian community, although many may have worried about relatives and friends in Europe fighting on the side of the Axis or Allied powers. Wartime, even for those not directly affected by the trench warfare, was nevertheless a time of high anxiety. Were the immigrants worried about food, shelter, and employment? About their children's future? About English-Canadian society's and the state's hostile responses to all things German? Were they afraid, cautious, defiant, or arrogant? Did they hasten or slow down their attempts at integration or even assimilation?

Even if one did not fight in the war or had a relative fighting in the trenches of France, Winnipeg's home front was busy. There was much that could have been remembered about this home front experience. But Grenke did not ask for any details and few particulars were volunteered. As Blanchard has shown, the Great War became a public spectacle in Winnipeg, and it was impossible to ignore. From the outbreak of the war in August 1914 until Armistice Day in November 1918, Winnipeg staged countless military and citizen parades, drawing up to 50,000 spectators at the beginning and up to 100,000 (two thirds of the city's population!) at the end. Only one interviewee volunteered information about the Armistice Day parades, which she described as "wonderful."[25] This tells us that Germans participated in, or at least knew about these

Figure 1.1. Peace Day Celebration, Winnipeg, c. 1919. Archives of Manitoba, Foote Collection, Nr. 354, P7393/7, digital image number PR18-000223.

events. No interviewee mentioned the annual "Patriotic Week" that drew in many of the city's businesses, associations, clubs, and other groups. There were demonstration trenches on Main Street to advertise war bonds, yet only one person talked about buying war bonds. Tens of thousands of Winnipeggers were mourning the heavy losses that began with the battle of Ypres in April 1915, and public memorial services became ubiquitous, yet only one interviewee spoke about hearing news of neighbours' fallen sons. No one talked about soldiers coming into the city from nearby training camps to frequent bars and other public places, or about visibly scarred veterans roaming the streets. Soldiers and civilians clashed with Winnipeg and military police in April 1916, leading to a riot involving thousands, but about this too the interviewees were mute. No interviewee recounted the increasing labour unrest and major strikes in 1917 and 1918 in advance of the General Strike of 1919. Even upon request by Grenke, few participants remembered the introduction of prohibition in June 1916.[26]

Figure 1.2. The former German Society building at 61 Heaton Avenue. Photo: A. Freund, 2020.

Even closer to home, no interviewee mentioned the silence that apparently dominated the North End—where most Germans lived—in August 1914 or the first accounts of vigilante violence against central European immigrants. According to Grenke, "rowdy elements in the city expressed their enthusiasm for the war effort by beating up German-speaking citizens, breaking windows and doors of the German Club on Heaton Avenue, and by attacking the German and Austrian consulates in the city."[27] There was no mention of this in any of the interviews. While some participants recalled being laid off, no one remembered Anglo-Canadian attempts to "boycott the sale of German goods."[28] No interviewee mentioned that in January 1915, local authorities, searching (in vain) for German spies, ransacked German bookstores, clubs, and churches. No one reported the growing surveillance by militia and police, who arrested Germans "for 'suspicious' behaviour, such as walking along railway tracks on their way home from work."[29] One interviewee mentioned the disenfranchisement, a few recounted having to register and report. None talked about the raid of five German and Austrian clubs by local military authorities on 25 January 1917.[30] No participant brought up the July 1917 raid on German churches and clubs, including the German Society wherein the caretaker's wife was injured.[31] Several interviewees claimed that Germans were left in peace during the war, that nothing happened, and that no one was bothered.[32]

In spite of all of this silence in the interviews, one story emerged that was shared by several narrators. It was the story of the flying piano. What happened? According to Grenke, returning soldiers, disgruntled at the postwar unemployment, rampaged through the North End for two days in January 1919. German businesses were looted and destroyed. Moreover, "German homes were broken into and their occupants on occasion beaten and forced to kiss the British flag. Soldier and hoodlum elements also broke into the German-Hungarian club, the only German club still in operation. . . . [There,] club windows and doors were broken and the piano was thrown out of the second floor [*sic*] window." Grenke explained: "Unlike in 1914, English-Canadian newspapers tended not to condemn this mistreatment of Germans and alien enemies. Rather, the attacks of the soldiers were seen as being justified by the Bolshevik and treasonable tendencies of the aliens."[33] Contemporary accounts painted a slightly different picture. According to the *Manitoba Free Press*, "mobs, which were composed of returned soldiers and youths," had rampaged through the city and attacked "aliens" (including Italians and Chinese) and "Reds." The newspaper and veterans organizations were critical of the rampaging "mob" and blamed the government for failing to intervene more forcefully and for veterans' high unemployment rates.[34]

Most participants did not narrate an elaborate tale, but offered only anecdotal fragments, often as asides, accompanied by chuckles. Unlike most of Grenke's interviewees, Fred Martin was from Germany and closely connected to the German Club on Heaton Avenue. Born into a middle-class family in Dresden sometime in the 1890s, he immigrated to Winnipeg in December 1913 and worked in paint manufacturing. After the outbreak of the war, he was "kicked out" of his job "because I had turned from a German into a Hun." At the time of the interview in 1971–72, Martin was still incensed about his treatment in 1914. He said, "when all of a sudden the opinion about a human being is dependent on when a government announces war and then you are

Figure 1.3. Great War Veterans Association parade lining up at Broadway and Main, Winnipeg, 4 June 1919. Archives of Manitoba, David Millar Collection, Winnipeg General Strike photographs, N12295, previously Winnipeg General Strike 4, P8232/5.

reduced to a Hun . . . well, it's impossible! That man is not changed by what they did somewhere else!" In his account of the war, Martin seemed to collapse the 1917 raid on the German Society and the 1919 trashing of the German-Hungarian club: "The German Club, they were also forced to close down in the war. They raided it. I mean they [unclear]. And they threw the piano through the first-floor window onto the street [chuckling] and it was disbursed." Martin believed the club closed in 1915.[35]

While most interviewees, if they mentioned culprits at all, blamed either soldiers or "hooligans," Mrs. Bernhardt believed it was Bolsheviks. A Volga German, born in 1905, she came to Winnipeg at the age of six. She spoke Low German at home, attended German school, and was a member of the German Christ Lutheran Church. During the war, when she turned ten years old, she began to help her mother clean houses. The German school was not affected by the First World War, but "they stopped the Germans. How they closed the German club down on McGregor and Mountain. They threw the piano out of the window and smashed it to a thousand pieces. . . . [to Grenke:] Of course you would not remember that, you were too young then. But we were not even free to say that we were German in them days. . . . We said we were Russians." When Grenke asked her if Germans felt depressed because Germany had been defeated, Mrs. Bernhardt responded:

> Our people did not because we were not actually Germans. Oh, I think the "high Germans," the ones that were actually the real Germans, they would have felt defeated. That is for sure, but they dared not show it here because they would have been thrown in. I will never forget, in the spring of 1919 . . . I think it was the Bolsheviks actually that went up to Mountain and smashed all the windows in that hall and threw the piano out onto Mountain Avenue. It went into a thousand pieces. I remember seeing it. It was pathetic. You were scared to go out of your houses in them days. You know, especially if you were a real German. It did not bother us because we did not declare ourselves as Germans—we declared ourselves as Russians. Well, we were! We were Russian-Germans. I wasn't born in Germany, I was born in Russia.[36]

No other story about the wartime was recalled as frequently as the story about the piano, yet it was almost always mentioned in passing, with confusion about basic details, and with dubious claims to being an eyewitness. There were a few exceptions. The following is an account given by Mr. and Mrs. Kendel. In many ways, the Kendels were representative of Grenke's interviewees. Henry Kendel's family emigrated from Austria in 1903, following a brother who had already settled in Winnipeg. In 1904, Henry's father bought a house. Mr. Kendel's wife, who participated in the interview but was not noted by Grenke as an interviewee, came to Winnipeg as a toddler in 1904.[37] In their childhood, the Kendels' playmates were all "German," as they said. Much of their social life revolved around Trinity Lutheran Church. The couple was active in the German and Austrian clubs and organized parties before the First World War. Mr. Kendel became naturalized in 1914. Early on in the two-hour interview the topic turned to social and club life. The exchange that developed was the most sustained and complex discussion in all of the interviews regarding what occurred to the German clubs in Winnipeg throughout the First World War. The drama that unfolded, however, was less about what actually happened during or after the war and more about who got to tell the story and how.

> Grenke: What happened to the [Austrian] club during the war?
>
> Henry Kendel: Well, they closed them up. Well, they closed up on their own, rather.
>
> Mrs. Kendel: [excitedly:] But, oh Henry, do you remember? When the war started and that? They really got nasty and they threw the piano—.
>
> Henry Kendel: [impatiently:] Just wait, just wait.
>
> Mrs. Kendel: Oh, excuse me.
>
> Henry Kendel: This was the Austrian club.
>
> Mrs. Kendel: Yes.
>
> Henry Kendel: But then when the war broke out, they had that German club right over here on Heaton Street [*sic*], right off [unclear], maybe you heard about it. Then you know some of the soldiers, they got pretty nasty, because [they allowed] the Germans to go into the army. Well, see, they were after me two or three times. [They'd grab me] [They used to have them at a hotel], used to have them [open]. Yes. [you came there for] a glass of beer. [unclear] over here. And then, [we used] to go for a glass of beer [after work]. And then there is recruiting officers, "Well, come on, why aren't you in the army?" Well, you couldn't be nasty because they had it in for the Germans. Well, you know that. So, asked you your name and everything and, "What nationality?" "German." "Well, we can't take you." So, that was it.

If interviewees were determined to tell a story that was important to them, they were distracted neither by the interviewer's concrete question nor by another interview participant's interjections. Before talking about the clubs, Kendel wanted to tell the story of failed recruitment and harassment. Indeed, other German Canadians reported similar experiences. Mr. Jochen "John" Plischke, born in Russia around 1900, arrived with his family in Winnipeg in 1902 and settled in the North End. He quit school after grade eight and began to work at Eaton's. Asked how he experienced the First World War, he said, "Well, they wanted to recruit me [about 1915/1916, before conscription] when I was sixteen. You couldn't go on Main Street. Soldiers would grab you and take you in. Says, 'How old are you?' 'Sixteen.' 'Oh, you're too young, yet.' Couple blocks on, they got you again. There were recruiting offices." Indeed, Blanchard wrote that recruitment strategies became more rigorous during the war, but more so in 1917 and especially in 1918, when even conscription failed to get enough recruits. In the spring of 1918, all exemptions to conscription were cancelled: "All across the country, desperate measures were taken to raise troops. Police raided pool halls looking for eligible men. All men had to carry their conscription papers at all times and men picked up on the street were sometimes taken directly to army camps."[38] By that time, conscription was no longer an issue for those immigrants who had been disenfranchised in 1917 because they could not be conscripted. For Henry Kendel, this seemed to be the only wartime experience worth mentioning. It is unclear whether the attack on the club on Heaton actually referred to the raid in 1917. Kendel quickly turned to the postwar period, now apparently correcting his earlier statement that the German Club was trashed at the beginning of the war, and he also got the location right (the German-Hungarian Society that was trashed in 1919 was on 386 McGregor on the corner of Mountain Avenue). Before telling the story of the flying piano, however, the Kendels told Grenke another story, one Grenke had been told by only one other interviewee—the attack on the Riedle Brewery:

> Henry Kendel: So anyway, when the war was over and oh, did they raise heck here. But I don't think it was the soldiers so much. It was just a bunch of young hooligans.
>
> Mrs. Kendel: They really wrecked this brewery over here, the Riedle's.
>
> Henry Kendel: They walked over Louise Bridge here and the brewery was here—[to Grenke:] you weren't here, heh?—on the corner of [unclear]—
>
> Mrs. Kendel: [to Grenke:] Would you be familiar with Riedle's Brewery on Talbot? No?
>
> Henry Kendel: They ripped it down last year. So they come over here and they smashed that place—smashed everything!
>
> Mrs. Kendel: Beer kegs rolling down the street.

> Henry Kendel: I know one fellow, he [unclear] beer [from] the brewery, right down to the next street here. Rolled it.
>
> Mrs. Kendel: But I mean even at the club, Henry, do you remember? They threw the piano—
>
> Henry Kendel: [testily:] Well, yes, so?
>
> Mrs. Kendel: Through the windows!
>
> Henry Kendel: From here, they went up Mountain Avenue to the Mountain German Club and they went upstairs there and decided to raising [unclear] there. So there is a piano up there, so he gets a hold of that piano and rrrrrupp right through the window, right through the window.
>
> Mrs. Kendel: [laughing] terrible.

Grenke ended the discussion of the club at that point with a question about Riedle's brewery. Despite all of Mr. Kendel's attempts to maintain sole authorship over the piano story, Mrs. Kendel prompted him to tell the story of Riedle's and she interjected twice with the piano-story cue before her husband was actually ready to share the story. He was audibly unhappy about this interference. At the same time, Mrs. Kendel prevented her husband from remaining silent in regards to the piano story. But is it a story? Mr. Kendel did not add any further information about the event. The story is simple: "they" went to the German Club on Mountain Avenue and threw a piano out of the second-floor window. A disagreement arose, however, about who was responsible for this riot. While Mrs. Kendel later in the interview clearly indicted the soldiers, her husband tried to protect them: "I don't think it was the soldiers so much. It was just a bunch of young hooligans."

As with the Kendels, several interviewees disagreed about who threw the piano (soldiers, hooligans, Bolsheviks) and whether this happened during or after the war. Here is how the discussion continued between the Kendels:

> Grenke: Why did they pick on Riedle's brewery? There were other businesses [unclear]. . .
>
> Henry Kendel: Oh, no, no, no—
>
> Mrs. Kendel: Because Mr. Riedle was German.

Henry Kendel: No, no, no, no. [unclear] [businesses] Because he was a German, see? And they had it in for the Germans and the Italians. Well, you know that. That was in 1914 to 18.

Grenke [incredulous]: They had it in for the Italians too?

Henry Kendel: Oh! Italians and Germans! We were afraid to go out, you know.

Mrs. Kendel: It was terrible to be German at that time, of German descent. It was really bad.

Henry Kendel: [unclear]. It was bad. So then, from there, well, they quieted down a little, and that same old Riedle, that had the brewery, he—these returned men, the veterans, when they came back, see, they opened up these legions. Well, see the first legion was opened up in '25.

Mrs. Kendel: I wouldn't know, Henry.

Henry Kendel: Yes, in '25 they opened up the first legion, for the returning men to have their beer. So the same old Riedle, he used to supply them with beer. He—[unclear] for nothing. Just to get on the good side in the day. As time went on, it got better and better. Riedle was the best man then. Well, you know. It was most of these young punks that had nothing to do.

Mrs. Kendel: It was a lot of soldiers too, Henry.

Henry Kendel: They [the hooligans/punks] were really the ones smashing everything. It wasn't the soldiers so much.[39]

The last lines of this interview segment intensified the Kendels' interpretive conflict over who was to blame for the riot. This disagreement was driven in part by Mr. Kendel's anxiousness about saying anything "political"—he preferred to blame unnamed punks and hooligans rather than veterans; to him, this seemed a safer interpretation. His statement, however, was undermined by the brewery story. The Kendels, together with Ed Horch and John Plischke, were the only interviewees to talk about Riedle's, and here the Kendels offered an ironic gem.[40] After looting the brewery because it was owned by "a German," a few years later the veterans bought his beer because "Riedle was the best man." The irony was watertight only if Kendel held the soldiers responsible but, nevertheless, he stuck to his version of blaming "punks." This caution not to say anything that could be seen as anti-patriotic was shared by several other male interviewees. It was another demonstration of most of the participants' disinterest in politics, which many admitted explicitly in Grenke's questions about German immigrants' involvement in political life.

It is unclear to what degree the Kendels drew on hearsay and to what degree they were eyewitnesses to these events. According to contemporary newspaper reports, the Edelweiss Brewery, owned by Arnold Wilhelm Riedle, was severely damaged, but several veterans also spoke out in favour of Riedle, who had been financially supporting returned soldiers.[41]

Among the interviewees, there were competing versions of the story about the riot. John Plischke remembered the riot, including the attack on Riedle's, differently. Asked whether other Germans were affected by the war, he said nothing happened to the church, but "they" planned to "wreck Riedle. . . . But the police stopped them." Plischke continued: "They were marching here from the barracks, you know, marching around McGregor." Plischke described the route of the mob: "About 200, 300 soldiers, right after the war. They brought the Germans down and if they didn't kiss the flag, they took them and asked them for their identification card and took them along on the march. It was awful. But the police stopped all of that." He claimed to have been an eyewitness to the trashing of the German Club: "They stopped at McGregor, at the German Hall, they—I'd seen it myself—they threw that piano out there of that second floor, they threw it right out, down to the pavement. It was wrecked." Mrs. Plischke added that the First World War was worse than the Second World War because "they were just out of control, they could not control them. All the damage they did to the German Hall here." She had heard about "the piano, out through the window. . . . Just kids, kids that had no intelligence, if you know what I mean, just mischief."[42]

Ed Horch added yet another version to the story about Riedle's brewery. Born in the Lutheran colony of Eichenfeld, Russia, in 1903, Horch had immigrated with his family in 1909. His mother bought a house in 1914. Horch attended German school at Christ Lutheran Church until, according to Horch, the school was closed down during the war. He told one of the few elaborate stories about the immediate postwar year, especially the "little upheaval . . . when the boys came back."

> Ed Horch: They went to Riedle Brewery, it used to be in Elmwood, Riedle Brewery, they went in there too, in the office. I heard that the man had his son's picture on the desk. And Riedle was a big man, you know. . . . So when they walked in they asked "Who is that Canadian soldier?" He said, "That's my son." They said, "Well, okay then. It's alright." But why they wanted to make trouble like that I don't know.
>
> Grenke: I heard they wrecked the brewery.
>
> Horch: Yes, no, they didn't. What they wrecked was the German hall on McGregor. They threw the piano out. I'd seen it myself. The piano lying on the street with all the wires torn. That was really a fight over there, really a fight. They smashed everything inside.[43]

Unlike the story of Riedle's brewery, which was shared by only three participants, most of Grenke's interviewees were familiar with the piano story. None, however, wove this memory fragment into a cohesive, elaborate story. Yet, even this memory fragment carried meanings. In whatever way Grenke's interviewees described the piano-flying incident, they all portrayed it as a senseless act of violence. As such, this story served as an allegory or parable for the larger experience of the German-Canadian community of Winnipeg. According to German Canadians, they had nothing to do with the war, and any violence they experienced at the hands of the state (registration, surveillance, searches, disenfranchisement, exclusion from military service, and internment) or individuals (rioting of veterans and vandalism of hooligans) was just as senseless as the destruction of a piano. It harkens back to Blanchard's assessment that anti-foreigner and anti-German sentiment escalated into a "collective insanity" at the end of the war.[44] Perhaps, this likeness of a flying piano was all that Germans in Winnipeg needed to remember in order to integrate this dark period into their life stories and the story of their community, to find comfort in forgetting and silence, and to progress in their individual (if not collective) projects of integration and upward mobility. No elaborate story was needed, just an image that had been polished by time and memory and deliberate, selective forgetting.

Conclusion

As Christine Ensslen shows in Chapter 8 of this collection, silences in German-Canadian memories about wartime were also present in other forms of reminiscing on the Canadian prairies. Just as did Grenke's interviews, the biographies of German pioneer women in Saskatchewan teemed with accounts of cultural practices, religious beliefs, and homestead memories but were silent about the two world wars. Similar to this chapter, Ensslen's piece shows that such silences were not simply a result of forgetting. They were explained in part by the historical experience of anti-German hostility, in part by the breakdown of intergenerational dialogue, and in part by the type of reminiscing that took place.

What do historians do with such silences about wartime? What are their meanings? Did the silence about the First World War mean simply that it was not a significant event in German Winnipeggers' lives? Or did the war trigger a self-silencing that was reinforced by ethnic gatekeepers (such as the editors of *Der Nordwesten* urging their readers to keep quiet, the leaders of German clubs that voluntarily restricted their activities, or the leaders of German churches that dropped "German" from their names); by Anglo-Canadian hostility; and, later, by the repeat experience of the Second World War? Did the silence simply mark the war's insignificance for individual or collective identities? Or had self-silencing become so ingrained over half a century of two wars and anti-German hostility that it had begun to shape identities at a profound but nearly imperceptible level?[45] Was this a silence that had begun during the First World War and, as Grenke suggested, "All that Germans of Winnipeg asked of the host society, even before the war had ended, was that they be left in peace"?[46] Or did this silence result from a lack of intergenerational dialogue? Perhaps, as Elliot Worsfold demonstrates in Chapter 5, such breakdown in intergenerational dialogue was far more widespread, revolving not simply around wartime memories but also around competing ideas of the best ways to integrate into Canadian society. Indeed, forgetting and silence are essential practices of Canadian society at large, as Robert Teigrob reminds us in Chapter 2: after the Second World War, Canadians, after all, were eager to forget that their prime minister had paid a visit to Nazi Germany in 1937.

Histories of discrimination and injustice are often researched and told by succeeding generations, whether in the case of Chinese Canadian exclusion, Ukrainian Canadian internment, or Japanese

Canadian relocation and dispossession. The sons and daughters of Grenke's interviewees, however, had no interest in their parents' history. No historian emerged from that generation to document their parents' lives. As Ensslen writes in Chapter 8, German-Canadian descendants writing biographies of their pioneer ancestors in Saskatchewan "failed to mention either war, let alone the impact it had on their ancestors. This absence seems to have been a choice on the part of the biographers."[47] It was newcomers like Grenke, whose parents had not lived through the events in Canada, who conducted the research. But unlike other ethnic groups in Canada, German-Canadian historians have been hesitant to research "their" group's wartime experiences. Historians, as Teigrob in Chapter 2 and Brglez in Chapter 4 remind us, have at times been at the forefront of selective silencing.

As this case study demonstrates, silence in projects of oral history, biography, and official history may stem not simply from a lack of experiences or memories, or from a dearth of documents, but from the absence of an intergenerational conversation about war. This may have been, in part, the result of the shadow of the Holocaust that made it impossible to view Germans (including German Canadians) as victims—a legacy Sara Frankenberger discusses in Chapter 7 in the context of later German-Canadian generations. To some extent, this scarcity of dialogue was perhaps also due to the hesitance of children and grandchildren to ask their parents or grandparents about difficult times in their lives, as Roger Frie reminds us in the Afterword. In that respect, at least, the German-Canadian experience was like that of other war-affected ethnic groups, many of whom have found intergenerational talk about troubling experiences to be difficult if not impossible.

Notes

1 Even though the experience was the same throughout Britain and its dominions, Britons came to remember the war as a meaningless carnage whereas Canada, Australia, and New Zealand came to commemorate the war as a national "rite of passage." Mark David Sheftall, *Altered Memories of the Great War: Divergent Narratives of Britain, Australia, New Zealand and Canada* (New York: I.B. Tauris, 2010); David Reynolds, "Britain, the Two World Wars, and the Problem of Narrative," *The Historical Journal* 60, no. 1 (2017): 197–231; Jeff Keshen, "The Great War Soldier as Nation Builder in Canada and Australia," in *Canada and the Great War: Western Front Association Papers*, ed. Briton Busch, 3–26 (Montreal: McGill-Queen's University Press, 2003). Canada's mythistory has long distracted from the

war's significant impact on Canadian society. See Jarett Henderson and Jeff Keshen, "Introduction: Canadian Perspectives on the First World War," *Histoire sociale/Social History* 47, no. 94 (June 2014): 283–90.

2 Jonathan F. Vance, *Death So Noble: Memory, Meaning, and the First World War* (Vancouver: UBC Press, 1997).

3 Timothy C. Winegard, *For King and Kanata: Canadian Indians and the First World War* (Winnipeg: University of Manitoba Press, 2012); and Cynthia Toman, *Sister Soldiers of the Great War: The Nurses of the Canadian Army Medical Corps* (Vancouver: UBC Press, 2016).

4 John Herd Thompson, *The Harvests of War: The Prairie West, 1914–1918* (Toronto: McClelland and Stewart, 1978); Robert Rutherdale, *Hometown Horizons: Local Responses to Canada's Great War* (Vancouver: UBC Press, 2004); Patrice A. Dutil, "Against Isolationism: Napoléon Belcourt, French Canada, and 'La grande guerre,'" in *Canada and the First World War*, ed. David MacKenzie (Toronto: University of Toronto, 2005), 96–137; Geoff Keelan, "The Forgotten Few: Quebec and the Memory of the First World War," in *The Great War: From Memory to History*, ed. Kurschinksi et al. (Waterloo: Wilfrid Laurier University Press, 2015), 235–59; Donald Avery, "Ethnic and Class Relations in Western Canada During the First World War: A Case Study of European Immigrants and Anglo-Canadian Nativism," in MacKenzie, *Canada and the First World War*, 272–99; Mary G. Chaktsiris, "The Enemy At Home: Defining Enemy Aliens in Ontario During the Great War," in Kurschinksi et al., *The Great War*, 287–302; and Amy J. Shaw, *Crisis of Conscience: Conscientious Objection in Canada during the First World War* (Vancouver: UBC Press, 2009).

5 Ian McKay and Jamie Swift, *The Vimy Trap: Or, How We Learned to Stop Worrying and Love the Great War* (Toronto: Between the Lines, 2016); and Tim Cook, *Vimy: The Battle and the Legend* (Toronto: Allen Lane, 2017).

6 A few studies interested in ethnic minorities' experiences have focused on internment, most recently and comprehensively Bohdan S. Kordan, *No Free Man: Canada, the Great War, and the Enemy Alien Experience* (Montreal: McGill-Queen's University Press, 2016).

7 Tim Cook, "Battles of the Imagined Past: Canada's Great War and Memory," *The Canadian Historical Review* 95, no. 3 (September 2014): 418.

8 Gerhard Bassler, *The German-Canadian Mosaic Today and Yesterday: Identities, Roots, and Heritage* (Ottawa: German-Canadian Congress, 1991), 61.

9 Arthur Grenke, "The Formation and Early Development of An Urban Ethnic Community: A Case Study of the Germans in Winnipeg, 1872–1919" (PhD diss., University of Manitoba, 1975/1978); Thompson, *The Harvests of War*, 76.

10 Three quarters of internees were unemployed Ukrainians. James Farney and Bohdan S. Kordan, "The Predicament of Belonging: The Status of Enemy Aliens in Canada, 1914," *Journal of Canadian Studies* 39, no. 1 (Winter 2005): 74.

11 Peter Moogk, "Uncovering the Enemy Within: British Columbians and the German Menace," *BC Studies* 182 (Summer 2014): 50.

12 Grenke, "The Formation and Early Development," Chapter 9; Arthur Grenke, "The German Community of Winnipeg and the English-Canadian Response to World War I," *Canadian Ethnic Studies* 20, no. 1 (1988): 21–44; and Arthur Grenke, *The German Community in Winnipeg, 1872 to 1919* (New York: AMS Press, 1991).

13 Cook, *Vimy*, Chapter 12, 320–22, 325, 334–36.

14 This also affected the writing of military history in Canada. See Tim Cook, *Clio's Warriors: Canadian Historians and the Writing of the World Wars* (Vancouver: UBC Press, 2006), Chapter 6.

15 Alexander Freund, *Oral History and Ethnic History* (Ottawa: Canadian Historical Association, 2014).

16 In his dissertation, Grenke stated that he had interviewed sixty-five Germans. The provenance of the collection is unclear. The Manitoba Museum has no record of the project. It is unclear whether Grenke donated all of his German interviews to the Museum, whether he conducted all of his interviews with Germans within the larger project for the Manitoba Museum, or how many of these interviews survived. In 2004, I was able to receive cassette tape copies of about ten interviews with German immigrants, all of which I digitized. By 2014, the Manitoba Museum had digitized more interviews. I purchased digital copies of all available interviews conducted by Grenke. These included interviews with non-Germans, but most of the interviews I had purchased earlier were not part of that collection. Further, it is not clear what kind of recorder Grenke originally used. The Manitoba Museum has "original" reel-to-reel tapes and cassette tape copies of the reel-to-reel tapes as well as some digital copies. In a survey of German-Canadian archival material in 1993, Grenke simply noted: "The Manitoba Museum of Man and Nature (Winnipeg), which collects materials on ethno-cultural groups in the prairie region, holds sound recordings as well as a few photographs relating to German immigration to Winnipeg and Manitoba generally." Art Grenke, "The Archival Record of German-Language Groups in Canada: A Survey," *Archivaria* 35 (Spring 1993): 224.

17 Cook, *Vimy*, 310–17.

18 Ibid., 312.

19 J.W. Beer, interview; and Mr. and Mrs. Jentsch, interview. All interviews in this chapter were conducted by Art Grenke for the Manitoba Museum in 1971 approximately.

20 In our personal correspondence, Dr. Grenke wrote that he could not provide further information about the interviews. Art Grenke, personal correspondence with author, 8 August 2017.

21 Jim Blanchard, *Winnipeg's Great War: A City Comes of Age* (Winnipeg: University of Manitoba Press, 2010), 8.

22 Grenke, "The German Community of Winnipeg," 22.

23 Blanchard, *Winnipeg's Great War*, 3.

24 Ibid., 341.

25 Mrs. A. Bernhardt, interview.

26 Blanchard, *Winnipeg's Great War*, 14–22, 36, 80–81, 92–95, 100–103, 116, 149–52, 192, 206–7, 256–57.

27 Grenke, "The German Community of Winnipeg," 24.

28 Ibid.

29 Ibid., 26.

30 "Five Clubs Raided," *Manitoba Free Press*, 26 January 1917, 27.

31 Grenke, "The Formation and Early Development of An Urban Ethnic Community," 425, 430.

32 On English Canadians' anti-foreigner sentiments in the Canadian West during the war, see Thompson, *Harvests of War*; Donald Avery, *"Dangerous Foreigners":*

European Immigrant Workers and Labour Radicalism in Canada, 1896–1932 (Toronto: McClelland and Stewart, 1979); and Howard Palmer, *Patterns of Prejudice: A History of Nativism in Alberta* (Toronto: McClelland and Stewart, 1982).

33 Grenke, "The Formation and Early Development of An Urban Ethnic Community," 430.

34 "Socialist Meetings Broken Up and Property Damaged Throughout the City," *Manitoba Free Press*, 27 January 1919, 17; "Veterans on Search For Alien Workers," *Manitoba Free Press*, 28 January 1919, 19; "Law or Lawlessness?" *Manitoba Free Press*, 20; and "Square Deal All Returned Men Ask," *Manitoba Free Press*, 31 January 1919, 1, 28.

35 Mr. F[red] Martin, interview. In German, first floor refers to what North Americans generally call the second floor.

36 Mrs. A. Bernhardt, interview.

37 While some file names provided the names of both spouses, the Kendel interview only refers to Henry Kendel.

38 Blanchard, *Winnipeg's Great War*, 234.

39 Mr. Henry Kendel, interview.

40 It is not clear whether he mentioned Italians because he confounded the two world wars or whether he remembered some of Winnipeg's Italians had been harassed after the Great War. See "Veterans on Search for Alien Workers," *Manitoba Free Press*, 28 January 1919, 19.

41 "Socialist Meetings Broken Up"; "Veterans On Search For Alien Workers"; "Brewery Founder Is Dead," *Winnipeg Free Press*, 12 July 1937, 1; "Friends Pay Final Tribute to Memory of Arnold W. Riedle," *Winnipeg Free Press*, 15 July 1937, 22.

42 Mr. J. Plischke, interview.

43 Mr. Ed Horch, interview.

44 Blanchard, *Winnipeg's Great War*, 238–39.

45 Historians hold different views on why German Canadians have been a historically "silent" group. See my discussion of the debate among Bassler, Hoerder, and Sauer in the Introduction.

46 Grenke, "The German Community of Winnipeg," 21; Grenke, "The Formation and Early Development of An Urban Ethnic Community," 420.

47 Christine Ensslen, Chapter 8 in this collection.

CHAPTER 2

One Führer, Two Kings: A Canadian Prime Minister in Nazi Germany and the Dilemma of Responsibility

ROBERT TEIGROB

Once again in public reckoning, William Lyon Mackenzie King, Canada's tenth and longest-serving prime minister, stands ascendant over his peers. In a 2016 *Maclean's* survey of Canadian academics, King regained the title of greatest prime minister that he claimed in a similar 1997 poll and then lost—by a slim margin—in 2011. Survey participants praised his longevity, ability to weather enormous domestic and international crises, masterful political judgment, and fixation on national unity. Respondents were particularly impressed with King's consonance with the public mood, operating as he did in an era before opinion polls and focus groups. King, the surveys revealed, "intuitively understood and responded to popular attitudes"[1] and demonstrated a "canny ability to detect opinion trends."[2] As a federal politician, King's reputation is without equal.

William Lyon Mackenzie King *the man*, however, has not aged nearly as well. Never beloved as a national leader to the degrees enjoyed by his contemporaries Franklin Delano Roosevelt and Winston Churchill—although King helped to steer his country through the same traumatic miasma of the Depression and the Second World War—Canadians nonetheless respected King and his fellow Liberals enough to grant him an unprecedented five electoral victories and twenty-one years in power. Yet a series of revelations and re-evaluations since his

1948 resignation have bruised his image to the point where this extraordinarily successful national leader offers little in the way of a usable legacy. Testimonials from his colleagues and staff (he had few friends) culled after his death in 1950 depicted a humourless, thin-skinned, Oedipal, and cravenly opportunistic glory seeker who was cringingly sycophantic to both the famous and those who might be of use to him. His reputational crown slipped further when post-mortem rumours (later confirmed in King's own bizarre diaries, published in stages between 1973 and 1980) suggested a man gripped and guided by the spirits of dead family members, world leaders, and pets, and preoccupied by certain angles of the hands of a clock and numerical coincidences (or "seeming coincidences," according to King). While historians continue to praise his considerable administrative and tactical skills—even as they often hunt in vain for the principles undergirding his many feats of political endurance—aspiring Canadian politicians gain little leverage by casting themselves as the guardians of the Mackenzie King legacy. FDR, Churchill, John F. Kennedy, Margaret Thatcher, Ronald Reagan, Wilfrid Laurier, Lester Pearson, Trudeau the elder—all boast candid disciples, exploitable coattails, and a commonly held understanding of their guiding political philosophies. King's name, rarely invoked even by members of the political party he helped build into twentieth-century Canada's "natural" governor, has become something of a national embarrassment, one that cannot be uttered without at least some leavening (and usually puckish) allusions to his manifold oddities.[3] This paragraph is but one case in point.

These collective reckonings of the "two Kings"—King I, the political sage, and King II the cabalistic buffoon—have helped Canadians mediate one of the most notorious episodes in the history of Canadian foreign relations: the prime minister's four-day excursion to Nazi Germany in June 1937. It was the only such visit by a leader from the Western democracies, and it led King to the calamitous and widely broadcasted conclusions that Adolf Hitler's program would remake Germany and indeed the world for the better, and that the Führer would not dare threaten his nation's progress by risking a foreign conflict.

While King's trip received extensive national and international press coverage and the prime minister himself considered it the most significant act of his life to that date, the affair took on irredeemable baggage as the full nature and intentions of the Nazi regime unfolded in all of their apocalyptic savagery. The visit was frequently ignored in even the most comprehensive, first-generation postwar Canadian accounts of the King era. The few analysts who did attempt to come to terms with the trip—or what would appear to be a tacit legitimation of the abhorrent regime—sought to reframe King's mission as a well-intentioned and bluntly delivered, though ultimately futile, warning to Hitler of the steely resolve of the English-speaking world in the face of Nazi aggression.[4]

Both strategies—evasion and reframing—constitute archetypical and plainly disingenuous efforts to rework King's Second World War legacy into a usable story suited to present needs, to paraphrase Alexander Freund in his Introduction to this collection. Through both approaches, inspiring images of Canada's greatest statesmen and his nation's determined defiance of fascist aggression are preserved. This general wartime storyline has proven especially dear to Canadians. Historian Jeffrey Keshen determined that, when compared to the social memory of the Second World War in Britain and the United States, Canada's collective remembrance of that conflict is markedly "sanitized and simplified."[5] While analysts from other countries have produced works that address frankly their own culpability in the conflict and their own nations' wartime atrocities, psychoses, racism, sexual violence, and class conflict, Canadian historians, Keshen argued, have clung doggedly to tales of righteousness and valour.[6] His own examination of the evidence surrounding Canada's Second World War experience, in *Saints, Sinners, and Soldiers: Canada's Second World War*, reveals a much more nuanced and less heroic image of wartime Canada than his colleagues in the field have cared to admit. The widespread evasion and reframing of Mackenzie King's encounter with Hitler must be appraised in the context of this collective "sanitization."

The simplest of the two approaches to the problem of King's fascist apologetics is, of course, evasion. The tactic is familiar, as Karen Brglez reminds us in her discussion of Gottlieb Leibbrandt in Chapter 4. Like Leibbrandt, the Ukrainian-born ethnic German whose calculated suppression of his Nazi past facilitated his emergence as the doyen of German-Canadian historical studies, King is not forced to confront his earlier flirtations with fascism. As in Leibbrandt's example, that silence is essential to the preservation of personal respectability and authority. But in the case of King, the willful forgetting has deeper roots and wider implications: the nation itself is on trial here. This truth is underscored by the fact that, unlike the Leibbrandt case, the purging of King's Nazi apologetics is effected primarily by others—the keepers of the nation's historical record intent on inoculating that record against the taint of Nazi sympathies.

Yet even the attempts to reframe King's trip—in accounts that acknowledge its existence but present a "tough" prime minister—are burdened with their own, rather glaring evasions. Absent in these analyses is any discussion of whether a tour of Fascist Germany was morally defensible, why others in King's position who had received similar invitations had demurred, and why King, by his own estimation, did not raise any concerns about the brutality of Nazi policies with his hosts. Indeed, one author cast the uniqueness of the prime minister's dalliance with Hitler as an accomplishment in and of itself. King "was well ahead of his time in applying this innovative diplomacy," wrote Brian Nolan, who pointed out that "none of the leading Allied war chieftains . . . ever met Hitler face to face. Only King achieved this."[7]

More recent interpretations, penned by a subsequent generation of historians privy to a far more unsettling description of the encounter in King's own diaries, have become considerably more candid and unsympathetic about this "achievement."[8] Here the affair, which saw King happily breaking bread with Hitler and other architects of looming racial war and genocide, was labelled as "one of King's most contested foreign policy decisions,"[9] "a central blemish on his record,"[10] "one of the strangest diplomatic missions in Canadian history,"[11] and "probably the most controversial of all his actions in external relations."[12] These interpretations have also placed much of the blame for the controversy firmly on King's shoulders: he was, historians have written, singularly "naïve,"[13] "absurd,"[14] "imperceptive,"[15] "innocent,"[16] and "blissfully unaware"[17] in his appraisal of and tolerance for fascism.

Much, too, has been made of the inflated sense of personal destiny and cravings for international adulation that motivated King's ill-famed trip. Prior to meeting Hitler, King, who had lived among Germans both in his Ontario hometown of Berlin (later Kitchener) and while a visiting student in "old-world" Berlin in 1900, confided in his diary, "I know the best sides of the German people. If I were talking to Hitler, I could reassure him what was costing him friends was the fear he was creating against other countries."[18] In June 1936 he wrote confidently that stability in Europe could be effected through the "personal individual effort" of "men of different countries," and saw himself as a fitting principal in these deliberations.[19] "At that moment," wrote a recent biographer, "King believed he might well be the one individual who could unite Britain, the U.S. and Germany in common cause and 'friendship.'"[20] These musings are offered as evidence that the prime minister was both delusional and in well over his head.

These more recent judgments of King's visit are fully warranted but potentially misleading on two counts. First, in drawing attention only to the episode's (undeniable) infamy, a modern reader might infer that Canadians of King's day also shared the condemnatory verdicts of later writers fully cognizant of the years of horror that would follow the prime minister's totalitarian holiday. In fact, in the Canada of 1937 King's mission was remarkably—and, to the modern observer, alarmingly—*uncontroversial*, or more accurately, widely applauded. Second, in these same recent accounts, the Mackenzie King who tours Hitler Youth and forced-labour camps, gambols with Hermann Goering, Rudolf Hess, and Joachim von Ribbentrop, and perceives an immediate spiritual bond with the Führer, is seemingly bereft of his otherwise-vaunted shrewdness and is lacking his genius for intuition and for personifying the public mood. Instead, King II—or "Weird Willie,"[21] as some authors have christened him—has taken the reins, a derisible, deluded, and self-important figure ostensibly alien to Canadian sensibilities.

The overwhelmingly positive public responses to the King visit among his pre-war contemporaries, however, suggest that the alleged personality defects underlying King's capacity to countenance Nazism—his strange amalgam of artlessness and seeming indifference toward the regime's abuses and victims—may not have been so strange or "un-Canadian" after all. In this instance at least, comforting rationalizations built primarily around the prime minister's peculiarities and psychoses will only take us so far. King may have served as Canada's longest-serving leader—literally and figuratively its first citizen—but this did not grant him any special capacity to manufacture personal sensibilities and traits independent of his social and cultural context. In fact, that very political durability suggests King's striking congruence with his time and place (as his more recent champions correctly point out in their response to the *Maclean's* surveys). As cultural theorist Rosine

Kelz observes, personal attributes like rationality and sovereignty "are not 'natural' properties of every human being"; instead, individuals "have to 'learn' or acquire certain abilities or traits by internalising social and linguistic norms."[22] King's political success suggests a man with a special capacity for that internalization, and one who should thus not bear the sole shame for his flirtation with the Führer. At the same time, I want to argue that the prime minister's diplomatic efforts do not warrant unreserved condemnation and ridicule, and that many of King's contemporaries lauded the effort or withheld criticism for reasons that also rehabilitate some aspects—though certainly not all—of the prime minister and his German initiative.

Memory, Responsibility, and Public Awareness of Nazism

Nineteenth-century French thinker Ernest Renan declared that in the service of nation building, members of a polity must simultaneously recall collective triumphs and forget "many things,"[23] especially those events that tear at the fabric of social harmony. Contemporary political theorist Ross Poole makes the conundrum associated with this axiom plain: in order to fulfill this demand, citizens must "remember what it is they are commanded to forget."[24] Poole offers a pathway out of this blind alley, arguing that forgetting under these circumstances "does not require the complete erasure of the past; what it prescribes is the erasure of the *responsibilities* that are associated with it"[25] (emphasis added).

In the context of King's mission to Berlin, responsibility is expunged when chroniclers of the era simply omit the event; when they recast the prime minister's approbation and servility as principled toughness; or when their narratives replace the statesman who skillfully shepherded Canada through trying times with the guileless, mystic clown who bumbled off to Berlin and whose patent weaknesses were no match for Hitler's cunning. The last approach accomplishes the feat of laying much of the blame for Canada's "softness" toward Nazism at the feet of a single and ostensibly unrepresentative figure. Under all three strategies, certain unflattering truths about the nation's response to totalitarianism are moderated: that Canada could have done more to expose and ameliorate the suffering of Nazism's victims; that the nation shared certain ideological affinities with fascism; that the "ideology of racelessness"[26] upheld as a mark of Canadian identity (especially in juxtaposition with the United States), one that represented Canada as a "haven of refuge" for groups fleeing persecution, cannot accommodate the collective response to the political extremism of the 1930s; that the "Good War" was in fact thrust upon a Canada that had few misgivings about doing business with Nazi Germany until Hitler's armies threatened the balance of power in Europe. None of these claims are absent from the historical record, but a more honest reckoning of the purpose and significance of the prime minister's visit gives these difficult truths a greater and more appropriate presence in the annals of Mackenzie King–era Canada.

Over the past several decades, scholars have dismantled the twin misconceptions that Canadians of the thirties lacked sufficient information to make sound judgments about Nazism and that the Dominion was largely free of the types of chauvinisms endemic to the fascist and other ultra-nationalist regimes and movements of the interwar period. Irving Abella and Harold Troper's landmark 1982 study of Canadian immigration policy in the Nazi era, *None Is Too Many,* shattered a half century of evasion and denial regarding the government's virtual ban on Jewish immigration, a policy that marked Canada as the least welcoming Western nation for Jewish refugees.[27] A surge of ensuing studies reinforced the fact that this was no "top-down" ailment. Rather, an especially virulent anti-Semitism proliferated in all regions of Canada during the Depression and manifested via discrimination in housing, education, and employment, via restriction of access to public spaces, and via growth of Canadian branches of the KKK.[28]

At the same time, the 1930s Canadian press provided extensive coverage of the disturbing excesses of the new German regime, including the liquidation of political opponents, the targeting of "unpatriotic" religious leaders, the massive spending on armaments and abrogation of the Treaty of Versailles, and (somewhat paradoxically, given the domestic anti-Semitism) the mounting proscriptions aimed at German Jews and other minorities.[29] Progressive newspapers like the *Winnipeg Free Press* and the *Toronto Star*—the latter the country's most widely read daily—denounced these developments with increasing alarm. More conservative publications joined in full-throated censure when the Nuremberg Laws stripped Jews of citizenship and most political and legal rights in the fall of 1935. As in the United States and Britain, in Canada a movement to boycott the 1936 Olympics—on the grounds the games would legitimize an abhorrent regime—made headlines, and

Figure 2.1. Prime Minister W.L. Mackenzie King with his personal secretary Edward Pickering, German Labour Front leader Robert Ley (waving), and German Sports leader Hans von Tschammer und Osten (right), inspecting tennis players at Olympiapark, Berlin, Germany, 1937. Credit: Library and Archives Canada, PA-119011.

the British and American press, frequently synopsized in the Canadian media, castigated Nazi tyranny from the early months of 1933 onward.[30]

By the time of King's 1937 visit, then, any Canadian claims of innocence regarding the true nature of Hitler's government represented either an astonishing lack of public engagement or an outright lie. This the mass-circulation weekly *Saturday Night* made clear in an issue released while the prime minister toured Berlin. Responding to German Canadians, attending a June 1937 convention in Regina, who had publicly criticized the negative Canadian media response to Nazism, *Saturday Night* charged the attendees with ignoring some incontrovertible and widely acknowledged facts. "The German-Canadians," editors wrote, "were demanding a more sympathetic attitude in the Canadian press towards a Government in Germany which has exercised the most ruthless intolerance that has ever been practiced by a modern civilized state against a racial minority of its population."[31]

Canada's parliament provided another conspicuous platform for airing such grievances. In April 1937, just two months prior to King's Berlin visit, the House of Commons debated Bill 89, a measure to ratify a bilateral trade deal negotiated with Germany in 1936. Samuel Factor, Liberal Member of Parliament (MP) for the Toronto riding of Spadina and Ontario's first Jewish MP, issued an extended, passionate denunciation of Nazi crimes for the parliamentary record. The Hitler regime's conduct, he maintained, was "offensive to human civilization. . . . Medieval barbarities have been perpetrated against hundreds of thousands of people which have shocked the moral conscience of the world. . . . The German government has passed ghoulish ordinances [against] human beings because of their religious profession." Citing energetic boycott-Germany campaigns underway in the United States and Britain, Factor implored that the House reject the deal brokered by his own party, asking, "what of our conscience?"[32] It was in part a measure of how mildly these protestations resonated that no parliamentarian offered a reply to Factor's plea; instead, the debate shifted abruptly to the economic prospects surrounding Bill 89, which subsequently passed by a wide margin.

The bilateral trade agreement would come to serve as something of a fig leaf for King's 1937 visit. The Canadian press made much of the fact that the prime minister would take up the issue with the Germans and seek to ensure that both parties upheld their end of the deal. But in truth, King had been contemplating such a visit for some time, and commercial matters were decidedly peripheral to his motivations. Concerns about the optics of calling on Hitler had already arisen when King proposed a similar meeting in 1936. O.D. Skelton, the prime minister's undersecretary of state for external affairs (King served as his own secretary on this file), had long expressed fear and revulsion toward fascism and Hitler. In a 1935 position paper drafted for foreign policy discussions in London, Skelton called the "Nazi religion and its prophet" the gravest source of danger in a Europe wracked with tension "in almost every corner."[33] Skelton did not share the delusions that other great powers bore a good deal of the blame for tensions or that German grievances were mostly legitimate—sentiments that underwrote the more sympathetic assessments of Hitler's pre-war provocations and the corresponding policy of appeasement.

Even so, in 1936 King considered a face-to-face meeting with the Führer. He recorded the reaction of Skelton, his most trusted foreign policy advisor, in his diary: "On talking the matter over with Skelton, he still feels very strongly that it would be resented in Canada; that it would only be flattering Hitler by having him feel some more persons were coming to him; that he was so much of an anglo-maniac, that nothing could influence him."[34] King heard similar warnings from British social reformer Violet Markham, with whom he had maintained regular correspondence since their 1905 meeting at the Governor General's residence in Ottawa. When King mentioned the possibility of meeting with the Nazi leader, Markham reminded King that Hitler "is the head of a detestable system of force and persecution and real horrors go on in Germany today for which he is responsible"; she advised that should King go, he should guard, above all, against the Führer's ability to "hypnotize" him.[35] King himself worried that "the Jingo press of Canada might misconstrue it all" and concluded in 1936 that "it might be better not to take the risk involved."[36]

King, Berlin, and the Canadian Media

King need not have worried. When he finally overcame his qualms and added Berlin to his itinerary following the 1937 Imperial Conference in London, mainstream Canadian press reactions ran from cautiously supportive to fawning. Both French- and English-language newspapers posted factual, dispassionate Canadian Press reports on King's activities that read as if this were a foreign trip like any other, *pace* the inclusion of some disturbing details and juxtapositions in the reportage. "Nazi Swastikas and Union Jacks Greet Premier's Arrival in Berlin," reported one *Globe and Mail* headline, explaining that King's was a noble mission aimed at "promoting international understanding";[37] further down the same front page, however, another story reported that twelve "Nazi pastors" were at that very moment facing trial for defying the regime.[38] Two days later, the *Globe* wrote that King sought only "to see something of modern Germany for himself and learn something of her rulers' viewpoints";[39] the plight of the insubordinate pastors appeared of little concern to the principals involved. An article in Ottawa's *Le Droit* noted, with no further discussion, that King "a visité un camp de concentration."[40] Its editors then praised the mission without qualification, writing, "Il est bon que les chefs de gouvernements visitent de temps in temps les autres pays."[41] Even the *Winnipeg Free Press*, Nazi Germany's most consistent and acerbic critic among mainstream Canadian media outlets, refrained from condemnation in its matter-of-fact reports on the meetings.[42]

Montreal's *La Presse* stressed the economic basis and benefits of the trip, stating that King was meeting "avec les chefs des gouvernements français, belge et allemande" in order to bolster trade with a range of partners.[43] The same paper included a story on a roundup of 102 German pastors, but again, no connection was made between this Gestapo sweep and any obligations the prime minister might have to speak out against the abuse of German citizens.[44] Canadian Press correspondent George Hambleton, citing as proof the bilateral trade agreement—so disparaged by parliamentarian Samuel Factor—held that "Canada's relations with Germany are of the friendliest."[45]

The *Ottawa Citizen* was the most steadfastly non-judgmental of Germany and impartial regarding European tensions, informing readers that the discord in Europe was purely economic in origin: "The German people," editors wrote, "refuse to accept [the] sentence of economic servitude or of national inferiority." The *Citizen* maintained that if only Britain would exhibit more flexibility regarding Germany's commercial interests (acknowledging the latter's right to colonies, for instance), London, like Prime Minister King, would grasp "the possibility of leadership along new economic paths away from war." According to the paper, failure to recognize the fundamentally economic basis of European friction meant that "public opinion is confused with arguments about race, religion, politics, Socialism, Fascism, and a multiplicity of side issues." The *Citizen* maintained that Hitler was supporting the Fascist Franco regime in the escalating Spanish Civil War, for instance, not out of any ideological consonance or aggressive agenda but simply because Germany needed Spanish ore.[46]

The silence from other media outlets on "side issues" like race, religion, and human rights seemed to confirm the *Citizen*'s stance: the Nuremberg Laws, censorship, the violations of civil rights and international treaties—these were ephemera unworthy of derailing the conversations in Berlin (a stance King obviously shared, since he, too, failed to broach them with the German leadership). To the few in

Figure 2.2. Prime Minister W.L. Mackenzie King as he exits the Reich President's Palace after meeting Hitler (there are no photos of the two of them together), Berlin, Germany, 1937. Credit: Library and Archives Canada, PA-119014.

Canada raising such concerns, the *Globe and Mail* argued that the visit "does not require, as some imply, any justification with the public at home." In his prepared statement to the press, King himself said only that he was impressed by Germany's postwar recovery and that his talks were "most interesting," "most informative," and "extraordinarily frank."[47]

Upon his return home, the prime minister continued to receive accolades for the visit in the House and in the press. When parliament resumed sitting in February 1938, the matter hit the papers again after politicians from rival parties offered congratulations for what they considered a fruitful visit. King's nemesis, Conservative opposition leader and erstwhile prime minister R.B. Bennett (ironically, an individual whom King had dismissed in public and private as "a dictator" and in his diaries as "a butcher, a tyrant and bully which he is"[48]), made a brief attempt to flummox his opponent over the issue. Bennett found it discordant that the Liberal leader would sit down with Nazi leaders despite previously warning "of the dangers that threaten the body politic from communism, on the one hand, and from fascism on the other."[49]

In what would appear to be a coordinated attack, Bennett's brother-in-law, Conservative Party apparatchik W.D. Herridge, had told an audience of Toronto Conservatives the day before that "Liberalism goes a long way from liberalism of freedom when it goes to Berlin."[50] Once again, these criticisms went nowhere, and once again, the *Globe and Mail* rose to defend King's trip and his right to not disclose the contents of the meetings.[51]

How can we bridge the considerable chasm between what was known of Nazism on the one hand, and the public commendations of King's initiative—abetted by the Canadian media's refusal to raise Nazi transgressions in coverage of the visit—on the other? After all, a similar visit by former British air force secretary Lord Londonderry a year before King's, which likewise saw Hitler's guest enthuse about the work done to reinvigorate the nation and its economy, received condescension and scorn in the liberal British press.[52] The anti-Semitic currents in Canadian policy and practice, alluded to above, certainly provide one answer, and as his diaries repeatedly reveal, the prime minister himself could be fairly regarded as an emissary of mainstream Canadian views on these matters. In the thirties, for instance, King purchased a neighbour's property for three times its appraised value "to prevent Jews or other undesirable people from getting in."[53] In reflecting on Nazi racial policies in a 1936 entry, the prime minister offered the remarkably weak "endorsement" that "there are good as well as bad Jews and it is wrong to indict a nation or race."[54] That such a statement need even be made *to oneself* says a great deal about the writer's own desultory opinions on the matter. Two years later, after hearing the reports of *Kristallnacht*, King's empathy appeared to grow. "The sorrows which the Jews have to bear at this time are almost beyond comprehension," he wrote. "Something will have to be done by our country."[55]

Canada's most significant potential contribution to the Jewish dilemma would have been to open its doors to Jewish refugees, but King's government, fully aware of the depth of its country's anti-Semitism, knew this would invoke a public outcry from anglophone and francophone alike and thus did nothing.[56] After the Anschluss in 1938, King wrote: "my own feeling is that nothing is to be gained by creating an internal problem in an effort to meet an international one."[57] As such, Jewish persecution in Germany did indeed constitute—in the estimation of both the Liberal government and canonical Canadian ethnic groups—what the *Ottawa Citizen* called a "side issue." It may have been a confusing, even troubling practice, but that did not translate into the conclusion that anti-Semitism should be permitted to interfere with the vital work of building bilateral goodwill.[58]

The idea that Jews served as agents of bolshevism—an ideology that many Canadians, including King, considered a more dire threat to liberal democracies in the thirties than fascism—also contributed to this collective lack of enthusiasm for a more tolerant immigration policy.[59] But as Jonathan Wagner has shown, socialism alone did not automatically bar a prospective immigrant's entrance to Canada: King's Liberal government knew full well that many of the 5,000 Sudetenland Germans offered asylum in 1938 sought refuge precisely because their socialist politics made them *persona non grata* in the expanding Reich.[60] Concerns over race thus clearly trumped those over ideology, no matter how reviled the political views. Renan wrote that because it forges kinship via the rejection of those deemed dissimilar, national unity "is always effected by means of brutality."[61] Canada's domestic history provides numerous examples of that brutality expressed toward First Nations peoples, the Métis, and non-European immigrants; here we find an internationalization of that dyad. To keep the country together, Canada would permit the perpetuation of a brutality against European Jews that the nation had at least some ability to temper.

There is something, too, of the perennial Canadian desire for greater international prestige underwriting the collective affirmation of the trip. Easily overlooked internationally and keen to demonstrate independence from both British and American policy makers, Canada now had an opportunity to take centre stage, perhaps even alter the plot, in the momentous drama that was interwar Europe. This impulse was certainly crucial to the prime minister. In order to reinforce the impression of Canada's sovereignty and international significance, King declined an invitation to stay at the Berlin residence of Sir Nevile Henderson, Britain's ambassador to Germany, and snubbed Henderson's request to join King in his visit to the Führer.[62] *Saturday Night* magazine was entirely justified in satirizing the many Canadian reporters who hailed the King visit as the dawn of their nation's global eminence and a resetting of European relations. In an article titled "Not Settling the World," staff writer "Rideau Banks" (a.k.a. Norman MacLeod) provided a sampling of the press hype surrounding the trip and lampooned the collective message that "the peace of the world has been placed in King's hand" (an expansive view that, as his diaries demonstrate, King fully embraced). It was patently absurd, Banks argued, to think "that British statesmanship has confessed defeat and abdicated in favour of the Prime Minister of one of the Dominions."[63]

That said, a certain measure of the salutary press reporting and attendant diffidence regarding Nazi wrongs was understandable: Canadian observers sought to avoid interfering with and perhaps sabotaging potentially delicate negotiations that could lessen the prospect of war. On this, the overall atmosphere in interwar Canada, the United States, and Europe was undeniable: citizens and governments alike were prepared to go to extraordinary lengths to avoid a return to the bloodletting of the Great War. The conflict was viewed as singularly horrific—and more and more, in the collective post-mortems of the twenties and thirties, it was believed that the war had been sparked by relatively petty grievances and that, in the end, it had settled little. While Hitler's domestic abuses were well documented by the mid-thirties, his foreign agenda was widely debated and subject to a broad range of contradictory interpretations and international approaches.[64] By 1936, King reflected these tensions, as he was both open to treating Germany as a favoured trading partner *and* expressing amazement "that Hitler has been permitted to go to the lengths he has."[65]

King's Appeasement in International Context

Where, then, does King sit on the continuum of outsiders' myriad reactions to Hitler? Citing the prime minister's above concerns over the leeway granted the Nazis, historian John MacFarlane wrote: "That King does not deserve the reputation of a naive appeaser is further suggested by the fact that his visit with Hitler was supported by such hard-line supposed opponents of appeasement as British Secretary of State for Foreign Affairs Anthony Eden and U.S. Secretary of State Cordell Hall."[66] This support grew out of King's private assurances that he would make plain to Nazi leaders Canada's support for Britain in any conflict with Germany, a message that, if his log entries of the trip are to be believed, the prime minister did indeed convey. (We have no other record of his private conversations in Berlin, but a reporter who discussed the trip extensively and privately with King in July 1937 doubts that King raised the issue of backing Britain in a world war.[67])

If King was open to virtually any approach or blandishment toward the Nazis that would forestall a British-German conflict, he was certainly not alone. Ian Kershaw notes that at the Imperial Conference preceding King's Berlin jaunt, "the Dominions (apart from New Zealand) had . . . favoured appeasing the dictators."[68] A war involving Britain would doubtlessly place extraordinary pressure on these nations to come once again to the Empire's defence, an obligation responsible for fresh and bitter memories of Great War carnage, debt, and controversy; the latter outcome was especially abundant in Canada, whose francophone citizens had begun to talk earnestly of separatism after being conscripted into an overseas war to preserve the Empire.

French Canadians were not alone in their indignation. While the idea that the Canadian nation was "born" at the Battle of Vimy Ridge gained mythological status in the decades following the conflict, this belief, as well as the nation's upbeat recollection of the Second World War, relies on some determined forgetting. Freund reminds us in Chapter 1 of this collection that the Great War exacerbated fissures beyond the frequently invoked French-English divide. By virtue of their wartime resistance or merely their identity, farmers, pacifists, racialized Canadians, "enemy aliens," and labour and women's organizations found themselves on the outside of a national identity constructed around First World War loyalty and heroics. If nationalism and national survival required, to again cite Renan, a collective memory of having "done great things together,"[69] wars for the British Empire amounted to decidedly awkward instruments for nation building. Indeed, another such conflict could hasten the unmaking of a bilingual Canada.

The prospect of reopening those First World War wounds traumatized King. Moreover, as King informed the House in debates over Germany's remilitarization of the Rhineland in March 1936, a broken Canada could not play a meaningful role in the peace and stability of Europe. King stated: "I believe that Canada's first duty to the league [League of Nations] and to the British empire, with respect to all the great issues that come up, is, if possible, to keep this country united."[70] British historian Nicholas Mansergh believes that King's overall response to Hitler was governed mostly by these domestic complications; he writes, "essentially it was the situation in Canada, not the situation in Europe that determined his approach."[71] Given the national tribulations assured by another potential continental war, the prime minister's forbearance for Nazi ills and international demands finds some basis here.

At the same time, it should be noted that in the spring of 1937 German leaders had earmarked King as especially hospitable, and therefore serviceable, to their cause. Ribbentrop, then Germany's ambassador in London, drew up a list of "eminent Britons" whose comparative warmth toward the regime warranted special invitations to visit Germany. He included one non-Briton on the list, "the Canadian prime minister, Mackenzie King who is very friendly towards Germany and whose visit I consider particularly important in view of the significance of the Dominions for British Foreign policy."[72] Historian Abraham Ascher included King, along with several "prominent Britons," on his own list of "leading appeasers," although Ascher observed that many of those most conciliatory toward Hitler expressed "comments about him [that] were often distinctly unflattering, sometimes not very different from those of diplomats who despised the dictator and urged condemnation of his repressive policies."[73]

The same could not be said of Mackenzie King. His affirmative public comments about his encounter with German Fascism were not sugar-coated diplomatic niceties meant to gloss over more unsympathetic personal impressions. Indeed, the prime minister's private comments about his first-hand look at the National Socialist experiment go much further, revealing a nearly universal empathy and admiration for the work undertaken since 1933 and for the individuals most responsible for that "progress." Upon meeting Ribbentrop at the 1937 Imperial Conference, King called the man even fellow Nazi leaders universally detested for his flagrant careerism, vanity, hypersensitivity, and obsequiousness toward elites "a man I could get along with quite easily"[74] (thus revealing something of his own personality traits). While there is no evidence that King initiated any talk regarding the Nazis' persecution of Jews, Germany's foreign minister Baron Konstantin von Neurath was happy to raise the matter in a lengthy conversation with King. "He said to me," the latter wrote in his diary that evening, "that I would have loathed living in Berlin with the Jews.... He said there was no pleasure in going to a theatre which was filled with them.... They were getting control of all the business, the finance.... It was necessary to get them out to have the German people really control their own City and affairs."[75] The prime minister, who had made considerable efforts to keep

Jews out of his own neighbourhood, offered no rebuttal to these views in conversation or diary. Their encounter ended at von Neurath's home for a luncheon party—"one of the pleasantest I have ever enjoyed," read his diary; King hoped that he would enjoy the confidence of his tremendously kind and affable host "through the rest of [his] days."[76] This blossoming friendship would do nothing to check the expansion of the German consular network headed by von Neurath throughout Canada, a process begun in 1936, but one which accelerated rapidly after King's discussions with the German foreign minister. "Given the nature of the Hitler regime," observed historian Graeme Mount, "King's government should not have permitted the expansion," but here again, this growing presence of Nazi agents in Canada failed to generate any controversy in the nation's media.[77]

Since the publication of the prime minister's diaries, as a host of writers have made clear, the story of King's excursion to Berlin gets far worse. He reserved his greatest admiration for the Führer himself, to whom the awestruck prime minister spoke privately for a little more than an hour. Here, King told Hitler that the Nazis' "constructive work . . . was bound to be followed in other countries to the great benefit of mankind." He believed his host's claim that, unlike Stalin who needed to shoot opponents in order to implement his programs, Hitler was simply an instrument of the will of the people—"exactly the same argument that I had used in the Canadian Parliament," wrote the smitten King. It was clear, he mused further, that Hitler was "one who truly loves his fellow man," and lauded the Führer's commitment to peace, as well as the dictator's comportment, "liquid" eyes, and smooth skin. King's overall conclusion? "I believe the world will yet come to see a very great man . . . in Hitler." King was entirely satisfied when he left Berlin. "Looking back on the German visit," he wrote on its final day, "I can honestly say it was as enjoyable, informative and inspiring, as any visit I have ever had anywhere. Indeed I doubt if I ever had four days which were more interesting or indeed comparable in significance." He was "tremendously relieved," he wrote, that Europe would be spared another conflict.[78]

Once back in Canada, King allowed himself to raise issues in the diary that he had evaded—both before his hosts and in his own reflections—while touring the barbarous state. At the same time he made it clear that, like the *Ottawa Citizen*, he regarded the inhumanity of Nazi

Germany a "side issue." "His dictatorship is a means to an end," he wrote, "needed perhaps to make the Germans conscious of themselves—much I cannot abide in Nazism—the regimentation—cruelty—oppression of Jews—attitudes toward religion etc., but Hitler . . . the peasant—will rank some day with Joan of Arc among the deliverers of his people, & if he is only careful may yet be the deliverer of Europe."[79]

While Hitler's subsequent moves—the Anschluss with Austria, the seizure of all of Czechoslovakia—curbed much of King's enthusiasm for the Führer, the prime minister continued to cling to the belief that Hitler's goal was peace, even after the start of the Second World War. In a séance with his lifelong friend Joan Patterson the day after war broke out in Europe, King's grandfather, the politician and 1837 Upper Canada Rebellion leader William Lyon Mackenzie, told his progeny that "Hitler did not want to have war" but had been driven to desperation. In the course of that same session, the earthly King was informed by his deceased parents that Hitler had been "shot [dead] by a Pole" and that "War would be averted."[80] When these assurances proved false, King's diary entry read, "this all makes perfectly clear either that a lying spirit has come in somewhere, or that sub-conscious wishes dictate the words expressed."[81] He swore off any further attempts to gain counsel from the dead for the duration of the war.

More Recent Verdicts on the Visit and King's Leadership

Recent historians' assessments of King's encounter with the monstrous engineers of the Holocaust, rendered with the full knowledge of his private reflections about the affair, are entirely justified in their damnations of the prime minister and his stunning political credulity. Terry Reardon gives King too much slack when he writes that "King's thoughts were written soon after the meeting, and he can be forgiven for his enthusiastic assessment," but the writer is on surer ground in noting that "it is baffling that he could have written in that vein when he knew that the Nazis were operating concentration camps for political prisoners, and that laws had been placed on the books since 1933 to deny Jews the freedoms which the rest of the citizens enjoyed."[82] Claude Bissell argues: "Of all the innocents abroad, King was the most innocent. Whereas his British predecessors had refrained from praising the Nazi regime, King sounded, in his summing up, like a disciple of Oswald Mosley."[83] Larry Rose concedes that the "comments King confided to his diary are cringe-inducing," and Tim Cook concurs, noting that "King's schoolgirlish description [of Hitler] still has the power to make one squirm."[84] Jonathan Wagner reports that even German diplomats stationed in Ottawa found the depth of the prime minister's fervour for Hitler "amusing."[85] King I, the judicious statesman and political savant, never made it to Berlin, and his grave misreading of the most critical issue of his era—and a servile infatuation with Hitler that would have heartened the most ardent Canadian fascist—should prompt at least some attenuation of the praise for his formidable political acumen.

What, then, of the Liberal leader's other celebrated administrative gift—his capacity to divine the public mood? As reporters of King's era and historians writing prior to the mid-1970s had no access to the diaries, their coverage and opinions of his trip to Germany lack the sense of disbelief and mortification present in modern accounts. Even so, the public response of 1937 is conspicuously bereft of any criticisms of the unprecedented decision by a democratic leader to be feted by Nazi leaders or of the prime minister's refusal to raise even the slightest public (and as it turns out, private) objections to the intensively documented ruthlessness that had, by that point, marked more than four years of Hitler's reign.

Those conspicuous absences, placed in the context of the broader societal forbearance for the types of repression that found their fullest expression in Nazism, suggest that King's amalgam of myopia, timidity, and callousness was not merely a personal failing but that the responsibility for and consequences of this diplomatic miscarriage are not King's alone to bear. This is not to say that the prime minister should have spurned the invitation to talk to Third Reich officials. His visit was undertaken in an era wracked by fear and uncertainty and lacking many of the modern mechanisms and institutions aimed at preventing war and mass violations of human rights. King could have made it plain that talk did not amount to legitimization or endorsement and that talk would include a forthright disavowal of the policies that liberal democracies claimed to abhor. He failed to voice any such qualifications, and many Canadians of his era and beyond failed to call out the oversight.

Modern, ethnically diverse Canada has adopted official multiculturalism and championed its reputation as a leading sanctuary for refugees. As several other authors of this volume point out, that progressive identity evolved in often painful fits and starts, and remains only partially realized today. For instance, the few "Yekkes" Jews who managed to emigrate to Canada faced the double exclusion endemic to their Jewish and German heritage, and confronted scorn for their cultural particularisms even from fellow Jews. Similarly, a national identity built on the mythology of Great War valour drew rigid lines around who truly belonged, excluding those deemed insufficiently loyal to King and the Empire. The anointing of Mackenzie King, a one-time devotee of Hitler and principal architect of policies meant to preserve an Anglo-Saxon Canada, as the nation's greatest leader under these circumstances requires a generous capacity to forget, one that may strike the descendants of those he failed to protect in the 1930s as excessive and unmerited. Additional research into how racialized groups, religious minorities, the disabled, and the political left responded to King's close relationship with Nazism—both at the time and in the ensuing decades—will give us a clearer ability to render judgment on the prime minister's vaunted contributions to nation building and national unity.

Notes

1 Stephen Azzi and Norman Hillmer, "Ranking Canada's Best and Worst Prime Ministers," *Maclean's*, 7 October 2016.

2 Matthew Hayday, cited in Norman Hillmer and Stephen Azzi, "Canada's Best Prime Ministers," *Maclean's*, 10 June 2011.

3 Ian Stewart, "Names Written in Water: Canadian National Leaders and Their Reputations among Party Members," *Journal of Canadian Studies/Revue d'études canadiennes* 41, no. 1 (Winter 2007): 34, 36. On the trajectory of King's reputation since his death, see Christopher Dummitt, "The Importance of Not Being Earnest: Postwar Canadians Rethink Mackenzie King's Christian Manhood," in *Canadian Men and Masculinities: Historical and Contemporary Perspectives*, ed. Christopher J. Greig and Wayne Martino (Toronto: Canadian Scholars' Press, 2012), 61–75.

4 Prior to the 1980s, the vast majority of accounts fell into these two camps, although similar assessments continue to the present. A random sampling of monographs and general surveys that conspicuously ignore the trip include Edgar McInnis, *Canada: A Political and Social History* (Toronto: Clarke, Irwin, and Company, 1959); H. Blair Neatby, *The Politics of Chaos: Canada in the Thirties* (Toronto: Macmillan, 1972); J.L. Granatstein, Irving M. Abella, David J. Bercuson, R. Craig Brown, and H. Blair Neatby, *Twentieth Century Canada* (Toronto: McGraw-Hill Ryerson, 1983); J.F. Finlay and D.N. Sprague, *The Structure of Canadian History*, 6th edition (Scarborough: Prentice Hall Canada Inc., 2000); John Herd Thompson and Stephen J. Randall, *Canada and the United States: Ambivalent Allies*, 3rd edition (Athens: University of Georgia Press, 2002); and Desmond Morton, *A Short History of Canada*, 6th ed. (Toronto: McClelland and Stewart, 2006). Accounts that include very brief, similarly worded, and generally laudatory descriptions of

King's "blunt" warning to Hitler include J.B. Brebner, *Canada, a Modern History*, rev. ed. (Ann Arbor: University of Michigan Press, 1970), 469; Henry Reginald Hardy, *Mackenzie King of Canada: A Biography* (Toronto: Greenwood Press, 1970), 165–66; H. Blair Neatby, *William Lyon Mackenzie King Volume III, 1932–1939: Prism of Unity* (Toronto: University of Toronto Press, 1976), 223; J.L. Granatstein, *Mackenzie King: His Life and World* (Toronto: McGraw-Hill Ryerson, 1977), 128; and Robert Bothwell, Ian Drummond, and John English, *Canada 1900–1945* (Toronto: University of Toronto Press, 1987), 313.

5 Jeffrey Keshen, *Saints, Sinners, and Soldiers: Canada's Second World War* (Vancouver: UBC Press 2004), 5.

6 Ibid., 9.

7 Brian Nolan, *King's War: Mackenzie King and the Politics of War, 1939–1945* (Toronto: Random House, 1988), 12.

8 Here I am drawing upon the idea that generations consist of cohorts shaped by their own particular historical and social contexts, as Freund discusses in his Introduction to this collection.

9 Ulrich Frisse, "The Missing Link: Mackenzie King and Canada's 'German Capital,'" in *Mackenzie King: Citizenship and Community*, ed. John English, Kenneth McLaughlin, and P. Whitney Lackenbauer (Toronto: Robin Brass Studio, 2002), 19.

10 Paul Roazen, *Canada's King: An Essay in Political Psychology* (Oakville, ON: Mosaic Press, 1998), 15.

11 Tim Cook, *Warlords: Borden, Mackenzie King, and Canada's World Wars* (Toronto: Allen Lane, 2012), 200.

12 Joy E. Esberey, *Knight of the Holy Spirit: A Study of William Lyon Mackenzie King* (Toronto: University of Toronto Press, 1980), 209.

13 Allan Levine, *King: William Lyon Mackenzie King, A Life Guided by the Hand of Destiny* (Vancouver and Toronto: Douglas and McIntyre, 2011), 297.

14 Bruce Hutchison, *The Incredible Canadian: A Candid Portrait of Mackenzie King* (Toronto: Longmans, Green and Company, 1952), 227.

15 Jonathan F. Wagner, *Brothers Beyond the Sea: National Socialism in Canada* (Waterloo: Wilfrid Laurier University Press, 1981), 122.

16 Claude Bissell, *The Imperial Canadian: Vincent Massey in Office* (Toronto: University of Toronto Press, 1986), 93.

17 W.A.B. Douglas and Brereton Greenhous, *Out of the Shadows: Canada in the Second World War*, 2nd ed. (Toronto: Dundurn, 1996), 11.

18 King Diary, 28 June 1936. Library and Archives Canada, "Diaries of William Lyon Mackenzie King," https://www.bac-lac.gc.ca/eng/discover/politics-government/prime-ministers/william-lyon-mackenzie-king/Pages/diaries-william-lyon-mackenzie-king.aspx.

19 Cited in Esberey, *Knight of the Holy Spirit*, 210.

20 Levine, *King*, 281.

21 Dummitt, "The Importance," 61.

22 Rosine Kelz, *The Non-Sovereign Self, Responsibility, and Otherness: Hannah Arendt, Judith Butler, and Stanley Cavell on Moral Philosophy and Political Agency* (New York: Palgrave Macmillan, 2016), 57–58.

23 Ernest Renan, "What is a Nation?" trans. by Martin Thorn, in *Nation and Narration*, ed. Homi K. Bhabha (London: Routledge, 1990), 11.

24 Ross Poole, "Enacting Oblivion," *International Journal of Politics, Culture, and Society* 22, no. 2 (June 2009): 154.

25 Ibid.

26 The term comes from Constance Backhouse, *Colour-Coded: A Legal History of Racism in Canada, 1900–1950* (Toronto: Osgoode Society for Canadian Legal History/University of Toronto Press, 2001), 14.

27 Irving Abella and Harold Troper, *None Is Too Many: Canada and the Jews of Europe, 1933–1948* (Toronto: Lester and Orpen Dennys, 1982).

28 See L. Ruth Klein's excellent edited collection *Nazi Germany, Canadian Responses: Confronting Antisemitism in the Shadow of War* (Montreal-Kingston: McGill-Queen's University Press, 2012).

29 Amanda Grzyb, "From Kristallnacht to the MS *St Louis* Tragedy: Canadian Press Coverage of Nazi Persecution of Jews and the Jewish Refugee Crisis, September 1938 to August 1939," in Klein, *Nazi Germany*, 82.

30 Richard Menkis and Harold Troper, "Racial Laws vs. Olympic Aspirations in the Anglo-Canadian Press of Fall 1935," in Klein, *Nazi Germany*, 58–63, 67; Ian Kershaw, *Making Friends with Hitler: Lord Londonderry, the Nazis and the Road to World War II* (New York: Penguin, 2004), 32.

31 "The Front Page," *Saturday Night*, 3 July 1937, 1.

32 Canada, House of Commons Debates, 1937, vol. III, 2737–39.

33 O.D. Skelton, "Foreign Policy Discussions in London, 1935," External Affairs Correspondence and Position Papers, n.d., 1935, Folder 3 of 3, O.D. Skelton Fonds, MG 30/D33/13, vol. 4, Library and Archives Canada.

34 Cited in Esberey, *Knight of the Holy Spirit*, 210.

35 King Diary, 11 March 1936.

36 Cited in Esberey, *Knight of the Holy Spirit*, 211.

37 "Nazi Swastikas and Union Jacks Greet Premier's Arrival in Berlin," *Globe and Mail*, 28 June 1937, 1.

38 "Nazi Pastors to Face Trial for Defiance," *Globe and Mail*, 28 June 1937, 1.

39 "Premier Gets Hitler's Views," *Globe and Mail*, 30 June 1937, 1.

40 "King Attend Berlin L'Arrivée De Hitler," *Le Droit*, 28 June 1937, 10.

41 "M. King en France et Allemagne," *Le Droit*, 29 June 1937, 3.

42 "Nazi Camp Visited by King," *Winnipeg Free Press*, 28 June 1937, 1; "King Greeted in Berlin," *Winnipeg Free Press*, 29 June 1937, 6.

43 "L'hon. M. King et la question de nos tarifs," *La Presse*, 28 June 1937, 14.

44 "102 pasteurs allemands écroués en huit jours," *La Presse*, 29 June 1937, 11.

45 George Hambleton, "Premier in Berlin, to Meet Hitler Tomorrow," *Ottawa Citizen*, 28 June 1937, 21.

46 "For Peace with Germany," *Ottawa Citizen*, 29 June 1937, 6.

47 "Mr. King's Conversations," *Globe and Mail*, 3 July 1937, 6; "Premier Gets Hitler's Views.

48 Cited in Levine, *King*, 217.

49 Canada, House of Commons Debates, 1938, vol. I, 471.

50 "A Jolt for Mr. Herridge," *Globe and Mail*, 12 February 1938, 6.

51 "King Won't Tell What He Talked About with Hitler," *Globe and Mail*, 15 February 1938, 1.

52 Kershaw, *Making Friends*, 142.

53 Cited in Levine, *King*, 169.

54 Ibid., 286.

55 Ibid.

56 Ibid., 292.

57 Cited in Neatby, *William Lyon Mackenzie King*, 304.

58 For a similar view of Lord Londonderry's take on Nazism, see Kershaw, *Making Friends*, 147.

59 Amy Knight, *How the Cold War Began: The Gouzenko Affair and the Hunt for Soviet Spies* (Toronto: McClelland and Stewart, 2005), 113.

60 Jonathan Wagner, "Saskatchewan's Sudetendeutsche: The Anti-Nazi Germans of St. Walburg," *Saskatchewan History* 33, no. 3 (1980): 90–101.

61 Renan, "What is a Nation?" 11.

62 Pierre Berton, *The Great Depression, 1929–1939* (Toronto: McClelland and Stewart, 1990), 412.

63 Rideau Banks, "Not Settling the World," *Saturday Night*, 3 July 1937, 5. Richard Kottman reveals the holder of this waggish pseudonym in *Reciprocity and the North Atlantic Triangle, 1932–1938* (Ithaca: Cornell University Press, 1968), 163 n21.

64 Kershaw, *Making Friends*, 25–27.

65 King Diary, 14 June 1936.

66 John MacFarlane, *Ernest Lapointe and Quebec's Influence on Canadian Foreign Policy* (Toronto: University of Toronto Press, 1999), 109.

67 Hutchison, *Incredible Canadian*, 227.

68 Kershaw, *Making Friends*, 200.

69 Cited in Maurice Vernes, *Ernest Renan* (New York: Twayne Publishers, 1968), 101.

70 Canada, House of Commons Debates, 23 March 1936, 1333.

71 Nicholas Mansergh, *The Commonwealth Experience, Volume II: From British to Multiracial Commonwealth* (London: Palgrave Macmillan, 1982), 218.

72 Cited in Max Beloff, *Imperial Sunset: Dream of Commonwealth, 1921–42* (London: Palgrave Macmillan, 1989), 273.

73 Abraham Ascher, *Was Hitler a Riddle? Western Democracies and National Socialism* (Stanford: Stanford University Press, 2012), 8.

74 Cited in Levine, *King*, 281; on Ribbentrop, see Kershaw, *Making Friends*, 160.

75 King Diary, 30 June 1937.

76 Ibid.

77 Graeme Mount, *Canada's Enemies: Spies and Spying in the Peaceable Kingdom* (Toronto: Dundurn, 1993), 53.

78 King Diary, 30 June 1937.

79 Ibid., 14 July 1937.

80 Ibid., 2 September 1939.

81 Ibid., 4 September 1939.

82 Terry Reardon, *Winston Churchill and Mackenzie King: So Similar, So Different* (Toronto: Dundurn, 2012), 83. While Reardon is certainly justified in calling out King's seeming forbearance for concentration camps and anti-Jewish legislation, here again the prime minister's response to these policies may have been tempered

by the fact that Canada and the Empire were no strangers to such practices. The British had deployed notorious concentration camps against the Boers in the South African War, Canada had interned recent immigrants from the central powers in the First World War, and King himself would oversee similar measures against Japanese Canadians in 1942. It's granted that the Nazi roundup occurred in peacetime and saw the murder, not merely detention, of leading "enemies of the state," but King obviously concurred with the notion that, in the interests of national security, the state had a right to deploy the mass incarceration without trial of entire groups suspected of disloyalty. Likewise, the Canadian interdictions against Jews cited above, while not as comprehensive or infamous as those of the Nazis, would have undermined principled objections to Germany's chauvinism. In other words, Reardon may be asking King to express qualms that the prime minister was unwilling or unable to entertain.

83 Claude Bissell, *The Imperial Canadian: Vincent Massey in Office* (Toronto: University of Toronto Press, 1986), 93.

84 Larry D. Rose, *Mobilize! Why Canada Was Unprepared for the Second World War* (Toronto: Dundurn, 2013), 137; Cook, *Warlords*, 200.

85 Wagner, *Brothers Beyond the Sea*, 122.

CHAPTER 3

A Transnational Yekkish Identity? Comparing German Jews in Canada and Israel

PATRICK FARGES

Migrants from German-speaking countries or regions form a global diaspora in which forms of "Germanness" are transmitted and (re)produced.[1] Within this diaspora, socio-cultural distinctions may include dialects, geographical origin, date of immigration as well as cultural and religious backgrounds—aspects that lead to the creation of subsequent in-groups. One such in-group are the German-speaking Jews who throughout the nineteenth century had intellectually shaped German culture and formed an integral part of the emerging bourgeois middle class,[2] despite the permanence of a deeply rooted anti-Semitism in German and Austrian societies. In German (and Austrian) urban and industrial centres, the proportion of "assimilated," and sometimes converted, Jews was high, to the extent that Judaism was only marginally part of some families' social practice and identity. At the same time, the German language, (high) culture, and education were important means of integration into the bourgeois middle class, and hence they became identity markers for Jews even after they left Germany. Notwithstanding, German-speaking Jews and their transnational post-migration identities in particular remain under-researched.[3]

In 1933, half a million Jews—those who claimed to be Jewish and viewed themselves as a religious minority—were living in Germany.[4] However, although the "German-Jewish symbiosis" was revealed as an illusion after the brutal rupture of 1933 when Adolf Hitler and his party came to power, the cultural heritage of German Jewry was not completely eradicated by Nazism and the Holocaust. After 1933, many German-speaking Jewish refugees fled to a number of countries where they grew new roots. According to German historian Wolfgang Benz, approximately 250,000 Jews left Germany between 1933 and 1939. In addition, over 100,000 Austrian Jews became refugees after Austria's annexation in 1938.[5] In some host societies—most prominently in Mandatory Palestine/Israel—the German-speaking Jews became known as "Yekkes," a term that connotes cultural difference and formal stiffness. Corresponding to the dominant etymology, the word comes from German *Jacke* and Yiddish *yekke* for "jacket." The label allegedly plays on the Yekkes' inadequate clothing as a trace of their bourgeois past. In a 1943 article published in the *Menorah Journal*, Hannah Arendt—herself a German Jew in exile—used the term to demonstrate the German-Jewish refugees' distinct ethnicity abroad.[6] Like the term "Ostjuden," which "assimilated" Jews in Germany used to designate Jews who had emigrated from Eastern Europe, "Yekke" was originally meant as a derogatory term in order to ridicule German-speaking Jews and mock their deeply habitual formal manners. Such usage seems to have originated in Eastern European, Yiddish-speaking communities. The Yekke was not a "pariah" (Arendt's terminology); that is, a Jew rejected by non-Jews. The Yekke was a Jew who was being ostracized by other Jews because of a mocked social status and grandeur.[7] Yet, over time, the term's connotation gradually changed and became a positive marker of "ethnic" cultural difference.

The purpose of this chapter is to show how the German-speaking Jewish refugees who came to and stayed in Canada and Mandatory Palestine/Israel after 1933 reconstructed their individual identities; how they interacted with their socio-cultural environment; and how they created and transmitted their distinct collective memory within the larger frame of a reconfigured postwar Jewish diaspora. How did these refugees cope with memories of persecution, expulsion, flight, war, and genocide? Far from being shielded from ostracism after they had escaped Nazi Europe, the German-speaking Jews were confronted with various forms of rejection and hostility in their host societies. For instance, they experienced forms of anti-Semitism and cultural denigration within the Jewish community in Canada and rejection of an abhorred "Germanness" in Mandatory Palestine/Israel. The

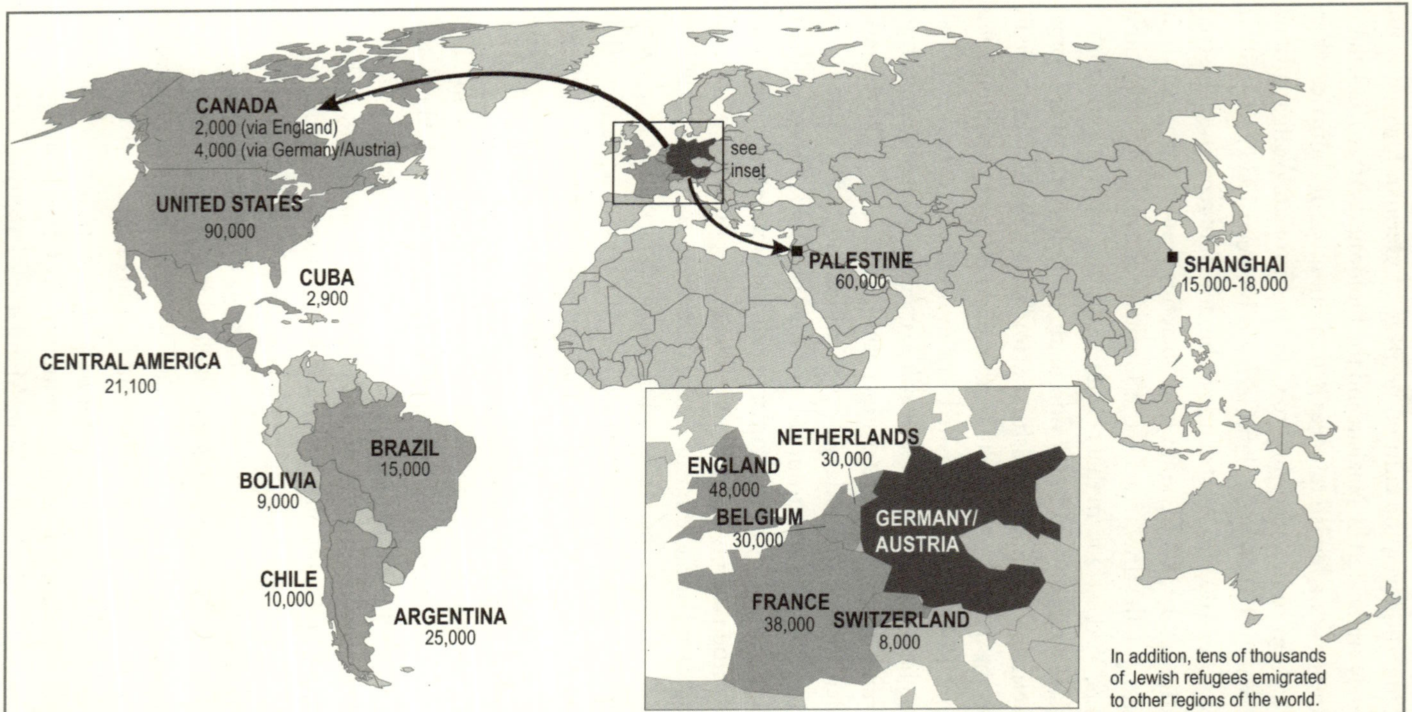

Map 3.1. Jewish emigration from Germany (and Austria), 1933 to 1940. Adapted from United States Holocaust Museum, https://encyclopedia.ushmm.org/content/en/gallery/refugees-maps.

transnational "Yekkish" identities were thus profoundly reconfigured according to local socio-cultural environments. The Yekkes' distinctive selfhood was largely situational, and depended on their relations with other groups in multicultural societies. Understanding the interactions and frictions at the margins of ethno-cultural group definitions unveils the mechanisms that lead to such imagined group formations in the first place. Subsequently, such understanding helps us to grasp multicultural dynamics. Moreover, challenging the dichotomy of "ethnic retention" and "acculturation,"[8] the intense and selective use of "Yekkishkeit"[9]—as a specific form of "symbolic ethnicity"[10] expressed in language use, everyday practices, values, and narratives—proves that the Yekkes strategically saw these elements of identification as something "worth holding onto."[11] Yekkishkeit, Yekkes' way of being, I shall argue, can be seen as one of many memory options available for German-speaking Jews in Canada and Israel.

In "comparing the uncomparable," to use Marcel Detienne's phrasing,[12] or the Canadian and Israeli society, I will discuss the transnational heritage of German Jewry as it is preserved in social networks, values, and socialization approaches. By doing so, I wish to integrate German Jewish Canadian issues into a larger historical context and answer Alexander Freund's call to open up a "German-Canadian bubble that is too small to sustain dialogue" (Introduction). My research during the last fifteen years in both Canada and Israel was conducted, to a considerable extent, by the way of ethnographic oral history. In addition to personal interviews, my sources also include personal papers, testimonies, correspondences, memoirs, and autobiographical accounts found in archival or private collections.[13] Consequently, my research is a qualitative study of mostly everyday acculturation and identity work of German-speaking Jewish immigrants, based on the interpretation of personal and largely narrative data.

The Yekkes as Canada's "Accidental" Immigrants

In Canada, the official policy of multiculturalism sets an institutional framework in which ethnic cultures are granted recognition. Theoretically, therefore, multiculturalism promotes the "acculturation" over the "assimilation" paradigm thought to be prevalent in other societies, most prominently in the United States. Canadian multiculturalism, however, embodies the paradox that cultures can be recognized and gain visibility only if they correspond to institutionalized and socially accepted norms of multiculturalism. As a result, there is little allowance for in-between or interstitial identities. One of those interstitial "blind spots"[14] in German-Canadian historiography is the story of the German-speaking Jewish refugees, a story that falls in between the cracks of the Canadian mosaic—in between German-Canadian historiography and Jewish-Canadian historiography.[15]

As a consequence of Nazism, between 4,900 and 6,000 German-speaking refugees came to Canada, most of whom were Jewish. Some gained entry into Canada because they had relatives who vouched for them, others were able to demonstrate proficiency in a profession favoured by immigration officials, while others, still, settled as farmers. During the 1930s, however, Canada did not have a welcoming policy toward Jewish refugees, despite the fact that Canadians were well informed about the violent excesses of the Nazi regime at the time, as Robert Teigrob shows in Chapter 2. Consequently, Canada in the 1930s was not a haven for groups fleeing persecution.[16] In 1940, Canada also took in civilian internees from Great Britain, referred to as the "camp boys." This group consisted for the most part of Germans and Austrians residing on British soil. In view of Germany's growing military successes in the Second World War, the fear of a "fifth column" of saboteurs spread over the United Kingdom, reaching a peak in the spring of 1940. In reaction, Winston Churchill decided to register and categorize all "enemy aliens" and to intern some of them.[17] Among those interned, there were numerous Jewish refugees. About 2,000 male internees were then sent overseas to Canada (and Australia) where they spent several months in internment camps. As Ernest Robert Zimmerman has illustrated, the incredible micro-history of "Camp R," located in Red Rock, Ontario, was part of the larger history of Canada's handling of approximately 35,000 prisoners of war and civilian internees, and of Canadian participation in the Second World War. In Camp R, as in other "ethnic" Canadian internment camps, the detainees' composition was mixed: among them were Nazis, anti-Nazis, soldiers, merchant seamen, Italians, and German-Jewish refugees whom London saw as "high security risks."[18] In her recent dissertation, Christine Whitehouse has demonstrated that this episode was part of Canada's larger practices of war internment, wherein the detainees were moulded according to the nation state's normalizing project.[19] After finally being released,

Figure 3.1. German Jewish refugees arrive in Montreal, *The Gazette,* 19 November 1938. LAC, PA-156125.

Figure 3.2. "Some Victims of Nazi Oppression." LAC, MG30, c192, vol. 2. Eric Koch Fonds.

they became Canada's "accidental immigrants."[20] About half of the internees returned to the United Kingdom, while the rest permanently settled in North America.

In Canada, the German-speaking Jewish refugees were sometimes stigmatized as Germans (and thus considered enemies), or as Jews by anti-Semites, and in some cases as "German Jews" within the Jewish community. Canadian society was generally not welcoming toward those who did not approximate the dominant model or were not of "native stock." In English-speaking Canada, the main concern of "nativists" who opposed immigration was that the "British" character of Canada would be seriously threatened by a massive immigration of people who seemed to defy assimilation, especially Asians, Blacks, and Jews.[21] When, after being released from internment, Gerd Waldstein was not hired for several jobs in 1944, he assumed that it was because his name sounded German, Jewish, or both German and Jewish. He then decided to change it to Gerry Waldston and quickly found a job in the advertising field in Montreal.[22] In his memoirs, Eric Exton (born Erich Eckstein) recalled that his first Canadian boss overtly suggested a name change in 1943: "'We're at war with Germany, so a German and Jewish sounding name just won't do,' he said. 'How about something more Canadian, like, say, Elliott?'"[23]

When entering Canada, the German-speaking Jewish refugees were burdened with the weight of their cultural and experiential "heavy baggage" (Freund, in Introduction), which included racial stigmatization, estrangement, and displacement (sometimes several displacements). In order to avoid discrimination, their preferred strategy was to blend in as much as possible. If one could not possibly hide a German accent, one could at least pass as a non-Jew. Anti-Semitism was a widely accepted, normal aspect of everyday life in the late 1930s and 1940s. When endorsed by immigration officials or civil servants, it would lead to a form of institutional anti-Semitism based on simple prejudice, as well as elaborately constructed economic and social theories in order to justify anti-immigration measures. This explains why some refugees decided to adopt English-sounding names, to marry non-Jews, or to convert. The anti-Semitism at schools and universities—still largely denominational Christian institutions at the time—was rampant. Alfred Bader, who studied at Queen's University in the 1940s after being released from an internment camp, explained that "a protracted discussion went on at the university's Board of Trustees meetings regarding the increasing number of Jewish students. Before the war, 2 or 3 percent of the students were Jews, by 1944 this had risen to 10 percent. They came mainly from Montreal where McGill enforced a *numerus clausus*. Jews had to have higher marks than Christians to be admitted."[24]

Moreover, after the Second World War the German-Jewish identity could no longer be referred to within the Canadian Jewish community unproblematically. Eric Koch stated in an interview in 2003: "German Jew. Do you know what irritates me most? Before the Nazis, we used to be Germans. There existed something like that. We were Germans, we were Jews, we were Germans. It's unimaginable today."[25] "Canadian Jewry," the American historian Jonathan Sarna argues, "never experienced a 'great German period' in the sense in which the term is used in the United States. For this reason, the community is both more homogeneous and more heavily East European than in the United States."[26] American urban centres, like Philadelphia, Cincinnati, and especially New York, had been characterized by ongoing frictions between German-Jewish "uptowners" (old immigrants) and Eastern European Jewish "downtowners." In Canada, the small wave of post-1933 refugees bore alone the weight of the "German" tradition. This was the case of Emil L. Fackenheim (born in Halle), a German-Jewish refugee, who came to Canada as a "camp boy" and later became the Rabbi of the Anshe Sholom Congregation in Hamilton. He was one of the most distinguished Canadian scholars of Reform Judaism, a religious practice that was consolidated in Germany in the nineteenth century. Another example was Rabbi W. Gunther Plaut (born in Münster), who had first-hand experience of the differences between Jewish culture in the United States and Canada. In 1935, his first destination when he came to North America as a refugee was the American Reform Seminary (Hebrew Union College) of Cincinnati, where he encountered modern Judaism—the continuation in the United States of German Jewish Reform practices. After twenty-five years in the United States, Plaut moved to the Holy Blossom Temple in Toronto in 1961 and became a leader of Reform Judaism in Canada.

For the most part, German-speaking Jews did not fit into a Canadian-Jewish community that largely embodied a culture they had looked down upon in the old *Heimat* (home). Rabbi Erwin Schild recalls that he first had to learn Yiddish in order to address his congregation at the Adath Israel synagogue in Toronto.[27] By doing so, he earned the respect of the congregation's members. Most refugees, however, remained strangers in the local community. Well-educated, worldly, and sophisticated, they were assimilated Jews who spoke German—sometimes along with French—and they clashed with a working-class milieu dominated by Polish and Galician Jews. In the sharp and ironic tone so characteristic of his writings, Mordecai Richler portrayed the arrival of the refugees, as embodied by an archetypal Yekke Mr. Bamberger:

> The war in Europe brought about considerable changes within the Jewish community in Montreal. To begin with, there was the coming of the refugees. These men . . . were to make a profound impact on us. I think we had conjured up a picture of the refugees as penurious *hassidim* with packs on their backs. We were eager to be helpful, our gestures were large, but in return we expected more than a little gratitude. As it turned out the refugees, mostly German and Austrian Jews, were far more sophisticated and better educated than we were. They had not, like our immigrant grandparents, come from *shtetls* in Galicia or Russia. Neither did they despise Europe. On the contrary, they found our culture thin, the city provincial, and the Jews narrow. This bewildered and stung us. But what cut deepest, I suppose, was that the refugees spoke English better than many of us did and, among themselves, had the effrontery to talk in the abhorred German language.[28]

Richler depicted the mixed feelings toward German-speaking Jews, which fluctuated between animosity, envy, and reluctant respect. Some of the refugees recalled being perceived as "arrogant know-it-alls who were not properly grateful for the marvellous opportunity afforded to them in the New World."[29] Helmut Kallmann confessed: "I guess everyone went through a little bit of '*zuhause war alles besser*' [everything was better at home] attitude, perhaps as a self-defence, even when you came from Nazi Germany!"[30] Erwin Schild also remembered the difficult relations with Jews of Eastern European origin: "We certainly had fun, Jewish religious fun. Modern Westernized Jews rubbed shoulders—and sensitivities—with 'Ostjuden,' mutually suspicious and quaint; the

Figure 3.3. Helmut Kallmann, "Camp I with netmakers outside barbed wire." Ontario Jewish Archives, *Ex-Internees Newsletter,* 1969, Fonds 93, Box 1, file 9.

'Yekkes' with their stiffly formal, punctilious style of Jewish observance clashed with the informality of the Yeshivah spirit."[31]

In Canada, the low numbers of German-speaking Jews made it almost impossible to locally recreate "Little Jewish Germanies."[32] It was also not possible to envision close relations with the German-Canadian community that developed a culture of victimization and stigmatization over time (see Freund's Introduction), for which the German-speaking refugees and their descendants had little understanding. The dominant impression among German-speaking Jews was that in the 1930s and even after the Second World War, most German Canadians were largely anti-Semitic.[33] With the exception of the German Society of Montreal (twice chaired by Jewish refugees from Germany in the past forty years), there was hardly any common ground for a German-Jewish dialogue in Canada. Cultural transmission of the German-Jewish heritage was thus relegated to private practices among family and friends.

Consequently, the Yekkes in Canada were separated from the cultural environment in which they had been socialized. They were the heirs of an impossible cultural heritage for which there was little understanding after Auschwitz. For a long time, the stories of those who had escaped the Nazi regime *before* the final solution could not be told, as they were incommensurable with the horrors of the Holocaust. While German-Jewish culture was not completely annihilated in the Holocaust, the German-speaking Jews were largely silenced after the Second World War.

In the postwar period, a dominant narrative emerged within the Canadian Jewish community. As Canadian historian Abella summarizes: "The world had become too dangerous a place for Jews to allow themselves the luxury of internal dissent and divisiveness. . . . Jewish energies were now totally devoted to protecting the State of Israel, to welcoming the influx of Holocaust survivors and to breaking down the barriers in Canadian society. One Yiddish pundit labelled postwar Jewry the 'sha shtill' generation, literally the silent generation, afraid to rock the boat for fear of sinking with it."[34] Postwar Canada opened its doors to approximately 20,000 Holocaust survivors. Though the Holocaust had a "delayed impact" on Jews in Canada, it became a structuring memory for the Jewish community in the 1970s and 1980s. According to Franklin Bialystok, "by 1985, most Canadian Jews felt that the destruction of European Jewry was *their* loss as well. . . . [The Holocaust] had now become an important marker of ethnic awareness."[35] Within the "silent generation," the Yekke voice inevitably became even fainter.

Little by little, the prevailing memory within the Jewish community in Canada reinforced the rupture between Jewish-Canadian and German-Canadian postwar memories, and later between Jewish-Canadian and German-Canadian historiographies, which contradicted the Yekkes' deepest feelings of self-identification. Though they did not identify with German Canadians (or Austrian Canadians), the Yekkes kept an emotional and cultural link to Germany (or Austria). The impossible dialogue with "Germans" was a recurrent theme within the Jewish community. Another prominent characteristic was the symbolic boycott of German things. These aspects even became narrative features of a collective Jewish-Canadian memory. This, however, put the Yekkes in an untenable identity and memory position. Similarly, it was unimaginable for a long time that Jews would want to return to Germany or Austria. The son of a Yekke said: "You know, when people say to me: 'How could your father go back after what they did to the Jews,' you know, after that, it's inconceivable, it's crazy. I don't feel that way. I understand fully that my father at some level believes he is German and still feels connected."[36] Rabbi Erwin Schild also repeatedly reflected on this very issue: "Why did it take so long to tell the story? How could you speak of suffering when you had escaped from the Nazi continent, when you knew only too well what your brothers and sisters were experiencing? And how could you help feeling guilty when your contemporaries were undergoing the agonies of a horrible war while you were enjoying the security and the abundance of Canada?"[37] The German-Jewish refugees who survived through their migration were Holocaust survivors of a *different* kind.[38] Erwin Schild wrote: "Our internment was a minor event, dwarfed by the Holocaust,"[39] signalling his sentiment of an illegitimate right to testify. In his text titled "A Canadian Footnote to the Holocaust," Schild equates his life-changing and traumatic experience as a refugee to a mere footnote in history, an infrapaginal co-text in the history of Jews in the twentieth century.

After attending the funeral of a Yekke in Montreal in the late 1990s, Chaim Vogt-Moykopf wrote a nostalgic article in the New York–based German-Jewish magazine *Aufbau* about "the last Yekkes."[40] The article underlined that Yekke culture in Canada had died away with the passing of its bearers. There is no third generation of Yekkes in Canada. Yet some sense of a distinct Yekkish "symbolic ethnic" memory has been transmitted on a small scale and almost secretly to children and grandchildren in private circles. Remarkably, as in German-Canadian families, silences were transmitted to the next generations, even when the German language was not (see Sara Frankenberger in Chapter 8). Wendy Oberlander, the daughter of Peter Oberländer (born in 1923 Vienna), always knew that *something* had been transmitted to her, but she needed time to figure out what that something was. In 2013, she wrote about her efforts to make sense of the scarce traces her father left behind: "How to find words in the silence? How to make something from nothing? Luckily, the time was right. During the late 1980s and '90s, other children of immigrants [in Canada] started to narrate their parents' past. . . . We started with questions, asked from the privilege of here, not there, looking tentatively at the geographies of displacement: what could they tell us that our parents could not?"[41] Currently, the German embassy in Ottawa receives applications for re-naturalization from former German citizens who lost their German citizenship under the Nazi regime and from their children who feel some connection to Germany. Unlike other Jewish families, Yekkes and their descendants have the possibility to obtain dual citizenship and hence a German passport, which in a way materializes their transnational identity.

The Yekkes in Israel: At the Margins of the Centre

To some extent, the German-Jewish refugees in Mandatory Palestine/Israel had similar experiences to those in London, New York, Toronto, and Montreal: finding a job, learning a new language, adjusting to the climate, coping with a foreign administration, and dealing with loss and rupture. These experiences cannot be specifically defined as "Zionist"—they are at the core of most immigrants' lives. However, the immigration of Jews to Eretz Israel had a somewhat different connotation: it was considered an "Aliyah," a mythical return and ascent to the Promised Land that ended the state of exile "Galuth" and dispersion "Diaspora." Whereas prior to 1933, fewer than 3,000 German-speaking Jews had immigrated to Palestine under British administration, between 1933 and 1941, nearly 55,000 Jews emigrated from Germany to Palestine (among those, 6,000 had a non-German—often Polish—passport). In addition, 9,500 Jews left Austria for Palestine after the "Anschluss" in March 1938, and 11,000 Jews escaped from Czechoslovakia to Palestine after the Munich Agreement in September 1938, some of which were German-speaking. In total, approximately 90,000 German-speaking Jews found refuge in Mandatory Palestine in the 1930s and 1940s.[42] They constituted nearly 15 percent of the "Yishuv" (settlement) or 15 percent of all the Jewish residents in Eretz Israel. The newcomers were hence a significant minority. At the time, the Yishuv was already in a process of social and cultural formation and though it was never a homogeneous community, but one of "Olim" (immigrants who made Aliyah), it did not easily absorb the influx of German-speaking Jews who brought their lifestyle and culture with them.

In Zionist historiography, this migration was labelled "Fifth (or German) Aliyah," which postulated a form of continuity with previous Aliyot since the end of the nineteenth century. Yet, a majority of the German-speaking Jews who settled in Jerusalem, Tel Aviv, Haifa, Nahariya, or in various kibbutzim during the Fifth Aliyah (1930s to 1940s) had not planned on "ascending" to the Promised Land. Most of them would have stayed in Europe had the Nazis not come to power.

This generated specific acculturation problems. Most of these refugees were not committed Zionists but had been forced into exile by the radicalization of anti-Semitism and the brutalization that took place in Nazi Europe. Inhabitants of the Yishuv sometimes called them "Hitler-Zionists," and a common quip about them was voiced as the question: "Do you come out of conviction or do you come from Germany?" (*Kommen Sie aus Überzeugung oder kommen Sie aus Deutschland?*). In fact, most German-speaking Jews lived their migration as a form of exile—similarly to the refugees in Canada.

In the early years of Israel, the Zionist movement, dominated by the Labour Party (Mapai), sought to unite all Jews from the diaspora in the form of a "melting pot" (*mizug galuyot*) that did not leave room for transnational identities. Zionism combined a socialist discourse, collectivist values, and a secular national ethos. As a national movement, it advocated for a pioneering spirit, the use of modern Hebrew, and the redemptive aspect of physical labour, agricultural settlement, and military defence.[43] These injunctions translated into political power and socio-ethnic hegemonic models. The Zionist archetype of the "New Jew," characterized as a man and a citizen in arms, was one such example. The New Jew had to free himself from his diasporic roots.[44] In practice, however, Israeli society was multi-ethnic and, like many other multi-ethnic states (e.g., Canada), Israel was faced with dilemmas stemming from this multicultural reality, as cultural, linguistic, religious, and ethnic minorities struggled for distinctive forms of recognition. Since the 1970s, the divisions in Israeli society had begun to become salient, revealing the growing discontent of previously marginalized groups.

By and large, Ashkenazi Jews positioned themselves at the centre of the Yishuv and, later, at the centre of Israeli society, holding key positions in administration, the army, and politics. In doing so, they excluded a number of other groups such as Sephardic and Oriental Jews as well as the Arab population. The German-speaking Jews, however, who were predominantly Ashkenazi, did not exactly meet Zionist demands. In particular, they voiced their reluctance to endorse militaristic and nationalistic defence values because they had witnessed, first-hand, the dangers of exacerbated militarism in Europe.[45] In the oral history interviews and self-narratives that I have analyzed, many complained retrospectively about the pressure to integrate, the imposed process of absorption into the Israeli melting pot, and, most prominently, about the symbolically violent process of Hebraicization. Performing the role of a New Jew and *Daber Ivrit* (speaking Hebrew) were imperious Zionist injunctions. The Israeli writer and translator Michael Dak, son of German Jewish parents, wrote: "Hebrew? Some of the [German-speaking] immigrants turned away from the new language. *Ivrit saffa kasha*, Ivrit difficult language, they said, in a syntax that was unmistakably German. Strange sounds encountered closed lips."[46]

The Yekkes experienced rejection and prejudice that was based on being seen as conservative, European, and alienated from Judaism as well as being arrogant and utterly bourgeois. When compared to the reputation of German-speaking Jews in Canada, this seemed to be the most common way Yekke identities were perceived. The cultural link to Germany and the German language were vehemently discouraged. Even before the horrors of the Holocaust became fully known and discussed in Israeli society, the Yekkes' "Germanness" and the cultural heritage they clung to were perceived as problematic. While the German language was banned from public life in Israel,[47] some Yekkes kept their cultural heritage in private circles, cafés, and amongst friends and families. In fact, the interviews of Yekkes in Israel that I consulted were entirely in German (with occasional cases of code switching into English or Hebrew)—over fifty years after migration. In comparison, the twenty-five interviews I conducted in Canada between 1999 and 2004 were mostly in English, occasionally in French, with rare instances of German. In Israel, German language and culture retention became a coping mechanism for some. Contrary to Canada, in Israel there were "German" cultural enclaves wherein Yekkishkeit was born.

The high level of cultural capital within this group sometimes delayed German-speaking families' economic integration into Israeli society. The German-speaking Jews were well-educated, professionally skilled, and often in possession of economic resources; in other words, they were a high-status immigration group. At the same time, they were "inside outsiders" in their society, located at the margins of the centre, and they experienced hostility and contempt. Their response was to found an "ethnic" organization in the 1930s, which eventually became the Organization of Immigrants from Central Europe (Irgun Olei Merkaz Europa or Irgun), and a political party, the New Immigration (Aliyah Hadashah), that was established in 1942. The party's leaders, such as Pinchas Rosen (Felix Rosenblüth), campaigned for Yekke recognition but also for urban planning, social services, education, and, most critically, for an understanding (*Verständigung*) of Arab political and territorial claims.[48] This call for compromise and negotiation did not correspond to the dominant Zionist militaristic view, which the New Jew had to follow. The Aliyah Hadashah was short-lived: after the Israeli Declaration of Independence in 1948, the party merged with several other liberal parties to form the Progressive Party.

Inner Jewish political and socio-cultural conflict was rife and the Yekkes were ideal scapegoats. They embodied what the Israeli Jew should not be. During the creation of a young Jewish nation of Israel, Yekkishkeit was a strategic response to specific socio-cultural dynamics. Like other ethnic groups after migration, the German-speaking Jews in the nascent state of Israel created a socio-cultural sphere with specific internal hierarchies, codes, and rules of distinction. "Be(com)ing a Yekke" was a complex process of identity negotiation involving a cultural European heritage as well as a strategic positioning within the Israeli arena.

Over the years, the connotation of "Yekke" and even the Yekke jokes have changed. This originated in Israeli society and then spread to Canada, the United States, and other countries. Whereas the term "Yekke" had been derogatory in the 1950s, at the climax of anti-German sentiment in Israel, it had become a distinctive ethnic attribute a decade later.[49] In 1979, Haim Hermann Cohn (himself a Yekke, born in Lübeck in 1911), a Supreme Court of Israel judge, even declared the term to be an honorary title. To be a "real" Yekke meant to maintain a certain distance from the Zionist ideal of Hebraicization.

Above all though, Yekkishkeit was not Yiddishkayt, the Yiddish-speaking Jews' way of being. To identify as a true Yekke was to reject *Ostjudentum*, or the culture of traditionally Eastern European Jews, a point that has already been observed for Canada. This had something to do with embodying the master narrative of *Verbürgerlichung* and displaying distinctive bourgeois habits, which involved distinct cultural practices. For instance, Josef Burg (born in Dresden in 1909) insisted on the Yekke lineage of a friend of his, a former member of the Knesset: "Moshe Unna was a *true* Yekke. His father was [a] Rabbi in Mannheim, his great-grandfather was a Rabbi in Würzburg, the famous Rabbi Bamberger in Würzburg, one hundred and thirty, one hundred and forty years ago: Yekke ben [son of] Yekke ben Yekke ben

Yekke!"[50] This form of "symbolic ethnicity" sometimes led to paradoxes. Even families with an "ostjüdisch" past were keen on displaying real, "kosher" Yekkishkeit,[51] precisely because it was a distinctive feature that could in part be self-proclaimed. This worked both ways: the former director of the Leo Baeck Institute in Jerusalem (a core institution in preserving the memory of German Judaism), Joseph Walk (born in Breslau in 1914), never considered himself a "full" Yekke because his father was born in Lithuania.[52]

Over the years, Yekkishkeit became a unifying feature among German-speaking Jews. It made them a more cohesive ethnic group in Israel than they had been in Germany before migration. The Yekkes' inclusion into Israeli society is thus a paradigmatic case of "integration through distinction."[53] Through ethnic organizations, gatherings, publications, and even the inauguration of a Yekke Museum in Tefen (Galilea) in 2005, Yekkishkeit has been transmitted to the second and third generations, while the German language has not (or only partly).[54] Israel or, to be more precise, certain neighbourhoods in Tel Aviv, Jerusalem, Haifa, and Nahariya developed as important centres of a transnational Yekkishkeit, with antennas reaching all the way to the United Kingdom, the United States, and Canada.

Transnational Dynamics: New Geographies of Yekkishkeit?

Displacement, both geographical and cultural, is the common feature of migrant trajectories. Hence, the comparative dimension is at the core of migrant experience. Comparison takes place between "here" and "there" and between "here" and other possible destinations one could have gone—destinations to which family members, friends, or former neighbours may have migrated. Transnationalism as a research agenda that profoundly reconfigures migration studies offers tools to grasp the socio-cultural dynamics that take place in diasporic communities. Instead of focusing on rupture and trauma, transnational studies focus on *longue durée* continuities, long after the actual migration takes place, and also on transversal ties migrant families forge between host societies. Transnationalism thus helps us to rethink societies as they are created. Scholars show in particular how migrants maintain and establish social ties within fluid transnational spaces. These spaces are constantly being reworked through migrants' simultaneous embeddedness in more than one society: in fact, they are created through migration by migrants.[55] In migration studies, I argue for a broad approach of transnationalism that includes formal as well as informal social, cultural, and intergenerational family practices, which simultaneously connect various levels of social experience and "ways of belonging."[56] The sites of identity negotiation are multi-layered and include not just the home and host societies but other places around the world that link migrants to the people they feel connected to. This definition of transnationalism is particularly relevant in societies like Canada and Israel where multiculturalism and diversity offer multiple identity options.

The forced out-migration of German-speaking Jews after 1933 led to a new form of diaspora. The Israeli historian and journalist Tom Segev, himself the son of Yekke parents, called it a "Yekkish diaspora."[57] The remnants of German-speaking Jewry were indeed scattered across different parts of the world, and the examples of Canada and Israel I presented here are just two of their many destinations. Other important places on the map of post-1945 German Jewry include New York, London, Sidney, Buenos Aires, and, more recently as the grandchildren of Yekkes "return" to Germany, Berlin. German-Jewish families maintained transnational ties between Jerusalem and Toronto and between Tel Aviv and New York. They visited family members and friends, wrote letters, sent packages, and, above all, kept abreast of what was going on in their relatives' and friends' lives abroad. In a way, the Yekkish postwar diaspora is a paradigmatic Jewish experience of dispersion, and it seems particularly fitting for a transnational research approach. This transnational diasporic Yekkish space, however, was not free of internal contradictions: German and Austrian Jews of the first generation did not mingle; nor did Zionists and non-Zionists mix; bourgeois German Jews who lived in Jerusalem's Rehavia neighbourhood looked down on those Jews from Germany with an *ostjüdisch* background; Orthodox German Jewish families in Montreal did not socialize with non-religious German Jews; and those who migrated in the 1930s (i.e., before the horrors of the Holocaust) were distinct from Holocaust survivors who immigrated to Canada and Israel after 1945. The Yekkes as a transnational ethnic group are not homogeneous: they come from different social backgrounds, voice different political opinions, and have different levels of religiosity. In addition, their very migration differed greatly due to their financial conditions, age, gender, and profession, and they settled in different places in societies with diverse potentials.

As early as 1955, German Jewish émigrés, among them Martin Buber, Ernst Simon, Hannah Arendt, and Robert Weltsch, were determined to preserve the cultural legacy of German Judaism and founded the Leo Baeck Institute (LBI) in Jerusalem. At the first conference, most participants were Yekke personalities who, in the interwar period, had been members of the Central-Verein deutscher Staatsbürger jüdischen Glaubens, the Zionistische Vereinigung für Deutschland, and the Reichsvertretung der Deutschen Juden. The Institute was named after Rabbi Leo Baeck (1873–1956). He represented the tradition of Liberal Judaism and had been the last leader of Germany's Jewish community under Nazism. Baeck, who settled in London after the war and chaired the World Union for Progressive Judaism, was appointed as the Institute's first president. In 1955, the LBI established centres in Jerusalem, London, and New York. In the late 1990s, the LBI-New York opened an office in Berlin, which became an administrative branch in 2013. Also, since 1956, the LBI-London has been publishing the *Leo Baeck Institute Year Book* (Oxford University Press), a renowned journal in the field of the history of German-speaking Jews. These branches of LBI have been engaged in preserving a transnational memory of German Jewry by collecting material, doing research, and presenting historical narratives.[58]

For the Yekke diaspora, the question of a centre became particularly crucial after the Second World War, when the Zionist response to the Holocaust was to impose Israel as the unique place of reference for all Jews. In return, Yekkes made claims on alternative centres like London, New York, and even, more recently, Berlin and Vienna. Building on the historical "distinctive path" of German Zionism,[59] many voices critical of Zionist injunctions came from Yekkes scattered around the world. In spite of the difficulties linked to embodying Germanness, reaffirming one's Yekkishkeit (hence one's emotional ties to things German), and resisting the host societies' cultural injunctions, these practices can be seen as strategies for defining what it means to be Jewish after the Second World War. In the context of a critical contemporary re-evaluation of Zionist injunctions, new Jewish ethnicities are being discussed, and Yekkishkeit is one of them. This is why the historiography of the Yekke phenomenon has been flourishing for over a decade. In 2004, the cultural centre Mishkenot Sha'ananim in Jerusalem hosted a conference on Yekkes. Against all odds and much to the surprise of the organizers, a crowd of second- and third-generation Israelis attended the conference, commencing vivid debates about the intergenerational nature of collective memory. It is also noteworthy that the conference proceedings were published in Germany and in the German language.[60] The second and third generation showed a deep personal and familial identification with the legacy of German Judaism and the urge to preserve this legacy. Those involved in keeping the Yekke identity alive wanted to underline a humanistic dimension of German history, in which the Jews were an integral part of German culture and society.

In recent years, a new occurrence is affecting third-generation Yekkes. Germany in general and Berlin in particular have become destinations for young Jews who want to experience, temporarily or permanently, the country of their ancestors. This is also part of a more general trend that leads young Israeli citizens of Ashkenazi descent to apply for European passports. Owning a European passport is as a security measure in view of the geopolitical situation in the Middle East, an intergenerational gift, and a distinctive "inner-Jewish" (Ashkenazi) feature. It signifies one's (high) cultural background, which is constructed in opposition to Sephardic or Mizrahi (Oriental) Jewish origins. Being an Ashkenazi, and—even more so—being of Yekke descent, holds specific connotations in regard to one's position on the contemporary Jewish map. This certainly holds true in Israel and, to some extent, in the United States. However, in this regard, more research is needed in Canada.

New forms of transnational circulations are thus made possible within a fluid Yekkish space. Currently, Berlin is becoming a new centre of Jewish life and culture, especially since the influx of Russian Jews in the 1990s, a phenomenon that also characterizes Russian Jewish migrations into Israeli and Canadian cities.[61] Moreover, new "German Jews" continue to build new Jewish networks and communities. Decades after the Holocaust, it appears that Jewish life and culture indeed have a future in Germany. In 2012, an English-language newspaper, the *Jewish Voice from Germany*, was founded to document the diversity of German-Jewish life. Its readers are scattered around the world; they reside in Berlin, New York City, Chicago, Toronto, London, Haifa, and Tel Aviv.

Conclusion

This chapter provides one example of a "divergent migration research agenda."[62] It offers a focus on the various destinations of migrants who share the same cultural background. The Yekkes in Canada and Israel maintained emotional ties with German culture, and some of them with their actual countries of origin (Germany and Austria). They also became an integral part of the countries that received them, and some developed a sense of belonging to a transnational German Jewish diaspora. In each setting, Yekkes have carved out a unique form of ethnic belonging that translated into specific ways of remembering that were profoundly shaped by national and family narratives, by traumatic events, and by silences.

By and large, there is a gap between the Yekkes' overall economic integration in their host societies and their personal sense of belonging. Whereas success stories abound—of Yekkes in academia, the arts, in libraries and museums, Yekkes also voice a feeling of being apart. From a macro perspective, the period between 1945 and 1974, in which the first generation of Yekkes was professionally active, is one of tremendous economic boom in the Western world. It is a period in which success stories proliferate *in general*. But a sharper lens shows that the Yekkes as first-generation immigrants did not fit into the dominant socio-cultural categories in Canada and Israel.[63] They certainly represented a strange voice within the Jewish community and often transmitted specific and distinctive memories to their children and grandchildren. Today, more than seventy years after the Holocaust almost destroyed German Jewry, those who identify with their (grand)parents' Yekkishkeit have the option of living a transnational German-Jewish life and of feeling connected to a polycentric diasporic space. We need more research on intergenerational memory cultures, on the actual networks of this new form of "Germanness," and on the emotional consequences of these transnational connections. We also need to compare the family memories, the transmitted silences, and the heavy burdens within Jewish *and* non-Jewish German-speaking families in order to enrich our understanding of the "polyphone history" (discussed by Freund in Introduction) of the twentieth century as the century of refugees.[64] In 1955, Martin Buber, the well-known Austrian-born philosopher, stated that German Jewry was one of the strangest phenomena in Jewish history.[65] His view certainly holds true to this day. Still, the Yekkes are not simply an odd curiosity, but an important case study that explores questions of diaspora and transnational as well as intergenerational identity formation. Yekkes in Canada, Israel, and elsewhere developed distinct identities that depend on local contexts. They have and continue to share emotional, institutional, and family ties that make Yekkish identity a transnational one.

Notes

1 Mathias Schulze, James M. Skidmore, David G. John, Grit Liebscher, and Sebastian Siebel-Achenbach, eds., *German Diasporic Experiences: Identity, Migration, and Loss* (Waterloo: Wilfrid Laurier University Press, 2008).

2 Shulamit Volkov, "Die Verbürgerlichung der Juden in Deutschland: Eigenart und Paradigma," in *Bürgertum im 19. Jahrhundert: Verbürgerlichung, Recht und Politik*, vol. 3, ed. Jürgen Kocka (Göttingen: Vandenhoeck und Ruprecht, 1995), 105–33.

3 Elke-Vera Kotowski, ed., *Das Kulturerbe deutschsprachiger Juden: Eine Spurensuche in den Ursprungs-, Transit- und Emigrationsländern* (Berlin-Munich: De Gruyter/ Oldenbourg, 2014); Jay Howard Geller and Leslie Morris, eds., *Three-Way Street: Jews, Germans, and the Transnational* (Ann Arbor: University of Michigan Press, 2016); and Hagit Lavsky, *The Creation of the German-Jewish Diaspora: Interwar German-Jewish Immigration to Palestine, the USA, and England* (Berlin-Boston/Jerusalem: De Gruyter/Magnes Press, 2017).

4 Wolfgang Benz, ed., *Die Juden in Deutschland 1933–1945: Leben unter nationalsozialistischer Herrschaft* (Munich: Beck, 1988).

5 Wolfgang Benz, *Das Exil der kleinen Leute: Alltagserfahrung deutscher Juden in der Emigration* (Munich: C.H. Beck, 1991), 9.

6 Hannah Arendt, "We Refugees," *Menorah Journal* (January 1943): 69–77. Reprinted in *The Jew as Pariah*, ed. Ron H. Feldman (New York: Grove, 1978), 55–66.

7 Curt D. Wormann, "German Jews in Israel," *Leo Baeck Institute Year Book* 15 (1970): 73–103; and Neima Barzel, "The Attitude of Jews of German Origin in Israel and Germans after the Holocaust, 1945–1952," *Leo Baeck Institute Year Book* 39 (1994): 271–301.

8 Herbert Gans, "Toward a Reconciliation of 'Assimilation' and 'Pluralism': The Interplay of Acculturation and Ethnic Retention," *International Migration Review* 31, no. 4 (1997): 875–92.

9 Dani Kranz, "Being a Yekke Is a Really Big Deal For My Mum! On the Intergenerational Transmission of Germanness Amongst German Jews in Israel," *Austausch* 2, no.1 (2013): 43–66.

10 Herbert Gans, "Symbolic Ethnicity: The Future of Ethnic Groups and Cultures in America," *Ethnic and Racial Studies* 2, no. 1 (1979): 1–20.

11 Richard Alba, *Ethnic Identity: The Transformation of White America* (New Haven: Yale University Press, 1990), 76.

12 Marcel Detienne, *Comparing the Incomparable*, trans. Janet Lloyd (Stanford: Stanford University Press, 2008).

13 Patrick Farges, *Bindestrich-Kanadier?: Sudetendeutsche Sozialdemokraten und deutsche Juden als Exilanten in Kanada: Studie zu Akkulturationsprozessen nach 1933* (Bremen: Edition Lumière, 2015); Patrick Farges, *Le Muscle et l'Esprit* (Brussels: PIE Peter Lang, 2020). In my research about German-speaking Jews in Palestine/Israel, I used 150 oral history interviews conducted in the 1990s by a German-Israeli team under the supervision of Anne Betten (University of Eichstätt, later University of Salzburg) and Miryam Du-nour (Bar-Ilan University). For a presentation of the interviews, see Archiv für Gesprochenes Deutsch, Institut für deutsche Sprache (Mannheim): http://agd.ids-mannheim.de/IS--_extern.shtml (accessed 20 June 2018).

14 Angelika E. Sauer, "The 'Ideal German': Politics, Academics and the Historiographical Construction of German-Canadian Identity," in *A Chorus of Different Voices: German-Canadian Identities*, eds. Angelika E. Sauer and Matthias Zimmer (New York: Peter Lang, 1998), 228.

15 Patrick Farges, "'What Church Do You Go To?' The Difficult Acculturation of German-Jewish Refugees in Canada, 1933–2004," in *Beyond the Nation? Immigrants' Local Lives in Transnational Cultures*, ed. Alexander Freund (Toronto: University of Toronto Press, 2012), 187–210.

16 See also the groundbreaking study of Canada's response to the rise of Nazism: Irving Abella and Harold Troper, *None Is Too Many: Canada and the Jews of Europe 1933–1948* (Toronto: University of Toronto Press, [1983] 2012).

17 Tony Kushner and David Cesarani, eds., *The Internment of Aliens in Twentieth Century Britain* (London: Frank Cass, 1993).

18 Ernest Robert Zimmerman, *The Little Third Reich on Lake Superior: A History of Canadian Internment Camp R*, eds. Michel S. Beaulieu and David K. Ratz (Edmonton: University of Alberta Press, 2015).

19 Christine Whitehouse, "'You'll Get Used to It!': The Internment of Jewish Refugees in Canada, 1940–43" (PhD diss., Carleton University Ottawa, 2016). See also Franca Iacovetta, Roberto Perin, and Angelo Principe, eds., *Enemies Within: Italian and Other Internees in Canada and Abroad* (Toronto: University of Toronto Press, 2000); Elise Bigley, "Creativity, Community, and Memory Building: Interned Jewish Refugees in Canada During and After World War II" (Master's thesis, Carleton University Ottawa, 2017); and Patrick Farges, "Masculinity and Confinement: German-Speaking Refugees in Canadian Internment Camps (1940–1943)," *Culture, Society and Masculinities* 4, no. 1 (2012): 33–47.

20 Paula Jean Draper, "The Accidental Immigrants: Canada and the Interned Refugees" (PhD diss., University of Toronto, 1983); and Eric Koch, *Deemed Suspect: A Wartime Blunder* (Toronto: Methuen, 1980).

21 Franca Iacovetta, *The Writing of English Canadian Immigrant History* (Ottawa: Canadian Historical Association, 1997).

22 Gerry Waldston, personal interview, Toronto, 13 May 2004.

23 Eric Exton, *Zaidie Exton's Odyssey*, vol. 1 (Toronto: privately published, 1986), iii.

24 Alfred Bader, *Adventures of a Chemist Collector* (London: Weidenfeld and Nicolson, 1995), 41.

25 Eric Koch, personal interview, Toronto, 22 April 2003.

26 Jonathan D. Sarna, "The Value of Canadian Jewish History to the American Jewish Historian and Vice Versa," *Canadian Jewish Historical Society Journal* 5, no. 1 (1981): 20. There were, however, a few exceptions, like the German-Jewish Shaar Hashomayim Synagogue [Gateway to Heaven] in Westmount, or Hamilton's Jewish community, both founded in the 1850s by immigrants from Germany.

27 Erwin Schild, personal interview, Toronto, 10 May 2004.

28 Mordecai Richler, *The Street* (1969; repr., Toronto: McClelland and Stewart, 2002), 58–59.

29 W. Gunther Plaut, *Unfinished Business: An Autobiography* (Toronto: Lester and Orpen Dennys, 1981), 58.

30 Helmut Kallmann, Letter to Eric Koch [22 Jan. 1979], Library and Archives of Canada, MG30-C192, Eric Koch Collection, vol. 1.

31 Erwin Schild, "A Canadian Footnote to the Holocaust. A Review Essay of *Deemed Suspect: A Wartime Blunder*, by Eric Koch," *Canadian Jewish Historical Society Journal* 5, no. 1 (1981): 36.

32 Canadian German Jewish communities were unlike the German-Jewish neighbourhood in Washington Heights (NYC) that became known as "Frankfurt on the Hudson." See Steven M. Lowenstein, *Frankfurt on the Hudson: The German Jewish Community of Washington Heights, 1933–1983, Its Structure and Culture* (Detroit: Wayne State University Press, 1989).

33 While Wagner convincingly demonstrates that pro-Nazi activities had in fact a limited influence on the German community in the 1930s, Meune shows that within the German-Canadian community, there consistently existed a small but vigorous minority voicing tendentious ideas, especially among immigrants from the 1950s. See Jonathan F. Wagner, *Brothers Beyond the Sea: National Socialism in Canada* (Waterloo: Wilfrid Laurier University Press, 1981); Manuel Meune, *Les Allemands du Québec: Parcours et discours d'une communauté méconnue* (Montreal: Éditions du Méridien, 2003), 135–53.

34 Irving A. Abella, *Coat of Many Colours: Two Centuries of Jewish Life in Canada* (Toronto: Lester and Orpen Dennys, 1990), 226.

35 Franklin Bialystok, *Delayed Impact: The Holocaust and the Canadian Jewish Community* (Montreal and Kingston: McGill–Queen's University Press, 2000), 6, 13.

36 Daniel Iggers, personal interview, Toronto, 24 April 2003.

37 Schild, "A Canadian Footnote," 40.

38 On the difficult postwar adaptation of Holocaust survivors in Canada and their uneasy interactions with the established Canadian Jewish community, see Adara Goldberg, *Holocaust Survivors in Canada: Exclusion, Inclusion, Transformation, 1947–1955* (Winnipeg: University of Manitoba Press, 2015).

39 Schild, "A Canadian Footnote," 42.

40 Chaim Vogt-Moykopf, "Die letzten Jeckes—deutsche Juden in Kanada," *Aufbau: Deutsch-jüdische Zeitung* 9 (1999): 11.

41 Wendy Oberlander, "Once It Was Written: The Story After *Nothing To Be Written Here*," Vancouver Holocaust Education Centre's publication, *Zachor* (Spring 2013). 7–8.

42 Yoav Gelber, "The Historical Role of the Central European Immigration to Israel," *Leo Baeck Institute Year Book* 38 (1993): 323–39.

43 Anita Shapira, *Land and Power: The Zionist Resort to Force, 1881–1948* (Stanford: Stanford University Press, 1999).

44 Yitzhak Conforti, "The 'New Jew' in the Zionist Movement: Ideology and Historiography," *The Australian Journal of Jewish Studies* 25 (2011): 87–118. I have retained the masculine pronoun here to signal a gender bias of the "New Jew" figure. This topic is actually the focus of my current research on German Jewish masculinities in Israel.

45 Patrick Farges, "'Diese meine Sprache, die so männlich geworden ist.' Jeckes in Palästina/Israel im Spannungsverhältnis zwischen Sprachen und Geschlecht," *L'Homme: Zeitschrift für feministische Geschichtswissenschaft* 26, no. 1 (2015): 63–78.

46 Michael Dak, "Israelis aus Not," *MB Yakinton. Mitteilungsblatt der Vereinigung der Israelis mitteleuropäischer Herkunft* (2007), http://www.irgun-jeckes.org/?CategoryID=254&ArticleID=211 (accessed 20 June 2018).

47 Na'ama Sheffi, "Rejecting the Other's Culture: Hebrew and German in Israel 1933–1965," *Tel Aviver Jahrbuch für deutsche Geschichte* 27 (1998): 301–20.

48 Anja Siegemund, "Eine Bürgergesellschaft für den Jischuw: Deutsche liberalnationale Zionisten in Palästina," *Tel Aviver Jahrbuch für deutsche Geschichte* 41 (2013): 60–81.

49 Limor Shifman and Elihu Katz, "'Just Call Me Adonai': A Case Study of Ethnic Humor and Immigrant Assimilation," *American Sociological Review* 70, no. 5 (2005): 843–59. The authors show that the ethnic superiority implicit in Yekke jokes and humour turns the tables on earlier inner-Jewish frictions in which *Ostjuden* were denigrated for embarrassing "established" (or assimilated) Jews.

50 Josef Burg, interview with Miryam Du-nour, Israel-Corpus, Jerusalem, 27 January 1994.

51 Micha Limor, "Was ich noch sagen wollte: Wer ist Jecke?," *MB Yakinton. Mitteilungsblatt der Vereinigung der Israelis mitteleuropäischer Herkunft* 79, no. 246 (2011): 2.

52 Joseph Walk, interview with Anne Betten, Israel-Corpus, Jerusalem, 27 April 1991.

53 Rakefet Sela-Sheffy, "Integration through Distinction: German Jewish Immigrants, the Legal Profession and Patterns of Bourgeois Culture in British-Ruled Jewish Palestine," *Journal of Historical Sociology* 19, no. 1 (2006): 34–59; and Rakefet Sela-Sheffy, "'Europeans in the Levant' Revisited: German Jewish Immigrants in 1930s Palestine and the Question of Culture Retention," *Tel Aviver Jahrbuch für deutsche Geschichte* 41 (2013): 40–59.

54 Anne Betten, "Familiales Gedächtnis und individuelle Erinnerung," in *Emotionsausdruck und Erzählstrategien in narrativen Interviews: Analysen zu Gesprächsaufnahmen mit jüdischen Emigranten*, ed. Simona Leonardi, Eva-Maria Thüne, and Anne Betten (Würzburg: Königshausen and Neumann, 2016), 85–121.

55 Peggy Levitt and B. Nadya Jaworsky, "Transnational Migration Studies: Past Developments and Future Trends," *Annual Review of Sociology* 33 (2007): 129–56.

56 Peggy Levitt and Nina Glick-Schiller, "Conceptualizing Simultaneity: A Transnational Social Field Perspective on Society," *International Migration Review* 38, no. 3 (2004): 1002–39.

57 Tom Segev, "Ach, gäbe es doch noch einmal Karpfen wie an der Rehwiese!" in *Die Jeckes. Jüdischer Almanach des Leo Baeck Instituts*, ed. Gisela Dachs (Frankfurt: Jüdischer Verlag im Suhrkamp Verlag, 2005), 30.

58 Christhard Hoffmann, ed., *Preserving the Legacy of German Jewry: A History of the Leo Baeck Institute, 1955–2005* (Tübingen: Mohr Siebeck, 2008).

59 Hagit Lavsky, *Before Catastrophe: The Distinctive Path of German Zionism* (Detroit: Wayne State University Press, 1996).

60 Moshe Zimmermann and Yotam Hotam, eds., *Zweimal Heimat: Die Jeckes zwischen Mitteleuropa und Nahost* (Frankfurt: beerenverlag, 2005).

61 Larissa Remennick, "Russian Jews in the Global City of Toronto: A Pilot Study of Identity and Social Integration," *Espace populations sociétés* 3, no. 1 (2006): 61–81.

62 Nancy L. Green, "The Comparative Method and Poststructural Structuralism: New Perspectives for Migration Studies," *Migration, Migration History, History: Old Paradigms and New Perspectives*, eds. Jan Lucassen and Leo Lucassen (New York: Peter Lang, 1999), 69–71.

63 There is an interesting point of comparison with Hans Werner's work on ethnic Germans from Russia who immigrated to Canada in the 1950s and to Germany in the 1970s. Integration seems to have been more successful in Canada because there were no expectations of a "homecoming." See Hans Werner, "'Germans Only in Their Hearts' Making and Breaking the Ethnic German Diaspora in the Twentieth Century," in Freund, *Beyond the Nation?*, 211–26.

64 See Gabriele Rosenthal, ed., *The Holocaust in Three Generations: Families of Victims and Perpetrators of the Nazi Regime* (New York: Continuum, 1998); and Dan Bar-On, *Fear and Hope: Three Generations of the Holocaust* (Cambridge, MA: Harvard University Press, 1998).

65 Quoted in Avraham Barkai, "Deutsch-jüdische Forschungsinseln. Die Leo Baeck Institute in Jerusalem, London und New York," in Dachs, *Die Jeckes*, 13.

CHAPTER 4

The Roots of Ethnic Fundamentalism in German-Canadian Studies: The Case of Gottlieb Leibbrandt

KAREN BRGLEZ

In August 1989, the *Kitchener Waterloo Record* published an obituary of Gottlieb Leibbrandt (1908–89) of Kitchener, Ontario describing him as author, businessman, historian, and researcher. Summarizing his professional accomplishments, the obituary highlighted his contributions to the German-Canadian community in the postwar years, particularly his founding of the Kitchener-Waterloo German-Canadian Business and Professional Association, his role as lecturer at the University of Waterloo, and the writing of his most notable work, *Little Paradise: The Saga of the German Canadians of Waterloo County, Ontario, 1800–1975*.[1] An ethnic German from Ukraine, Leibbrandt had immigrated to Canada in 1952 and become actively involved in several German-Canadian organizations in the postwar years. Leibbrandt, who held a PhD in political science (*Staatswissenschaften*) from the University of Vienna (1934), authored numerous books and articles in German-Canadian studies over his close to four decades in Canada. He was determined to uphold his reputation as a respectable scholar in the postwar period by firmly establishing himself as an authority on the history of Germans in Canada. This in turn meant that, from 1945 until his death in 1989, Leibbrandt withheld biographical details from his past that connected him to the Nazi cause and its expansionist goals for Eastern Europe. He remained silent about his pre-war scholarly activities that actively supported the aims of the Nazi regime.

Leibbrandt fled civil war in the Soviet Union in the 1920s and became a leading member in the Russian-German émigré community in Berlin in the interwar period. In Germany, this group of educated émigrés worked to foster a pan-German national identity that included Eastern Europe's ethnic German minorities. Isolated from the German national consciousness before the First World War, émigrés sought to expand the scope of Germanness to include their compatriots and connect them to a German state that saw an increasing desire to unify the *Volk* (the people).[2] They envisioned a national community, defined not in cultural but in racial and biological terms.

This was achieved with the Nazis' rise to power and the ushering in of a new racial order that categorized individuals according to racial purity. Based on "blood," Soviet Germans were increasingly viewed as members of the *Volksgemeinschaft* (ethnic community.) In her work on the *Volksdeutsche* (ethnic Germans living outside of Germany) of Eastern Europe, Doris Bergen argues that the Nazi racial policy was double-sided: while those who were considered "alien," "hereditarily ill," or "asocial" were excluded from the national community, ethnic German minorities came to be perceived as "valuable Aryans" that legitimized the Nazi mission to obtain so-called *Lebensraum* (living space) in the East. According to Nazi thinking, ethnic Germans' struggles under foreign rule outside of the German borders served as justification for invasion and occupation; ethnic Germans needed to be liberated so they could play an important role in Germanizing the East.[3] The Nazi plans for spatial expansion created a demand for professional experts on Eastern affairs. The transnational network of Russian-German émigrés in the Reich willingly provided academic and administrative support for the regime's goals and established themselves as professionals ready to aid in the regime's plans to occupy the eastern territories.[4]

As an émigré scholar in Germany, Leibbrandt's contributions to advancing the Nazi state were primarily academic. A fervent anti-Bolshevik and anti-Semite, Leibbrandt worked in various agencies as a Nazi propagandist, furthering the myth of the interwar period wherein the German people struggled against various enemies who wished to destroy the German Reich. In this narrative, Russian Germans, together with their Reich counterparts, were cast as victims of a "Jewish Bolshevik" threat that intended to annihilate all things "German." As a producer of racist scholarship, Leibbrandt participated in the crafting of Nazi propaganda that juxtaposed a victimized *Volk* in a fight against the racial "other."[5] He was supported in his academic pursuits by a community of like-minded thinkers; two of Leibbrandt's closest confidants in Germany, his brother Georg and their associate Karl Stumpp, produced similar Nazi-era scholarship.[6] With the onset of the Second World War, these educated Russian-German émigrés found new roles to support the Nazi machine; Leibbrandt joined the Wehrmacht's eastern campaign, whereas Georg and Stumpp served in administrative positions as part of German occupation forces in the Soviet Union. By 1941, Georg was a senior official in the political sector of Alfred Rosenberg's Reich Ministry for the Occupied Eastern Territories (Reichsminister für die besetzten Ostgebiete or RMO). In addition, he oversaw Stumpp's *Sonderkommando* ("special action" unit) on the Eastern Front, which was responsible for racially categorizing and documenting ethnic Germans in Nazi-occupied Ukraine.[7] In the decades following the Second World War, Gottlieb remained in close contact with both men.

Several important studies have examined the role of academics and their contributions to the Nazi state. Beginning in the mid-1980s, scholarship such as British historian Michael Burleigh's *Germany Turns Eastward: A Study of "Ostforschung" in the Third Reich* (1988) and Karen Schönwälder's *Historiker und Politik: Geschichtswissenschaft im Nationalsozialismus* (1992) began to dissect the role of historians in Germany's plans for eastern expansion. A pivotal study by Götz Aly and Susanne Heim, *Architects of Destruction: Auschwitz and the Logic of Destruction*, published in German in 1991 and in English in 2002, revealed how historians, demographers, economists, and geographers became Hitler's planners for ethnic cleansing and genocide. The most recent books to examine the academic elite's collaboration with the Nazi regime include essay collections by Ingo Haar and Michael Fahlbusch, *German Scholars and Ethnic Cleansing, 1919–1945* (2005), and Wolfgang Bialas and Anson Rabinbach, *Nazi Germany and the Humanities: How German Academics Embraced Nazism* (2007).[8] This chapter seeks to contribute to the criticism by illuminating the role of a Russian-German émigré academic's coordination with the Nazi establishment and its impact on his professional scholarship after 1945.

As a postwar immigrant to Canada, Leibbrandt did not simply abandon his ethno-national past that was marked by his experiences in the war years. Instead, he reproduced his ethno-national ideas in a Canadian context through the writing of German-Canadian historiography. The political awakening of multiculturalism in Canada, beginning in the late 1960s, provided academics with the opportunity to author ethnic studies and ethnic histories. As an expellee immigrant to Canada, Leibbrandt used the burgeoning field of German-Canadian studies as a space to reproduce his ethnic historiography within a Canadian framework. My argument echoes Pascal Maeder's theory that postwar expellees did not discard their ethno-national ideals upon arrival in their new environments but rather reconstructed their national identities to fit the new nation state.[9] Intent on preserving his ethno-identity, the central purpose of Leibbrandt's writing was ethnic preservation. His additions to German-Canadian scholarship were "contribution pieces,"[10] that is, publications that highlighted the positive developments that German immigrants made to their adopted nation, written to advocate for the importance of Germans as an ethnic group in Canada. This filiopietistic approach frequently praised the achievements of German immigrants and marked them as a unique and exemplary ethnic group in Canadian society. Furthermore, throughout his work, Leibbrandt recurrently wove a narrative of victimization—an account in which ethnic German suffering was emphasized due to their displacement in the Second World War or as innocent immigrants who had endured unjust persecution in Canada during the war years. His writings helped foster what Angelika Sauer came to define as a "culture of complaint" amongst the German-Canadian community.[11]

As the concept of multiculturalism was taking root in Canada, Leibbrandt was of course not the only academic to emphasize the importance of his ethnic group in Canadian society. In light of his pre-war work, however, his devotion to producing German-ethnic historiography in Canada demands further examination. Notably, Leibbrandt's academic scholarship from the 1930s was based on racially motivated Nazi ideology that glorified the German *Volk* as an ethnic community superior to others both culturally and biologically. In the postwar period, he made no attempts to confront his Nazi past and chose to keep quiet about his earlier racist writings. As Sara Frankenberger notes in Chapter 7, the generation of Germans that directly experienced the war dealt with the past through a collective silence regarding National Socialism and the Holocaust. Throughout his German-Canadian scholarship, Leibbrandt's *völkisch* (ethno-racial) attitude persisted as he continued to perpetuate the myth of German cultural superiority.

Gottlieb Leibbrandt: A Nazi Past

Gottlieb Leibbrandt was born in the German Lutheran village of Hoffnungsfeld, near Odessa, Ukraine, on 30 July 1908. He received his primary education from the village school and then the central school in a nearby colony. In 1925, with two of his brothers having already fled to Germany, Leibbrandt left the Soviet Union and began studies at the Francke Foundations school in Halle, a Pietist educational complex that prepared him for university education. In 1927, he studied agriculture at the University of Leipzig, and one year later he transferred to the University of Hohenheim near Stuttgart. In Stuttgart, he worked closely with the German Foreign Institute (Deutsches Ausland-Institut[12] or DAI), a research centre that gathered information and offered support to Germans abroad. Over the course of that year, Leibbrandt established numerous contacts with other German-Russian émigrés in Germany. His brother Georg, who had just received his doctorate, had recently published his first monograph on the German colonists in Russia, which was based on archival sources that Leibbrandt had smuggled out of the Soviet Union. Wanting to further his own studies, but short of funds, Leibbrandt travelled to Canada and from 1929 to 1931 worked at a number of odd jobs across the country. He was employed as a farm labourer in Prince Edward Island, as a bartender in Montreal, as a CNR tour guide for Chinese tourists and businessmen travelling between Montreal and Vancouver, and he worked at a sawmill in Sudbury. He returned to Europe in the spring of 1931 and stayed briefly in Berlin, where he came under the influence of the *völkisch* theories of sociologist Max Hildebert Boehm. During that same year, he switched academic disciplines and enrolled in the doctoral program in the faculty of political science at the University of Vienna.[13]

Leibbrandt's doctoral advisor, the Viennese professor Othmar Spann, was a leading theorist and advocate for a return to a *Ständestaat*—an authoritarian state and society in Germany and Austria. Appealing to *völkisch* circles in Germany, Spann gave an address to the Kampfbund für deutsche Kultur (League of Struggle for German Culture) in the

Figure 4.1. The Leibbrandt brothers, Tübingen, Germany, 1928. While the Russian civil war raged, Georg fled the Soviet Union for Germany in 1920. His brothers followed, Reinhold in 1924, and Gottlieb in 1925. From left to right: Reinhold Leibbrandt, Georg Leibbrandt, Gottlieb Leibbrandt. Private Collection of Wolfram Leibbrandt.

presence of Hitler, Rosenberg, and other Nazi leaders in 1929. As an intellectual who offered a "third way" for the society, based on a corporate structure for the German *Volk* that was beyond democracy and Marxism, Spann appealed to the young conservative and nationalistic idealists within the university.[14] Leibbrandt became a convinced follower and joined the Spann *Kreis*, a circle of admirers who embraced Spann's philosophies. Leibbrandt's dissertation, "Der Begriff des Standes und seine Funktionen in Staat und Volk" (The Concept of the Estate and its Functions in State and Nation) was based on Spann's theories and later published in the Viennese journal *Ständisches Leben*. Leibbrandt was one of the first to write about Spann and his work in a short book published in 1933.[15]

Leibbrandt was also an active political student leader for the Nazi party at the University of Vienna. By the early 1930s, the Nazi student organization was the largest student group on the school's campus. Like other Austrian institutions, universities too were being heavily influenced by the National Socialist German Workers' Party (NSDAP) at that time. The party waged aggressive propaganda campaigns against Jews, monarchists, Communists, and Social Democrats whom they perceived to be their central opponents.[16] As Nazi radicalization increased across the country, the Engelbert Dollfuss government banned the party in June 1933. Although the party was now illegal, that did not stop Leibbrandt from becoming actively involved in its efforts. On 1 October 1933, he signed up to become a member of the Nazi party and the Sturmabteilung (SA) or "Brownshirts."[17] A few months later, he was commissioned by the NSDStB (National Socialist German Students' League) to hold political leadership seminars on National Socialism and Bolshevism for the National Socialist student union at the University of Vienna. Due to his committed involvement with the party, the police conducted numerous searches of his house.[18] On 25 July 1934, terror escalated when Austrian Nazis stormed the chancellery and shot Chancellor Dollfuss in a *coup d'etat* attempt to take over the government. The coup failed and hundreds of Austrian Nazis were arrested. On 27 July, police arrested Leibbrandt and interrogated him for four hours about his association with the party. On the day of his release, he fled to Berlin.[19]

In Berlin, Leibbrandt found immediate employment with the Anti-Komintern, an organization under Josef Goebbels's Reich Ministry of Public Enlightenment and Propaganda, which was devoted to disseminating anti-Soviet and anti-Jewish information around the globe. It is difficult to ascertain the organization's exact activities since most of its files were destroyed in an Allied air raid in 1943, but two documents from the NSDAP Office of Foreign Affairs written in the fall of 1934 provide some insight. Both documents were written by Georg Leibbrandt, who had been promoted as early as 1933 to director of the Eastern Division of the NSDAP's Foreign Policy Office under Alfred Rosenberg. On 2 October 1934, he claimed that the essential aim of the Anti-Komintern was to "advertise the dangers of Bolshevism to the world and to counter the machinations of the Comintern."[20] It attempted to achieve this through books, study circles, exhibitions, films, conferences, and publicity campaigns. The organization even had its own publishing house, the Nibelungen Verlag.[21] The second file, dated 10 October 1934, detailed the Anti-Komintern's undertakings for the immediate future, which included a series of exhibitions across

Europe to advertise the atrocities of the Soviet regime and a special operation in France to help combat the "governing Jewish Masonic clique."[22] That same year, the head of the Anti-Komintern outlined in a secret memorandum that Bolshevism was the world's greatest enemy and that Germany's defence action against the Russians should also be directed against the Jews.[23] Leibbrandt was an ideal candidate for the organization since the majority of the employees were young idealists, most of them Russian-born, with firmly established anti-Bolshevik positions.[24] In his unpublished autobiographical papers, Leibbrandt explained that he was particularly valued in this organization for his knowledge of Marxism and his involvement with the Pro-Deo Commission, an anti-Soviet committee in Switzerland that had been established and then managed by the Anti-Komintern from Berlin.[25] While the functions of the Anti-Komintern were often modest in scope, the organization played an important part in Nazi propagandists' attack on Bolshevism and Jews.

Although several Russian-German émigrés were already working within Nazi agencies by the mid-1930s, the German government was struggling to coordinate the activities of the different Russian-German organizations throughout Germany. By 1935, Georg Leibbrandt of the Foreign Office merged competing Russian-German groups into one body, the Association of Germans from Russia (Verband der Deutschen aus Russland or VDR), with the goal of organizing Russian Germans at home and abroad in preparation for the planned Nazi project of eastward expansion.[26] The association worked to publicize the experiences of the German communities that were situated in Soviet territory, and it lobbied the German government to provide financial support to the VDR as well as to new Russian-German immigrants to the Reich.[27] The VDR hosted cultural events, presentations, and lecture series to foster connections between the Reich and Soviet Germans, in the hopes of creating a national identity that spanned borders. With the VDR being financially supported by the Foreign Office and the Anti-Komintern, Rosenberg intended to use the organization as a political weapon to cultivate Nazi propaganda against the Bolsheviks.[28] The primary method to achieve this aim was through the *Deutsche Post aus dem Osten* (*DPO*), a periodical published monthly by the VDR for the Russian-German communities in Germany, the Soviet Union, and the Americas.

In 1937, after having left the Anti-Komintern, Leibbrandt was named Organizational Director of the VDR in Berlin. It was in this position as director that Leibbrandt actively contributed to Nazi propaganda. A committed, ideological Nazi, he praised Hitler in an essay for the *DPO*, stating that the four characteristics that most defined the German leader were "his racial and ethnic purity, his imagination, his power to create, and his unselfishness" and that because of him the German nation had "remembered its original power."[29] Leibbrandt's essays in the *DPO* were primarily devoted to perpetuating anti-Bolshevism. For Leibbrandt, Jews created Marxism, nurtured it in Europe, and delivered it to the Soviet Union in the form of Bolshevism. In a 1937 article for the *DPO*, Leibbrandt wrote: "Bolshevism is the deluge of a world conspiracy that has already conquered one sixth of the earth, a world monopoly for the benefit of parasitic criminal Jewry."[30]

In addition to his writings in the *DPO*, Leibbrandt published two monographs on the German struggle against Bolshevism. In 1936, written under the pseudonym Dr. Edgar Helmut Klein, *Das Verbrechen des Weltbolschewismus* (The Crime of World Bolshevism) was published as part of the *Schriften der Adolf-Hitler-Schule* series. Edited by Wilhelm Löbsack, the Nazi party ideologist of Danzig, the series was part of a propaganda campaign to educate the broad masses on the dangers of Bolshevism and the (falsely) purported Jewish origins of the Soviet state.[31] Three years later, Leibbrandt added to Nazi literature on the Soviet Union with the publication of *Bolschewismus und Abendland: Idee und Geschichte eines Kampfes gegen Europa* (Bolshevism and the Western World: The Idea and History of a Struggle against Europe). Building on Rosenberg's theories of a Judeo-Masonic conspiracy, Leibbrandt argued in a pseudo-scientific fashion that Germany was under attack from a "counter-race" that had emerged from the *Völkerchaos* (chaos of the peoples) of the Mediterranean. According to the book, the dissolution of races in the Middle East led to the rise of a Jewish "bastard culture" that had infiltrated Europe. These Syrian/Jewish carriers, which were contrary to the culture of Aryan Europe, had achieved global power through the ideas of Freemasonry, Liberalism, and Marxism, and they were now seeking to achieve world dominance through Bolshevism. In summary, Bolshevism was a political conspiracy in favour of a "Jewish world state."[32] Leibbrandt asserted that the "pure blood" of the German people had always been responsible for holding back the "alien blood" that attempted to destroy the German values of authority and order. He argued that through National Socialism, the Germans have once again restored their national strength to withstand the Jewish "mania for domination."[33] Upon publication of Leibbrandt's book in 1939, the *Contemporary Jewish Record*, an American Jewish periodical, labelled Leibbrandt's monograph a "Nazi propaganda blast" that placed the blame for Bolshevism on the Jews.[34]

Throughout his publications, Leibbrandt repeatedly referenced his brother Georg's Nazi scholarship. A prolific writer in the 1930s, Georg Leibbrandt wrote the foreword to the 1937 and 1944 editions of Rosenberg's book *Pest in Russland* (the first edition appeared in 1922). He also frequently contributed to the *Nationalsozialistische Monatshefte*, a Nazi party journal edited by Rosenberg. Just as blatantly anti-Semitic and anti-Bolshevik as his brother, Georg embraced similar theories of an Asiatic racial chaos responsible for Jewish dominance in Moscow.[35]

As the Nazi authorities prepared for spatial expansion eastwards, these propaganda tactics employed by Russian-German émigrés became increasingly useful to the state. The narrative of a "Jewish Bolshevik" enemy against "Germanness" connected the German communities in Soviet territory to those living within the Reich. A common enemy also allowed for the German communities in the Soviet Union to be perceived as German spaces justifying Nazi ambitions to attain *Lebensraum* (living space) in the East.[36] However, these propaganda strategies had to be put on hold in 1939 with the signing of the Molotov-Ribbentrop Pact between Germany and the USSR. The anti-Bolshevik agenda of the Russian-German émigrés was of no use during this brief period of renewed Soviet-German relations. It was only with the Nazi invasion of the Soviet Union in the spring of 1941 that émigrés became beneficial to the state once again.[37] Several Russian-German émigrés were staffed in key administrative positions, notably Georg Leibbrandt, who was appointed as a senior official in Rosenberg's Reich Ministry for the Occupied Eastern Territories. In preparation for the occupation, Georg, alongside Rosenberg, had helped draft the plans for setting up a civil administration in the occupied territories, and by late 1941, he was helping coordinate the "Jewish problem" in the East.[38] On behalf of his ministry, Georg attended the Wannsee Conference on 20 January 1942, where the "Final Solution" (the plan to exterminate the Jews of Europe) was determined. Georg Leibbrandt's coordinating efforts led to the

Figure 4.2. Gottlieb (left) and Georg (right) in uniform visiting their former home in Hoffnungsfeld, near Odessa, Ukraine, May 1942. This area of southern Ukraine, located on the Black Sea Coast, immediately east of Bessarabia between the Dniester and Bug Rivers, had been Soviet territory before the Second World War. Hitler had convinced his ally, Ion Antonescu's Romania, to support him in his invasion of the Soviet Union in June 1941, and in return, Romania would get back the land that the Soviets had recently occupied, including this piece of southern Ukraine, which Hitler had renamed Transnistria. Following the invasion, the Romanians occupied Transnistria, and the large population of Soviet Volksdeutsche came under the control of the German authorities. From 1941 to 1944, Romanian and German officers applied their genocidal violence, and with support from the local Volksdeutsche, brutally worked to eradicate the Jews from southern Ukraine. Private Collection of Wolfram Leibbrandt.

execution of 50,000 Jews in Libau and 68,000 to 75,000 Jews from the ghettos of the Ostland (the Baltic States under Nazi occupation).[39]

In addition, Georg was responsible for Sonderkommando Stumpp, a "special action" unit designed to compile racial research on ethnic Germans in the Ukraine. Before the war, Stumpp had been the head of the Forschungsstelle des Russlanddeutschtums im Deutschen Ausland-Institut (FstR), a research office that had been established in 1938 by the DAI and VDR. Following the invasion of the Soviet Union, Georg turned the FstR into Stumpp's Sonderkommando. Working alongside Heinrich Himmler's organization, the Ethnic German Liaison Office (Volksdeutsche Mittelstelle), which was set up to identify and register all ethnic Germans in the occupied regions, Stumpp's unit was responsible for determining persons of German "blood."[40] His action unit, made up of eighty people, trailed behind the killing squads of Einsatzgruppen C and D. Once the villages had been purged of "undesirables," Stumpp's team conducted ethnographic research to determine the racial character of the remaining population. Those who were "racially German" could join the "ruling race" to re-Germanize the land, whereby those who failed to have "German blood" were likely eradicated.[41] Stumpp's reports were then sent back to Berlin and processed at the Publications Office East, a research agency that helped coordinate German settlement in the eastern territories.

Like his fellow compatriots, Gottlieb Leibbrandt participated in the German attack on the Soviet Union. Having volunteered for the Wehrmacht in 1938, he served briefly in Poland and France before being assigned to the Eastern Campaign in 1941 as a Lieutenant Company Commander for the Luftwaffe. Promoted to leader of the Interrogation Division of Luftwaffe I, he was entrusted to interrogate Russian prisoners of war and defectors, including Stalin's son, Yakov Dzhugashvili, and the captured Soviet General Andrey Vlasov.[42] Leibbrandt was part of the Nazis' attempt to use Russian-German émigrés as eastern "experts" in their war on the Soviet Union.[43] At the end of the war, Leibbrandt was arrested by the Americans and detained for eight days. Upon his release, he met up with his wife and children in Bavaria, where he worked as a farm labourer until 1948. Then he moved to Stuttgart and worked in a leather factory until 1950.[44]

While in Stuttgart, Leibbrandt took to the task of advocating for the displaced Russian-German expellee community in Germany. The mass expulsions of ethnic Germans from central and Eastern Europe forced millions to leave their homes and resettle in occupied Germany at the end of the war. With the Nazis' defeat, ethnic Germans either fled west in fear of the advancing Soviet armies in 1944–45 or were forcibly resettled by Allied-sanctioned deportations to West and East Germany between 1946 and 1955. In total, 12 million Germans were expelled from their homelands in the aftermath of war.[45] By 1950, Leibbrandt became the head of the Working Group of East Resettlers, the precursor

Figure 4.3. Gottlieb Leibbrandt in charge of a communications radio during the Second World War. Location unknown. Private Collection of Wolfram Leibbrandt.

Figure 4.4. Gottlieb Leibbrandt, Head of the Interrogation Agency for Luftflotte 1 in the Occupied East, with officers. Private Collection of Wolfram Leibbrandt.

organization to the Stuttgart-based Landsmannschaft der Deutschen aus Russland (LmDR), organized in the interest of Russian-German expellees. On 5 August 1950, he represented the organization by signing the Charter of the German Expellees; a document crafted by thirty expellee organizations outlining the goals of the expellee movement.[46] He also edited the LmDR's newsletter, *Volk auf dem Weg,* whose authors had once been regular contributors to the *DPO*. Merely a few years after the war, the transnational network of Russian-German émigrés was reorganized through the creation of the LmDR, with the intent of publicizing the narratives of German victimization and suffering in the postwar era.

The Canadian Chapter: Leibbrandt's Contributions to German-Canadian History

In 1952, Leibbrandt surprised his émigré associates when he left Germany to live in Canada. Germans had been barred from immigrating to Canada since the beginning of the Second World War; by 1947, however, some ethnic German expellee groups that had been displaced by the war became eligible for admission. Not later than March 1950, the doors were further opened when Canadian officials approved the immigration of ethnic Germans who had not held German citizenship on or after 1 September 1939. And by September 1950 any German national could apply to immigrate.[47] Canadian officials still refused entry to higher level Nazis and collaborators well into the 1950s, although changes on the international scene led to the easing of immigration restrictions for lesser offenders. With the outbreak of the Cold War, the principal threat to Canadian immigration was no longer Nazi infiltration, but rather communist subversion. In 1954, the Federal Republic of Germany (FRG) gained admission into the North Atlantic Treaty Organization (NATO), establishing itself as a reliable military ally for the western alliance and an important economic trading partner in the fight against communism.[48] Now that they were considered allies, Canadian officials were encouraged to treat West Germans like any other northern European immigrants. In addition, the FRG's decision to wind down the process of denazification for less prominent Nazis by the early 1950s also had an effect on the Canadian immigration screening process. West Germany's willingness to remove imposed sanctions and reinstate Nazis into their former positions prompted Canadian officials to relax immigration eligibility for former Nazi party members.[49] These developments lessened the constraints for ex-Nazis trying to enter postwar Canada.

Part of the large influx of German immigrants to Canada in the early 1950s, Leibbrandt settled in Galt, Ontario, before bringing his wife and two sons over in 1953. The family opened "Leibbrandt Imports," a European goods specialty shop in Kitchener that operated from 1957 until 1972.[50] Active in the community, Leibbrandt organized an International Folk Festival in Galt in 1953 that brought together newly arrived European immigrants and native-born citizens for a two-day cultural celebration.[51] Still keenly concerned with German expellee interests, Leibbrandt actively participated in a number of German-Canadian organizations in the postwar period. Unlike those in West Germany, expellee groups in Canada received no public funding to form homeland societies. Only a few groups organized: the Danube-Swabians, Transylvanians, and Baltic Germans—none of these groups represented the interests of expellees from territories east of the Oder–Neisse line (the border drawn in 1945 to separate

Germany and Poland). Many of the ethnic German immigrants in Canada identified more with their church denominations than with ethnic society associations. Immigrants that wanted to participate in ethnic societies turned to the larger German-Canadian organizations in order to achieve their aims.[52] Leibbrandt joined the Trans-Canada Alliance of German Canadians, the first national German-Canadian organization, which was made up mostly of German Canadians from Ontario, and he served as its vice-president and secretary from 1953 to 1960. He also became actively involved in the Canadian German Society, previously known as the Canadian Society for German Relief, a charitable organization established by Clive von Cardinal in 1946 that provided aid for German refugees abroad. Leibbrandt served as secretary and president of the Canadian German Society and was editor of its publication *The German-Canadian Review*. In 1962 he began to sell insurance for the Commercial Life Assurance Company of Canada, and five years later established the German Canadian Business and Professional Men's Association in Kitchener, Ontario.

Within Canada, Gottlieb established himself as a reputable scholar on Soviet Russia. In 1961, he was asked to teach a ten-week course on Russian and Chinese Communism at the University of Waterloo. In an introduction to the course, Dr. Edmund Heier, from the department of Germanic and Slavic Studies, described Leibbrandt as an authority on the subject and as an author of books on Russian history and Bolshevik problems. In the climate of the Cold War, Leibbrandt revisited the topic of communism, lecturing to his students that they were in the midst of a world revolution that threatened to destroy Western civilization. Removing any mention of a Jewish scheme, Leibbrandt now defined communism as a "conspiracy of fanatics, all over the world who lead the awakening of submerged people, who demand a better life, by means of dictatorship into a communist society [*sic*]."[53] He continued to articulate the notion that Marxism was a kind of disease that had inflicted the Soviet Union.

By the early 1970s, Leibbrandt shifted his scholarship to the writing of German-Canadian history. In 1971 Prime Minister Pierre Trudeau had just ushered in multiculturalism as official Canadian government policy. This opened up the door for immigrants to include their experiences in the Canadian nation-building narrative, which up till that point had been dominated by the Anglo-French perspective of Canada's past.

Figure 4.5. Leibbrandt Family Portrait in Canada, Galt, Ontario, 1955. From left to right: Elisabeth (née Bukowsky), Wolfram, Gottlieb, George. Private Collection of Wolfram Leibbrandt.

In order to stake their claim in the nation's fabric, competing ethnic groups strove to demonstrate their groups' contributions to Canada's founding.[54] On behalf of ethnic Germans, Gottlieb Leibbrandt, along with several other German-Canadian representatives, founded the German Canadian Historical Association in Toronto in 1973. Partially funded with government grants, the association intended to generate historical research on German-speaking groups in Canada. Its main mouthpiece was an academic journal, the *German-Canadian Yearbook* (*GCY*). Within the growing field of ethnic studies, Leibbrandt immersed himself in the writing of German-Canadian history. By the end of 1973, he had contributed three articles to the first volume of the *GCY*, published a history of the Canadian Society for German Relief, and written an account of the Concordia Club in Kitchener.[55]

Leibbrandt was not alone in having been able to re-establish his career as a scholar in the postwar era. His brother, Georg, after having been detained by the Allies for four years in prison and having been considered officially denazified by 1951, returned to his career in West Germany as a specialist on ethnic German minorities. Both Georg and his former associate Karl Stumpp played pivotal roles in the postwar period as ethnic German researchers and genealogists in West Germany's ethnic German organizations (*Landsmannschaften).* They assisted in establishing Russian-German heritage societies in the United States, and their genealogical research is still frequently referenced in the scholarship on the history of the Russian Germans.[56] Some of their publications are included in a special 1990 bibliography edition of the *GCY* that lists the most important works of German-Canadian history. In addition to their ethnic German research, Georg served as a lobbyist for the cities of Wilhelmshaven and Bonn,[57] and Stumpp worked with the West German government negotiating the release of German prisoners of war (POWs) and ethnic Germans in the Soviet Union.

Despite living on the other side of the Atlantic, Leibbrandt maintained close ties with both of these men. In a letter from October 1973, Georg encouraged Gottlieb in his work with the German Canadian Historical Association and promised he would speak on it at the LmDR's Culture Days in Germany. In return, Gottlieb encouraged Georg to submit his migration research to be included in the forthcoming *GCY* publication.[58] In addition, Leibbrandt helped organize Stumpp's summer of 1973 eight-week lecture tour across Canada on the subject of the ethnic German minorities that had been expelled from Ukraine. In discussions with Stumpp before his arrival, Leibbrandt encouraged him to consider the 1971 cultural policies introduced by Trudeau when preparing his lectures. He told Stumpp that he wanted the lecture in Toronto to be a big success for the German Canadian Historical Association and that Stumpp should present on the history of German migration to Russia. In his description of Russian Germans, he should cast them as "cultured colonizers" arriving on the Russian steppe.[59] Stumpp landed in Toronto at the end of May and travelled across Canada, speaking in over twelve cities on the history of the Russian Germans and the sufferings they had endured under the Soviets. On 23 June 1973 in the *Courier-Nordwesten*, a Winnipeg-based German-language newspaper, Leibbrandt summarized Stumpp's Ontario lectures, reminding readers that this group not only included "colonist pioneers" but a culture of people who had suffered the most "severe and tragic fate."[60]

Another undertaking in the field of German-Canadian historiography that was of primary concern to Leibbrandt involved the dissemination of German scholar Heinz Lehmann's texts. Influenced by *völkisch* theory in the 1930s, Lehmann conducted research on the German ethnic community in Canada for his doctoral dissertation at the University of Berlin. In 1931, he published in German his formative work *Zur Geschichte des Deutschtums in Kanada: Das Deutschtum in Ostkanada* (The History of Germans in Canada: The Germans in Eastern Canada) and in 1939, a second book, *Das Deutschtum in Westkanada* (The Germans in Western Canada). Lehmann's studies reached few audiences, however, because they had never been translated into English and most physical copies had been destroyed in the Second World War. In the 1980s, Gerhard Bassler of Memorial University translated Lehmann's texts and combined them into one comprehensive study for the German-Canadian community.[61] Yet, in a letter to Clive von Cardinal in 1980, Leibbrandt asserted that the impetus for this considerable project was due to his demands. He stressed that he had been in constant correspondence with Lehmann over the years, even visiting him in Tübingen in 1974. According to Leibbrandt, it was due to his advocating efforts with the Secretary of State in Ottawa that allowed for the project to be financed, and because of his pressuring, *Das Deutschtum in Ostkanada* was reproduced in microfilm and made available in university libraries all over Canada, the United States, and Germany.[62] Although Lehmann's texts are vital studies on the history of Germans in Canada, it cannot be ignored that they emerged out of the Nazi era of ethnic revivalism that narrowly defined who was included (or excluded) in the *Volksgemeinschaft*.[63] It is not surprising that Leibbrandt, whose pre-war ideological convictions were also founded on an idealized vision of the German Fatherland, strongly advocated for the inclusion of Lehmann's work as an important piece of German-Canadian historiography.

Leibbrandt's most important contribution to the field of German-Canadian history was the writing of his 1977 monograph *Little Paradise* about the German Canadians of Waterloo County. Published in English in 1980, his account is frequently referenced as a notable text in the field of German-Canadian studies.[64] Gerhard Bassler described Leibbrandt's history as "the most informative and richly documented regional history of any German Canadian community."[65] Focusing on the German-Canadian population in Waterloo County in southern Ontario, Leibbrandt provided a cultural and historical analysis of the group's developments in the region. Financed with a multicultural government grant from Ottawa, Leibbrandt believed he was writing a "scientific study" that was based on a firm scholarly foundation. In the foreword, he stressed that the book was well-suited for the academic field, as well as for the general Canadian population.[66] Endorsed by leading German-Canadian scholars in the field as well as the Minister of State for Multiculturalism, Jim Fleming, the text was cast as a comprehensive critical addition to the field of German-Canadian historiography.[67]

Although praised by German-Canadian historians, the text lacked a serious scholarly approach. Rather, the study was devoted to highlighting the successes of the German-Canadian community to emphasize the ethnic group's importance in Canadian society. Angelika Sauer rightly categorized it as a "contribution piece" of German-Canadian historiography because it was deliberately crafted to reveal only the constructive influences of the ethnic Germans in Ontario. Written in a narrative form, Leibbrandt's study argued that it was the "ethnic German pioneer and community spirit" of the newly arrived immigrants that transformed the region into a "model settlement" with its many accomplishments.[68] Any mention of inner-ethnic conflict was deliberately avoided to assert the image of a united ethnic group integral to the history of Canada's development. Intent on "strengthening the historical consciousness of the ethno-German community,"[69] Leibbrandt's book forwent a critical examination of the past and instead exhibited writing entrenched in ethno national posturing.

The most distressing aspect of Leibbrandt's study was the details he chose to omit. His chapter titled "Dark Times" centred on the years from 1914 to 1945 and highlighted the anti-German sentiment that German Canadians experienced over the course of this period. For Leibbrandt, the persecution of the German Canadians by English extremists during the war years was the calamity most deserving of attention in this chapter. He emphasized how in the First World War, German Canadians were exposed to mob violence, hatred, and suspicion, and had to endure a ban on the German language, and how in the Second World War they were accused of being pro-Nazi supporters.[70] Failing to mention his own involvement with the Nazi state, he explained why the Deutscher Bund, a pro-Nazi group in Canada, appealed to some German Canadians during the 1930s.[71] He wrote that "National Socialism had tried, at least outwardly, to identify itself with every decent concept linked with the name Germany" and that Germans abroad "felt a part of its fate, and that sentiment requires no justification!"[72] In his reflections on this period, he asserted that Canadians in general lacked an understanding of cultural ethnicity, which the Germans referred to as *Volkstum.* Labelling it a "German peculiarity," he wrote, "Anglo-Canadians simply could not comprehend how one could still be so attached to and so enthusiastic about the good old German fatherland."[73] Defending this German "characteristic," he quoted Kant, stating that a German "is always prepared to conform to the law of the land; his political conscience dictates civil obedience to the established government out of a sense of duty."[74] By appealing to civil obedience, Leibbrandt excused pro-Nazi supporters for blatantly ignoring the abhorrent ideology on which these groups were based. He avoided any discussion of the actual war waged by Hitler, and he ended his analysis of this period by writing about the millions of German refugees that were forced to flee from the advancing Soviet troops. Any mention of the suffering of any other people during the Second World War, particularly the victims of the Holocaust, was left out.

Furthermore, Leibbrandt stressed that German immigrants had a "close relationship" with Anglo-Saxons, unlike French or Slavic immigrants. He argued that intermarriage between Germans and Anglo-Saxons in Canada led to the rapid assimilation of German Canadians into the national fabric and that Germans had an innate ability to adopt Anglo-Canadian culture. The reasons for this, he explained, are "too numerous and complex" to divulge. Leibbrandt wrote: "The Slavs are more alien to Anglo-Saxon ways than the Germans who therefore acquire English social customs and habits much more easily."[75] Leibbrandt argued that the Germans' ability to absorb their neighbours' cultural heritage without compromising their own "inherited cultural values" allowed for them to "significantly contribute to the economic and social development of Canada."[76] Leibbrandt's ethnic generalizations in his postwar Canadian writings suggest that he made few, if any, departures from his previously held German-centric scholarly interpretations.

Conclusion

Academics in the Third Reich provided an intellectual rationalization for the Nazis' racial war that ultimately led to ethnic cleansing and genocide in Central and Eastern Europe. Leibbrandt was one of the many academics in the Nazi regime who used their scholarly expertise to further Nazi ideology—an ideology that was bent on imposing a new racial order on Europe. At the end of the Second World War, he chose to remain silent about his involvement with the Nazi state. His move to Canada allowed the historical truth to be further buried as he settled into his new role as a Russian-German immigrant in a new country. As Roger Frie writes in the Afterword to this collection, immigration to Canada not only "provided new possibilities, it also became a means to leave the past behind, and in many cases actually reinforced the process of forgetting and denial that had begun prior to leaving Germany." Intent on building a new life for himself in Canada, Leibbrandt carefully selected which narratives of his past would be used to construct his new Canadian identity. He allowed some details of his past to be known, but he kept the depth of his involvement with the Nazi regime hidden from his Canadian world. Leibbrandt conveniently withheld details of his involvement with the NSDAP, the SA, and his virulent propaganda writings from the 1930s that were littered with racist diatribes against the Jews. As he was vague about his wartime activities, his exact whereabouts on the Eastern front are still mostly unknown, though his position in intelligence organizations and personal connections to his brother Georg make one suspect that he was well aware of the Nazis' crimes in the East.

Yet in private spheres, Leibbrandt tentatively revisited the past. In correspondence with his brother Georg in the decades after the war, he asked for advice regarding compensation payments in Germany related to his freelance work as a Nazi propagandist in the late 1930s, and the two brothers frequently sent books to one another discussing how Georg's work for the Rosenberg Ministry was being analyzed by postwar scholars.[77] Although Georg's crimes in the Holocaust are conclusive, Leibbrandt's support for his brother never waned. Writing in his autobiographical papers in 1984, two years after Georg's death, Leibbrandt admitted that he visited Georg frequently during his prison sentence at Nuremberg and did everything he could to have him released. He proudly wrote that on the stand at Nuremberg, Georg came across "valiant and exemplary" and that after the war Georg became one of the most respected men in the political circles of Bonn.[78] By the time of his own death in the late eighties, Leibbrandt still had expressed no signs of remorse or readiness to accept his complicity in the Nazi regime.

In Nazi Germany, ethnicity was the boundary for an exclusive community that was based on a shared national vision. The regime was founded on an ethnic ideal that, combined with racial politics, created a lethal combination for anyone the Nazis deemed "undesirable." Shaped by this Nazi ideology of a *völkisch* ideal, Leibbrandt came to Canada with these beliefs deeply entrenched but knew well enough to extract the explicit destructive notions of "racial purity" from his Canadian scholarship. However, his Canadian writings remained grounded in the concept of ethnic solidarity. He desired to preserve *Deutschtum* amongst the German-Canadian population, and worked tirelessly to sustain this pan-German identity over the course of his career. Ethnic love in itself is not dangerous, but it becomes concerning when one ethnic group elevates its importance over others. As Claudia Koonz argues, "ethnic fundamentalism continues to draw its power from the vision of an exclusive community of 'us,' without 'them.'"[79] This twisted vision of an ideal community resulted in the atrocities of the Third Reich. Leibbrandt expressed little concern for these crimes in the postwar period, and in the writing of his ethnic history he continued to adopt a *völkisch* framework. In spite of his flawed research agenda, Leibbrandt's ethnic scholarship on the history of Germans in Canada should not be altogether abandoned, but rather it needs to be reconsidered and critically deconstructed based on the knowledge of his personal past and previous political motivations. Only then can Leibbrandt's scholarship fully contribute to the historical record of the German experience in Canada.

Notes

1 I am very grateful to Wolfram Leibbrandt, Gatineau, for allowing me access to his father Gottlieb Leibbrandt's personal papers, as well as historian Martin Munke, who kindly shared letters with me from the private collection of Hansgeorg Leibbrandt, the son of Georg Leibbrandt, in Berlin. Gottlieb Leibbrandt Obituary, *Kitchener Waterloo Record*, 18 August 1989.

2 James Casteel, "The Politics of Diaspora: Russian German Émigré Activists in Interwar Germany," in *German Diasporic Experiences: Identity, Migration, and Loss*, eds. Mathias Schulze et al. (Waterloo: Wilfrid Laurier University Press, 2008), 118.

3 Doris L. Bergen, "Tenuousness and Tenacity: The *Volksdeutschen* of Eastern Europe, World War II, and the Holocaust," in *The Heimat Abroad: The Boundaries of Germanness*, eds. Krista O'Donnell, Renate Bridenthal, and Nancy Reagin (Ann Arbor: University of Michigan Press, 2005), 269.

4 Eric Schmaltz and Samuel Sinner, "The Nazi Ethnographic Research of Georg Leibbrandt and Karl Stumpp in Ukraine, and Its North American Legacy," in *German Scholars and Ethnic Cleansing, 1919–1945*, ed. Ingo Haar and Michael Fahlbusch (New York: Berghahn Books, 2005), 52.

5 See Gottlieb Leibbrandt, "Führertum und Geschichte," *Deutsche Post aus dem Osten* 5 (1936): 19–20; Gottlieb Leibbrandt, "Die sowjetische Aussenpolitik und die Weltrevolution," *Deutsche Post aus dem Osten* 11 (1937): 1–7; Gottlieb Leibbrandt, "Bilanz über die weltgeschichtliche Erscheinung des Marxismus-Bolschewismus," *Deutsche Post aus dem Osten* 12 (1937): 4–7; Gottlieb Leibbrandt, "Deutschland—das europäische Schicksal," *Deutsche Post aus dem Osten* 5 (1937), 1–4; Gottlieb Leibbrandt, "Die Sintflut des Weltbolschewismus," *Deutsche Post aus dem Osten* 4 (1937): 4–6; Gottlieb Leibbrandt, "Die Wissenschaft im Rätestaat," *Deutsche Post aus dem Osten* 6 (1937): 5–7; Gottlieb Leibbrandt, *Bolschewismus und Abendland. Idee und Geschichte eines Kampfes gegen Europa* (Berlin: Junker and Dünnhaupt Publishing, 1939); see also Edgar Helmut Klein a.k.a. Gottlieb Leibbrandt, *Das Verbrechen des Weltbolschewismus* (Gdansk: A.W. Kafemann, 1936).

6 Samuel Sinner, "New Archival Discoveries on Wannsee Conference Participant Georg Leibbrandt and 'SS-Mann' Karl Stumpp," paper presented at the German Studies Association Conference (New Orleans, 20 September 2003), http://www.leibbrandt.com/leibbrandt_archive/dr_georg_leibbrandt/leibrandt2012.pdf (accessed 20 October 2016).

7 Schmaltz and Sinner, "The Nazi Ethnographic Research," 52–53.

8 Michael Burleigh, *Germany Turns Eastwards: A Study of "Ostforschung" in the Third Reich* (New York: Cambridge University Press, 1988); Karen Schönwälder, *Historiker und Politik: Geschichtswissenschaft im Nationalsozialismus* (Frankfurt am Main: Campus, 1992); Götz Aly and Susanne Heim, *Architects of Destruction: Auschwitz and the Logic of Destruction* (Princeton: Princeton University Press, 2002); Ingo Haar and Michael Fahlbusch, *German Scholars and Ethnic Cleansing, 1919–1945* (New York: Berghahn Books, 2005); and Wolfgang Bialas and Anson Rabinbach, *Nazi Germany and the Humanities: How German Academics Embraced Nazism* (London: Oneworld, 2007).

9 Pascal Maeder, *Forging a New Heimat: Expellees in Post-War West Germany and Canada* (Göttingen: V&R unipress, 2011), 248.

10 Angelika Sauer, "The 'Ideal German-Canadian': Politics, Academics and the Historiographical Construction of German-Canadian Identity," in *A Chorus of*

Different Voices: German Canadian Identities, ed. Angelika Sauer and Matthias Zimmer (New York: Peter Lang, 1998), 232.

11 Ibid., 236.

12 On DAI, see Grant Grams, *German Emigration to Canada and the Support of its Deutschtum during the Weimar Republic: The Role of the Deutsches Ausland-Institut, Verein fuer das Deutschtum im Ausland and German-Canadian Organisations* (Frankfurt am Main: Peter Lang, 2001).

13 Wolfram Leibbrandt, interviewed by author, Gatineau, 11 August 2016. See also Gottlieb Leibbrandt, Autobiographical Notes, 1984, Private Collection of Wolfram Leibbrandt.

14 John Haag, "The Spann Circle and the Jewish Question," *The Leo Baeck Institute Year Book* 18 no. 1 (1973): 95.

15 Reinhard Müller, "*Gottlieb Leibbrandt*," Archiv für die Geschichte der Soziologie in Österreich, July 2015, http://agso.uni-graz.at/sozio/biografien/l/leibbrandt_gottlieb.htm (accessed 13 October 2016).

16 John Lauridsen, *Nazism and the Radical Right in Austria, 1918–1934* (Copenhagen: Museum Tusculanum Press, 2007), 405–10. For more on the NSDStB, see Michael Stephen Steinberg, *Sabers and Brown Shirts: The German Students' Path to National Socialism, 1918–1935* (Chicago: University of Chicago Press, 1977); and Geoffrey J. Giles, *Students and National Socialism in Germany* (Princeton: Princeton University Press, 1985).

17 NSDAP Personal Questionnaire of Gottlieb Leibbrandt, 1938, Private Collection of Wolfram Leibbrandt. See also Müller, "Gottlieb Leibbrandt," http://agso.uni-graz.at/sozio/biografien/l/leibbrandt_gottlieb.htm (accessed 1 June 2017).

18 Ernst Ferber to the NSDAP Aid Organization regarding Gottlieb Leibbrandt, 8 January 1938, Private Collection of Wolfram Leibbrandt.

19 Müller, "Gottlieb Leibbrandt," http://agso.uni-graz.at/sozio/biografien/l/leibbrandt_gottlieb.htm (accessed 1 June 2017).

20 Lorna Waddington, *Hitler's Crusade: Bolshevism and the Myth of the International Jewish Conspiracy* (London: Tauris Academic Studies, 2007), 100.

21 Walter Laqueur, *Russia and Germany: A Century of Conflict* (Boston: Little, Brown and Company, 1965), 183.

22 Waddington, *Hitler's Crusade*, 101.

23 Hermann Fehst, *Bolschewismus und Judentum: das jüdische Element in der Führerschaft des Bolschewismus* (Berlin: Eckart-Kampf Verlag, 1934), 167, quoted in Max Weinreich, *Hitler's Professors: The Part of Scholarship in Germany's Crimes Against the Jewish People* (New Haven: Yale University Press, 1946), 113–14.

24 Waddington, *Hitler's Crusade*, 101.

25 Leibbrandt, Autobiographical Notes, 9.

26 Renate Bridenthal, "Germans from Russia: The Political Network of a Double Diaspora," in ed. O'Donnell et al., *The Heimat Abroad*, 198.

27 Casteel, "The Politics of Diaspora," 121.

28 Robert C. Williams, *Culture in Exile: Russian Émigrés in Germany, 1881–1941* (Ithaca: Cornell University Press, 1972), 358.

29 Gottlieb Leibbrandt, "Führertum and History," translated from German to English by Peter Hessel, *Deutsche Post aus dem Osten* 5 (1936): 19–20.

30 Gottlieb Leibbrandt, "Soviet Foreign Policy and the World Revolution," translated from German to English by Peter Hessel, *Deutsche Post aus dem Osten* 11 (1937): 7.

31 Edgar Helmut Klein, *Das Verbrechen des Weltbolschewismus.* Schriften der Adolf-Hitler-Schule, Landesführerschule Deutscher Osten, Danzig, Heft 8/9 (Gdansk: A.W. Kafemann, 1936) http://www.pbc.gda.pl/dlibra/docmetadata?id=18648 (accessed 1 June 2017); and Robert Edwin Herzstein, *The War that Hitler Won: The Most Infamous Propaganda Campaign in History* (New York: G.P. Putnam, 1978), 364.

32 Gottlieb Leibbrandt, *Bolschewismus und Abendland: Idee und Geschichte eines Kampfes gegen Europa*, translated from German to English by Peter Hessel (Berlin: Junker and Dünnhaupt Publishing, 1939), 154.

33 Ibid., 156.

34 "Recent Publications, Books, Pamphlets, and new Periodicals," *Contemporary Jewish Record* (Sept.–Oct. 1939): 108.

35 Sinner, "New Archival Discoveries."

36 Casteel, "The Politics of Diaspora," 123.

37 Williams, *Culture in Exile*, 360–61.

38 Alex J. Kay, *Exploitation, Resettlement, Mass Murder: Political and Economic Planning for German Occupation Policy in the Soviet Union, 1940–1941* (New York: Berghahn Books, 2006), 41.

39 Schmaltz and Sinner, "The Nazi Ethnographic Research," 67–68.

40 Kate Brown, *A Biography of No Place: From Ethnic Borderland to Soviet Heartland* (Cambridge: Harvard University Press, 2004), 197. On ethnic Germans and Nazi organizations, see Robert L. Koehl, *RKFDV: German Resettlement and Population Policy, 1939–1945: A History of the Reich Commission for the Strengthening of Germandom* (Cambridge: Harvard University Press, 1957); and Valdis O. Lumans, *Himmler's Auxiliaries: The Volksdeutsche Mittelstelle and the German National Minorities of Europe, 1933–1945* (Chapel Hill: The University of North Carolina Press, 1993).

41 Bridenthal, "Germans from Russia," 199.

42 Interview with Wolfram Leibbrandt, Leibbrandt, Autobiographical Notes, 10. See also Gerhard Bassler, "Zum Geburtstag von Dr. Gottlieb Leibbrandt," *Kanada Kurier*, 25 August 1988, sec. 5.

43 Williams, *Culture in Exile*, 361.

44 Interview with Wolfram Leibbrandt.

45 Maeder, *Forging a New Heimat*, 19–25.

46 Johann Kampen, "50 Years of the *Landsmannschaft* of the Germans from Russia," translated from German to English by Alex Herzog, *Heimatbuch*, Teil II (2000): 8–20.

47 Maeder, *Forging a New Heimat*, 128.

48 Howard Margolian, *Unauthorized Entry: The Truth about Nazi War Criminals in Canada, 1946–1956* (Toronto: University of Toronto Press, 2000), 180.

49 Ibid., 162–63.

50 Interview with Wolfram Leibbrandt.

51 Earl Werstine, "Around the Town," *The Galt Reporter*, 1953, Private Collection of Wolfram Leibbrandt.

52 Maeder, *Forging a New Heimat*, 193; Hans Werner, *Imagined Homes: Soviet German Immigrants in Two Cities* (Winnipeg: University of Manitoba Press, 2007), 212.

53 Gottlieb Leibbrandt, lecture notes from "A Course in Russian and Chinese Communism: Why Should We Fear Them," University of Waterloo, 1961, Private Collection of Wolfram Leibbrandt.

54 Franz A. J. Szabo, "Introduction: The Austrian Immigrant and the Canadian Multiculturalism Spectrum," in *Austrian Immigration to Canada: Selected Essays*, ed. Franz A. J. Szabo (Montreal: McGill-Queen's University Press, 1996), 6.

55 Gottlieb Leibbrandt, "Deutsche Ortsgründungen und Ortsnamen in der Grafschaft Waterloo," *German-Canadian Yearbook* (1973): 119–30; Leibbrandt, "Canadian German Society," *German-Canadian Yearbook* (1973): 255–62; Leibbrandt, "100 Jahre Concordia in Kitchener," *German-Canadian Yearbook* (1973): 263–74; Leibbrandt, *25 Jahre caritative und kulturelle Arbeit des Hilsfwerkes der Deutsch-Kanadier; Festschrift zum 25jährigen Bestehen der Canadian Society for German Relief* (Waterloo: Waterloo Print, 1972); and Leibbrandt, *Jubiläums Ausgabe: Centennial Issue* (Kitchener: Concordia Club, 1973).

56 Schmaltz and Sinner, "The Nazi Ethnographic Research," 73–76.

57 Martin Munke, "Georg Leibbrandt, Reich Ministry for the Occupied Eastern Territories: An Academic Radical," in *The Participants: The Men of the Wannsee Conference*, ed. Hans-Christian Jasch and Christoph Kreutzmüller (New York: Berghahn Books, 2017), 231.

58 Gottlieb Leibbrandt to Georg Leibbrandt, 9 October 1973, Literary Estate of Georg Leibbrandt, from the private collection of Hansgeorg Leibbrandt, Berlin; Georg Leibbrandt to Gottlieb Leibbrandt, 30 October 1973, Private Collection of Hansgeorg Leibbrandt.

59 Gottlieb Leibbrandt to Karl Stumpp, 18 March 1973, Private Collection of Hansgeorg Leibbrandt.

60 Gottlieb Leibbrandt, "Dr. Karl Stumpp über die Deutschen in Russland," *Courier-Nordwesten*, 21 June 1973.

61 Heinz Lehmann, *The German Canadians, 1750–1937: Immigration, Settlement, and Culture*, translated from German to English by Gerhard Bassler (St. John's: Jesperson Press, 1986).

62 Gottlieb Leibbrandt to Clive von Cardinal, Clive von Cardinal papers, MG30–E368, vol.1, Library and Archives Canada (LAC).

63 Sauer, "The 'Ideal German-Canadian,'" 229.

64 Gottlieb Leibbrandt, *Little Paradise: The Saga of the German Canadians of Waterloo County, Ontario, 1800–1975* (Kitchener: Allprint Company, 1980).

65 Gerhard Bassler, "Heinz Lehmann and German-Canadian History," in Heinz Lehmann, *The German Canadians, 1750–1937* (St. John's: Jesperson Press, 1986), xiii.

66 Gottlieb Leibbrandt to Clive von Cardinal, 9 December 1976; Leibbrandt to Cardinal, 22 January 1977; Leibbrandt to Cardinal, 29 May 1980, Clive von Cardinal papers, MG30–E368, vol.1, LAC.

67 See dust jacket of the book (1980 edition); see also advertising insert published by Allprint Company in 1977, in the author's possession. The leading German-Canadian figures that publicly backed "Little Paradise" included: Dr. Clive von Cardinal, Dr. Frank Epp, Dr. Heinz Lehmann, Dr. Herrmann Boeschenstein, Dr. Hartmut Froeschle, Dr. F.K Jacobsh, Dr. Edmund Heier, and Wilfred Bitzer, Honorary Consul of the Federal Republic of Germany.

68 Leibbrandt, *Little Paradise*, x.

69 Ibid.

70 Ibid., 253 and 267.

71 Founded in 1934, the German-Canadian *Bund* intended to spread National Socialist ideology amongst the German-Canadian community. The racially motivated vision of a German *Volksgemeinschaft* appealed to the group's approximately 2,000 members, who were mostly young, recent German immigrants to Canada, struggling to integrate into the Canadian society and economy. The group failed to garner mass support from the larger German-Canadian community, and it was eventually disbanded in 1939 with the onset of the war. For more on the pro-Nazi movement in Canada during the interwar period, see Jonathan F. Wagner, *Brothers Beyond the Sea: National Socialism in Canada* (Waterloo: Wilfrid Laurier University Press, 1981).

72 Leibbrandt, *Little Paradise*, 260.

73 Ibid., 269.

74 Ibid., 270. See also Sinner, "New Archival Discoveries," 27–29.

75 Leibbrandt, *Little Paradise*, 270.

76 Ibid., 271.

77 Gottlieb Leibbrandt to Georg Leibbrandt, 31 January 1969, Private Collection of Hansgeorg Leibbrandt; Gottlieb to Georg, 24 July 1963, Private Collection of Hansgeorg Leibbrandt; Georg to Gottlieb, 4 June 1970, Private Collection of Hansgeorg Leibbrandt.

78 Leibbrandt, Autobiographical Notes, 11.

79 Claudia Koonz, *The Nazi Conscience* (Cambridge: Belknap Press, 2003), 274.

CHAPTER 5

Gatekeeping in the Lutheran Church: Ethnicity, Generation, and Religion in 1960s Toronto

ELLIOT WORSFOLD

Almost 1.5 million European immigrants, refugees, and displaced persons arrived in Canada between 1946 and 1965. This large number transformed communities in Ontario, where over half of the postwar immigrants chose to settle.[1] The influx of so many European displaced persons (DPs) held particular significance for the Canada Synod, an organization of Lutheran churches located primarily in Ontario.[2] As German-speaking immigrants originally founded many Canada Synod congregations, their pastors continued to offer German- as well as English-language services in the postwar period. Lutheran and German-speaking DPs from Europe therefore attended Canada Synod churches so that they could worship alongside their coreligionists in their native language. DPs significantly altered the Canada Synod's demographic makeup, increasing their membership from approximately 38,000 to 64,000 between 1950 and 1960.[3] This increase in the synod's membership placed a heavy workload on its pastors, who now ministered to DPs and Canadians alike. In the summer of 1965, pastors associated with the Waterloo Lutheran Seminary devised an internship program that would send students from their seminary to work in congregations with significant DP populations in Toronto. The internship program, lasting from May to December 1966, was designed to help alleviate the burden placed on Toronto pastors while

Figure 5.1. Waterloo Lutheran Seminary building, 1963. Credit: Ellis Little Local History Room, Waterloo Public Library, C-1-12.

also preparing the young students for their future careers. The pastors' and students' involvement in the internship program inevitably brought them into close contact with the newly arrived DPs and subsequently raised questions about how the Lutheran church could best serve these "new Canadians."

Histories of postwar immigration to Canada tend to focus on the interactions between newcomers and their host society by exploring how immigrants assimilated into Canadian society.[4] Historian Franca Iacovetta provides one of the clearest examples of this theme in her work by exploring the interactions between immigrant newcomers and the Anglo-Canadian "gatekeepers" they met upon arriving in Canada. Although the term "gatekeeper" typically refers to immigration officials and those "who determine admission requirements and regulations for a country or institution," Iacovetta broadens this term as a useful shorthand to include the "wide array of reception, citizenship, and regulatory activities" that immigrants faced after they arrived in Canada.[5] She argues that Anglo-Canadian social workers, educators, journalists, and health professionals all worked to assimilate newcomers into a hegemonic Canadian culture based on British and middle-class "respectable" values. Gatekeepers monitored immigrant behaviour, including their language, parenting style, clothing, food, and mental and physical health, in an effort to coerce them to conform to Canadian cultural norms. These preoccupations reflected Cold War–era concerns that stressed the need for immigrant newcomers to embrace Canada's liberal democracy in contrast to the totalitarian and communist governments the DPs had left behind in Europe.[6]

Although Iacovetta's study focuses on Anglo-Canadian gatekeepers, examining the Canada Synod's 1966 internship program suggests that Iacovetta's "gatekeeper" concept can be broadened to include the young German-Canadian Lutheran students that participated in the program. The seminary students, who were often third-, fourth-, and later-generation German Canadians, espoused the merits of assimilation throughout the course of their internship program. They argued that the DPs in their congregations should speak English, conform to Canadian church customs, and engage with mainstream Canadian society. Unlike their Anglo-Canadian counterparts, however, the students were not motivated by the need to create upstanding citizens in order to ward off communistic influences during the Cold War. Instead, religious concerns and a belief that the Canada Synod's growth depended on speaking the English language motivated the students to encourage DP assimilation. Their tactics nevertheless mirrored the strategies of Anglo-Canadian gatekeepers and brought them into conflict with their pastors. Their pastors, often first- or second-generation immigrants from the early to mid-twentieth century, sympathized with the recently arrived DPs and rejected their students' attempts to assimilate them. Instead, they believed that their congregations should be preserved as sites of ethnic maintenance, where the DPs could continue to speak their native tongue. Ultimately, the question of immigrant integration divided participants in the internship program along generational lines.

While biological age separated the pastors from their students, generational theory provides a deeper explanation as to why the students acted as gatekeepers and their pastors opposed them. Sociologist Karl Mannheim argues that generational identity consists of more than simply one's date of birth. Instead, Mannheim proposes that "participation in the same historical and social circumstances" can prove more important than biological factors such as age in forming a generational identity.[7] Mannheim's emphasis on the role of historical experience over biology in determining generational identity holds particular promise for understanding the intergenerational relationships among immigrants. Despite their different biological ages, Toronto's Lutheran pastors and DP newcomers bonded over their generational status as first- or second-generation immigrants. Both groups either migrated to Canada or witnessed their parents' experiences of migration and faced the challenges of speaking German in a predominantly English society. Their participation in these events, albeit at different times, created a link between the pastors and DPs that became increasingly important in cultivating the same attitudes toward immigrant integration. As both groups directly or indirectly experienced the process of migration, they believed the Lutheran church should be maintained as a place of ethnicity, rather than function as yet another institution seeking to assimilate immigrants.

Implementing a generational perspective is particularly useful for revisiting several themes in postwar immigration history. First, a generational perspective demonstrates that it was not only Anglo-Canadians who acted as gatekeepers and sought to regulate immigrant lives. Looking at ethnic communities, in this case German-Canadian Lutherans, through the lens of generation shows that third-, fourth-, and later-generation members of the community also espoused the merits of assimilation and functioned as de facto gatekeepers within their communities, even if their motivations for integration differed. As Anke Patzelt demonstrates in Chapter 6, different generations of German immigrants did not always relate to their forebears despite sharing the same ethnic heritage. Just as the post-1990s German immigrants Patzelt interviewed did not relate to the previous wave of German DPs, young seminary students had difficulty relating to the ethnic traditions of their senior pastors.

Second, Mannheim's theory of generational identity explains how first- and second-generation Lutheran pastors from the early twentieth century created an informal alliance with postwar DPs. Their shared experiences and memories of migration helped formulate a generational identity that frustrated the ability of the seminary students to implement their assimilationist convictions. The joint generational identity between pastors and DPs ensured that their Lutheran churches continued to function as places of ethnicity, despite the threats the later generations posed. Examining Toronto's Lutheran community along generational lines reveals why the young third-, fourth-, and later-generation students acted as gatekeepers and sought to regulate the church's ethnic identity while the older first- and second-generation pastors allied with the DPs to preserve it. In this sense, I echo Sara Frankenberger's findings in Chapter 7 that reveal how German immigrants and their descendants may have grappled with similar issues, but responded to them differently based on their generational identities. While many German immigrants may have engaged in conversations about immigrant integration, their response to these debates and events diverged depending on their generation.

Debating Immigrant Integration

The seminary students who entered the internship program were trained in the context of 1960s North American Lutheranism. Their education at the Waterloo Lutheran Seminary reflected the Canada Synod's contemporary concerns, wherein an evangelistic drive to recruit and retain more members for the church was at the top of its priorities. Following the Second World War, Canadians started moving from rural and urban communities to newly developed suburbs. This population shift greatly troubled Canada Synod leaders, as it meant that Canadian Lutherans moved away from their established congregations into suburban areas without Lutheran churches. Synod leaders became determined to build new churches in these areas so that their membership would not decline.[8] This new focus on following their members to the suburbs prompted Canada Synod leaders to realize that they could pay equal attention to recruiting "unchurched" Canadians who had no religious affiliation. A young pastor in the synod noted that the synod should not "confine our home mission work to the 'Lutherans.' The Gospel is for all and we must minister to all that we can reach."[9] Many new neighbourhoods in North America's urban communities did not yet have established churches, thereby opening up the possibility of recruiting unchurched Anglo-Canadians into their Lutheran congregations. The seminary students received an education that stressed outreach to Lutherans and unchurched Anglo-Canadians alike.

In contrast, the older pastors that participated in the internship program received an education focused on ministering to immigrants and their descendants. Trained earlier in the twentieth century, these pastors were raised during a period of North American Lutheranism that emphasized reaching out to newly arrived immigrants.[10] The marginal status of Lutheranism in North American life, alongside the tendency to offer bilingual German-English services, meant that few Anglo-Canadians felt compelled to join the Canada Synod. Instead, early twentieth-century church growth depended on church leaders welcoming newly arrived immigrants into their congregations and retaining their membership. To that end, the pastors who later participated in the internship program received English as well as German, and occasionally Finnish, language instruction to prepare them to meet the needs of new immigrants as well as their current bilingual congregants.

The 1966 internship program brought the students and pastors together and forced them to confront the influx of postwar DPs in Canada Synod congregations. Otto Reble, a prominent leader in the Canada Synod who was heavily involved in the synod's evangelical outreach programs in the 1960s, constructed this plan deliberately. Reble was a second-generation German immigrant who retained strong ties to Germany. He spoke German fluently and even completed some of his graduate work in Germany before returning to Canada to assume responsibilities in the synod. Reble chose to place the seminary students in Toronto congregations due to the city's unique geography and sizable DP population. Toronto, and its rapidly expanding neighbourhoods, provided a rare opportunity for seminary students to gain experience working in diverse congregations. By working in Toronto, the students would gain experience in "an urban situation, a suburban situation, a bi-lingual [*sic*] situation" that could prepare them for a range of employment opportunities once they graduated.[11] By sending the seminary students to multi-ethnic and multilingual congregations in urban and suburban contexts, Reble hoped that the seminary students would gain practical knowledge on how to minister to DPs while helping the synod achieve its primary aim of postwar growth.[12]

Reble selected four students to participate in the internship program. He chose Wayne Holst, Gordon Schmidt, Barry Boeckner, and Peeter Vanker to participate in the program due to their "deep sense of the mission of the church" and for their evangelistic drive.[13] All four young men were born and raised in Waterloo County, Ontario, and they traced their lineage back to German immigrants who arrived in the region in the nineteenth century.[14] Reble paired Holst with the Reverend Eberhard W. Schwantes, the pastor of Martin Luther Evangelical

Lutheran Church, a suburban congregation composed almost entirely of postwar German DPs. Schmidt went to Agricola Lutheran Church, an urban congregation in Toronto composed of postwar Finnish DPs under the care of the Reverend Leslie Lurvey, while Boeckner worked alongside the Reverend Albert Lorch at Redeemer Lutheran Church. Unlike the students, the pastors in the program were, like Reble, first- or second-generation immigrants. Lurvey, for instance, was a second-generation immigrant but remained steeped in the ethnic culture of his parents. Born in the midwestern United States to Finnish parents, Lurvey spoke Finnish fluently and received his theological training at the Suomi Seminary, an institution that offered Finnish-language education and believed in bringing Finnish traditions to America.[15] Vanker's internship was the only exception to this pattern. He worked alongside the Reverend Mark Innes at Emmanuel Lutheran Church, which offered services only in English and had limited contact with DPs.

News that Reble paired the students with congregations that included German and Finnish languages initially disappointed the students. "Let it be known from the outset," Holst wrote to Reble, "I am not jumping with glee about my assignment."[16] The students could speak only English and felt unsure about what role they would play at congregations that overwhelmingly spoke German and Finnish. After a preliminary visit to Toronto in December 1965, Holst "discovered that the only English at the church is limited, a small service of about 15 families every week . . . I began to wonder just were [*sic*] my contribution there might be of value."[17] The pastors gave these comments more weight than they otherwise may have received because of the age gap that existed between the two groups. The students were all in their early twenties at the time of the internship program, whereas their middle-aged pastors ranged from the late thirties to fifties. The pastors saw the students as junior members of the synod, and they perceived the students' critiques as exhibiting "arrogance connected with the anxiety of their own identity crisis" as young men just beginning their careers. The pastors' seniority in the synod ensured, however, that they believed they "should be the more mature ones who can 'suffer and see through' the 'blocks' in interpersonal relationships" with the students.[18] This initial resolve of providing guidance to the students regardless of their hostility became severely tested once the internship program formally began in May 1966.

The students arrived in Toronto in the summer of 1966 without a clear indication as to what role each of them was to play at their individual congregations. Boeckner noted during the first month of his internship that he did "not really know where [he stood] in relation to the congregation and the pastor."[19] Holst had similar concerns. "Am I the 'assistant'?—seemingly not," he wondered. "Am I the student?—yes, but in what sense?"[20] As a result, the students operated under the assumption that they should begin to put into practice what their training prepared them for: to increase the number of English-language services at their congregations. During his first month in Toronto, Holst became convinced that "somehow there has to be established (sooner or later, and the sooner the better) the framework for transition" from German to English services.[21] Due to their unilingual training, the students believed that linguistic divisions threatened the church's ability to expand as one organized body. The students placed priority on speaking English so that the DPs would blend in more within the Canadian society. This would ensure that the DPs would not impede the students' evangelistic attempts to incorporate unchurched Canadians into their congregations.

Implementing English-language services, however, proved difficult in the first months of the internship program. Unable to speak German or Finnish, the students found it difficult to feel fully comfortable in their new congregations. Schmidt reported that adjusting to life at Agricola proved to be "a slow process since it must be done entirely on an individual basis. This is because most of the meetings are carried on in Finnish and thus I cannot participate."[22] Schmidt's poor language skills ensured that few members of the congregation wished to call on his services, thereby leaving him outside "the mainstream life of the congregation." He lamented throughout the summer of 1966 that the congregation "want[s] their Christianity in Finnish . . . I cannot give it to them like that, so I am out."[23] Their status as unilingual third-, fourth-, and later-generation members of their community prevented the seminary students from connecting with the new generation of Lutheran immigrants.

Hampered by their unfamiliarity with German and Finnish, the students turned their attention to working with the congregation's youth. While most of the people Schmidt encountered at Agricola spoke Finnish, some of the congregation's youth could speak conversational

English. Their age and ability to speak English gave Schmidt the impression that the young Finnish Canadians at Agricola were the only members of the congregation who fully accepted his presence.[24] Holst also found this to be true at Martin Luther Church. Holst initially spent most of his time around the congregation's "younger adult members" as he felt he could "better relate to the people in this category."[25] His experiences with the congregation's youth confirmed his reluctance about working alongside DPs. Holst concluded that the "german [*sic*] youth who have had any acquaintance with the canadian [*sic*] school system are prone to be uncomfortable with the vestiges of their german [*sic*] heritage. They want to be Canadians and they see in their parents and their church the influence of much of what would tend to separate them from the world they wish to enter."[26] Indeed, some Canadian children did bully and tease the children of German DPs by calling them derogatory terms like "Kraut" or "Nazi," and the immigrant children occasionally received strange looks if they spoke German in public.[27] Regardless of how widespread this feeling was among Martin Luther Church's youth, Holst clearly felt more comfortable around members of the congregation who felt as uncomfortable with their German heritage as he did. More significantly, the congregation's youth confirmed his belief in the importance and necessity of converting Martin Luther Church from a German to an English congregation.

Aligning with congregants of a similar age helped ease the anxiety the young students felt about their age. Also, working with young Lutherans freed the students of the perceived judgments that their congregations' adults placed on them. Holst believed that adult DPs at Martin Luther treated him as a "nice young man" but little else.[28] Boeckner also felt that the "youth factor may have a role to play" in why his congregation had yet to fully embrace his presence. He described how Redeemer's congregants treated him with an "isn't he a nice young not-yet-pastor" attitude that he personally resented.[29] Working with the congregation's youth of a similar age and generational experience helped remedy these sentiments. Moreover, the students already had some experience working with Lutheran youth. Prior to enrolling at the seminary, Schmidt was the president of the Luther League, the Canada Synod's youth group. Interacting with the congregation's youth therefore provided the students a sense of familiarity and comfort amidst the difficulties of living and working in new congregations.

Regardless of their reservations about working alongside DPs, the students initiated programs that sought to promote the English language among adult members of their congregations throughout the summer of 1966. Their attempts to convert the congregation's language to English mirrored the philosophies and strategies that were also employed by Anglo-Canadian gatekeepers in Toronto. Such Anglo-Canadian gatekeepers often stressed the importance of creating social events where DPs could interact with native-born Canadians. In theory, the Anglo-Canadians would informally "teach" the DPs how to become good Canadian citizens by acting as positive role models. Gatekeepers wanted to ensure that DPs did not interpret these social events and classes as a type of ethnic club that would further isolate them from mainstream Canadian society. By using these strategies, gatekeepers hoped DPs would leave their "old world" ties behind them and embrace their status as new Canadians.[30] Holst put this philosophy into practice in August 1966 when he started a Vacation Church School (VCS) at Martin Luther Church. The VCS, a type of summer camp that included introductory Bible lessons and socializing, functioned as a mechanism to encourage the congregation's German DPs to speak English. In order to ensure that the VCS students received maximum exposure to English, Holst invited Canadian-born children from other religious backgrounds to his VCS rather than just the German Lutherans from Martin Luther. By inviting both German Lutheran and Canadian children to his VCS, Holst sought to fulfill both the Canada Synod's goals of attracting unchurched Canadians as well as integrating DPs into the congregation. In typical gatekeeper fashion, Holst believed that promoting DP-Canadian interactions ensured that Martin Luther Church would not continue to function, in Holst's words, as a type of "ethnic ghetto" that prevented DP integration into Canadian society. In a subsequent report to Reble, Holst stated that the "V.C.S. Showed [*sic*] the members of the community that Martin Luther was not merely 'that German church'—as some referred to it,—but rather a Christian church whose majority of members may worship in the German language but who are seeking to fit into the Canadian social and religious scene."[31] Dismantling Martin Luther Church's German reputation was an important first step for Holst if he wished to draw unchurched Canadians to the congregation.

The VCS furthermore gave members of Martin Luther Church an opportunity to take on leadership roles in their church. Holst encouraged several German DP women to work alongside him at the VCS as his assistants. He deliberately asked women who already had some knowledge of English in the hopes that their volunteer work would increase their fluency in the English language.[32] Anglo-Canadian gatekeepers often used this method of encouraging DPs to run their own social events while supervised by a Canadian. Such opportunities, however, were not available to all DPs, and they only gave the appearance that the DPs were playing a leadership role when, in reality, the gatekeeper supervisor was ultimately in charge. By selecting women who already spoke some English, Holst conveyed the message that authority within the church was intrinsically tied to one's ability to speak English. Gatekeepers believed that letting DPs manage their own events conveyed the importance of the individual in a liberal democracy, in contrast to the communist political system most DPs were familiar with.[33] While Holst was not concerned about the potential communist backgrounds of DPs, he still practised Anglo-Canadian gatekeeping methods in order to achieve his personal aim of promoting English within the church.

The seminary students continued to function as gatekeepers in their community by embarking on a "door knocking" campaign in Toronto as a part of their efforts to recruit more unchurched Canadians. The students hoped to attract English-speaking Canadians to their congregations not only to expand the size of the church but also to increase the number of English-speaking congregants. Recruiting unchurched Canadians would have the dual impact of increasing church attendance and decreasing the need for German and Finnish language services. The students, however, were severely disappointed with the results of their foray into Toronto. They visited some of Toronto's large apartment buildings around their congregations and found their inhabitants largely uninterested in Lutheranism. Holst visited several buildings where "old stock" Canadians lived alongside more recent DPs "of multi-racial [*sic*] backgrounds." Holst quickly became disheartened over the apathetic attitudes of those he encountered. To Holst, these DPs were "welfare cases and others who seem to care little where they live" let alone take an interest in the church.[34] Schmidt found it equally difficult to get the Finnish DPs at Agricola to interact with their Anglo-Canadian neighbours. Their reluctance to speak English or engage with

Anglo-Canadians made him realize "that fellowship among members is much more important than a desire to be the salt of Toronto." "Perhaps," he wondered, "this is because many of the members find it difficult to communicate precisely in English."[35]

The pastors resisted attempts by their students to bring gatekeeper attitudes into their congregations and offered a different approach to the question of immigrant integration. Their generational identities, both in terms of biological age and time of migration, motivated the pastors to maintain their churches as spaces where DPs could continue to practise their ethnic identities. In contrast to their younger students, the first- and second-generation pastors had received their theological training in languages other than English and were more accustomed to the church's history of working with immigrants. As the pastors either migrated to Canada or had parents who did, they drew explicitly on immigrant origins of North American Lutheranism to justify their belief that the church was not responsible for assimilating the current generation of DPs. "It is a fact of history that our Lutheran church has made its beginnings in the New World in the many languages of immigrants," Lurvey argued, and added, "Seminaries and colleges that now serve millions with great blessings were begun in these languages." He believed that the church's efforts to help DPs should be carried out "in the same spirit, although in a much later setting."[36] Lurvey's statement directly tied together his experiences training in a Finnish-language seminary to minister to immigrants and the new generation of DPs currently attending Lutheran congregations. As a result of his training and identity as a second-generation immigrant, he did not find it surprising that a new generation of DPs wished to also continue speaking Finnish. Unlike Schmidt's, Lurvey's training emphasized the ethnic and religious heritage of Lutheranism. While he empathized with Schmidt's "plight" over his inability to communicate with the congregation's "post-World War II immigrant stock," he did not accept Schmidt's emphasis on assimilation.[37]

Schwantes also described Lutheranism in ethnic terms in his effort to advocate for Martin Luther Church's German DPs. He knew that most members of the congregation were ethnic Germans from "Poland and Russia" where "they had fought and died for their faith and language for centuries." As a result, "it is only natural that they want to worship in their mother tongue and maintain the[ir] heritage of centuries."[38] Schwantes recognized that the German DPs fought to preserve their faith and language while they lived under Soviet or Nazi-occupied Europe and would continue to do so in Canada. The immigrant backgrounds of the DPs ensured that the church functioned as a place where they could speak their language with their peers outside of the purview of their host society. The DPs' conception of Lutheranism and the role it played in their lives would not change, even if they moved to yet another nation. Accordingly, Schwantes informed Holst that he must "work within the existing frame work [*sic*] of the congregation" and not challenge Martin Luther Church's German heritage. As Holst could not speak German, Schwantes believed that "he would concentrate on the English speaking [*sic*] part of the congregation" until his linguistic skills progressed enough that he could start to serve the German congregants.[39]

Through initiatives such as the VCS and promoting English in their congregations, the students positioned themselves as gatekeepers within the church and provoked the anger of their pastors. Schwantes accused Holst of exhibiting an "almost feverish attempt to find fault" in the behaviour of the congregation's DPs. "He is obsessed with the idea that English must be furthered and strengthened at all costs," Schwantes observed, "which in my opinion would result in adverse repercussion to the main work of the congregation." Holst pursued his goal of assimilating German DPs to such an extent that Schwantes wondered whether Holst harboured a form of "hidden resentment towards" those who maintained a German ethnic identity.[40] Lorch had similar concerns about Boeckner's disregard for the church's ethnic traditions. "What had taken place in bringing the congregation to its present situation," he noted, was never given due consideration by Boeckner or the other students.[41] While the students believed that they could help the Canada Synod grow by assimilating the DPs, their pastors believed that providing a space where these immigrants could speak their native tongue would ensure their loyalty and, therefore, the growth of the synod. While both pastors and students wanted to assist the Canada Synod in achieving postwar growth, their generational identities ensured that they sought to carry out this task differently.

In contrast to those of the other interns, Vanker's internship occurred without controversy. Emmanuel offered only English-language services and had few, if any, DP congregants. Vanker therefore did not grapple with questions of immigrant integration during his internship program. Instead, he participated in the evangelical activities the four students were trained for. During the program's first month, Vanker made several visits to the homes of unchurched Canadians in an effort to increase Emmanuel's church attendance. He also took part in interfaith meetings with Toronto's other Protestant churches and conducted several services at Emmanuel, as a language barrier between Vanker and the congregation did not exist. Vanker reportedly did a commendable job and received satisfactory reports from the congregation.[42] His internship proved valuable and productive, as he received hands-on experience that directly connected to his training at the seminary. Vanker did not experience the same alienation during his internship as the question of immigrant integration never put him in conflict with his pastor or congregation.

The "Old" and "New" Theology

Perceived theological differences between the pastors and their students as a result of their generational identities further intensified the animosity between the two groups. Theories on generational identity, such as those proposed by Mannheim, explain why the pastors and students expressed their disagreements over immigrant integration in ethnic and theological terms. Mannheim's definition of generation proposes that members of a young generation form their identity in opposition to the older generation and vice-versa.[43] This conflict between the young students and middle-aged pastors mirrored broader social trends in 1960s Canada. Canadian youth throughout the 1960s increasingly defined themselves against their more traditional parents and participated in protests advocating for civil rights, world peace, and nuclear disarmament on university campuses.[44] While these events did not directly shape the internship program, the social discourses surrounding them did. Generational differences heightened the religious and ethnic tensions between the students and pastors that were expressed against the backdrop of the 1960s.

The relationship between Schwantes and Holst in particular mirrored the broader tensions between Canadian youth and adults throughout the 1960s. The pastor of Martin Luther Church criticized Holst for embodying the rebellious generation of Canadian youth. In fact, Schwantes believed that the student-pastor relationship should consist of the pastor exerting "his authority and the student 'submit[ing]' to his authority." It is no wonder, then, that Schwantes felt Holst expressed "an almost defiant attitude to accept the pastor and his word" when he continued his gatekeeping efforts against Schwantes's wishes.[45] The older man reflected contemporary discourses on troubled youth when he commented that the seminary students came from a "fatherless society" that produced "aimless, frightened and fearful" students who could not adequately face the challenges of the modern world. "To come into an established congregation to experiment and play havoc with the congregational life are indications of immature behaviour and childish rebellion," Schwantes believed. He stated, "Their reluctance to submit to authority and discipline are further indications that something has gone amiss in their training and instructions. Wayne Holst, at the age of 24, is still very immature and emotionally unstable." On the whole, Schwantes's characterization of Holst as "fatherless" echoed the dominant postwar discourses on troubled youth. Traditional understandings of fatherhood situated fathers as the powerful head of their families who, if neglectful, could produce delinquent and disobedient children.[46] As a mentor in the internship program, Schwantes took on a parental obligation to authoritatively criticize Holst for his gatekeeping ways. He believed that the students needed "to be corrected or else they will never grow up."[47] The synod leadership agreed with Schwantes. Reble believed that the students often behaved immaturely and that the Waterloo Lutheran Seminary more generally was dealing with a "rebellious generation" of students.[48]

Out of the four students, Boeckner most clearly embodied the "rebellious" spirit of the seminary students and overtly challenged the "traditional" church practices of the older generation. Boeckner performed what he termed a "hottenanies and folk"-styled service at Redeemer after Lorch granted his request to preach a guest sermon. Boeckner believed that this "new form of worship" helped convey to the congregation that the pastor was "real" and "alive" in contrast to Lorch's more stationary and removed approach.[49] Holst made similar critiques of Schwantes throughout the internship program. He believed that Schwantes was too unfamiliar with the "modern" and "democratic" style of pastoral care to provide him with an effective role model. While Schwantes preferred a hierarchal church structure that situated the pastor as the authority figure in the congregation, Holst agreed with Boeckner that the pastor needed to be more available and accessible to his congregation.[50] In fact, rather than receiving guidance from his pastor, Boeckner drew inspiration for his experimental style of preaching from attending the Beatles concert at Maple Leaf Gardens that summer. Boeckner reportedly "loved every minute of it" and noticed the enthusiastic way that the teenage audience responded to the band. Boeckner believed the way teenagers responded to the Beatles "shows a whole new world about which we as adults of the Church know very little. I can truthfully describe my attendance at the Beatle's [*sic*] concert as worship in the full sense of the word."[51] The students tended to prioritize these approaches as a result of the importance they placed on the congregation's youth. As young members of the church, the students believed that both they and their peers would constitute the church's future. Retaining their membership and ensuring that the church appealed to them became an important goal for all the students throughout the program.

The differences in religious practice and theology became yet another way for the students to advance their gatekeeper aims and discredit the views of their pastors. Generation and ethnicity sat at the crux of their critiques. In contrast to his own modern approach, Boeckner criticized Lorch's mentorship by stating that he expected the internship program to teach him more than how to discuss the "Word and sacraments as they have been ministered ever since the 17th century."[52] Holst and Schmidt also portrayed Schwantes and Lurvey as part of Lutheranism's distant ethnic past by accusing them of practicing "the old liturgy" by speaking German and Finnish to their congregations. They believed speaking these languages "was not up-to-date enough and that people who were coming new into the church should not be asked to involve themselves in something that would be pretty meaningless." They "felt that pastors should have the opportunity to let the old liturgy go and develop new norms of the expression of congregational cohesion" based on the English language.[53] These critiques of their pastors' theology allowed them to extend their gatekeeper roles in their congregations by critiquing their pastors' ethnic identities alongside the DPs'. If the Canada Synod faced a "DP problem," their pastors were certainly a part of it. Promoting multiple languages within the church, the students believed, would only hurt the Canada Synod's goal of postwar growth. The students therefore situated Schwantes and Lurvey within the German and Finnish communities they aimed to assimilate. Holst attributed both Schwantes's traditional theology and sympathy for German DPs as a product of "his german [*sic*] cultural heritage."[54] Schmidt also attributed difficulties in his internship to the fact that he was "too different than [*sic*] the Finns." He could not minister effectively, in his opinion, because he was forced to "teach them Lurvey style Finnish theology instead of remaining true to [his] convictions" that he had learned at the seminary.[55] As third-, fourth-, and later-generation members of their communities, the students saw the ethnic traditions of their pastors as antithetical to their attempts to help their congregations grow. Since they conceptualized their generation as the future of the church, they inevitably constructed their pastors as embodying the church's outdated ethnic history.

Conversely, the pastors also used religious differences to combat their students' gatekeeping efforts. They criticized their students for being more concerned with worldly matters than spiritual matters. They believed that the concern over integrating immigrants into Anglo-Canadian society fell under the purview of the state, not the church. Schwantes perceived Holst's gatekeeper attitudes as "unsound theologically" and not based on what was best for the German DPs. Schwantes suggested that Holst's push for assimilation could be "interpreted as a misguided but ebullient nationalism BUT THIS IS NOT CHRISTIANITY."[56] Reble, as a second-generation German immigrant, agreed with the pastors. According to him, the gatekeeper attitudes exhibited by the students came from a Canadian, rather than Christian, point of view. While the seminary students saw it as necessary for immigrants to speak English in order to encourage the synod's growth, Reble and the other first- and second-generation pastors did not agree. Reble, for instance, urged Holst to clarify his views on why the congregants at Martin Luther Church needed to speak English for the congregation to thrive.[57] Speaking English was not a theological necessity for the first- and second-generation pastors who were raised among church members that largely spoke German. Since Reble and Lurvey attended German- or Finnish-language churches and seminaries in their youth, they saw nothing unusual about a new generation of immigrants worshipping in their own language.

The pastors furthermore drew on their own experiences and memories of migrating to Canada to strengthen their position in resisting

DP integration. Schwantes, for instance, declared that he understood "the German immigrant and the whole ethnic problem" in ways that Holst could not.[58] The pastors drew direct comparisons between being raised in the synod's German or Finnish culture and the lives of the new influx of DPs. Lurvey recognized the unique insight that they, as first- or second-generation immigrants, had into understanding the experiences of postwar DPs: "Imagine if you will the feeling of the immigrant hearing an English sermon when all his life he has heard the Gospel preached in Finnish. There is a certain theological vocabulary that must first be learned before the message breaks through. . . . We who have 'the gift of tongues' feel that we have something to offer these people not only basically for their spiritual well-being but also for their mental well-being. To speak another language is a gift of the Spirit, not to be regarded lightly. Its use, too, is a stewardship."[59] Unlike the students who portrayed the German and Finnish languages as a part of the synod's outdated theological and ethnic traditions, Lurvey advocated for its continued relevance. Knowledge of German and Finnish, he argued, would continue to be useful in growing the Canada Synod as long as DPs continued to arrive in Toronto without the ability to speak English. In contrast to the students, the pastors argued that the Canada Synod's future depended upon retaining the loyalty of DPs by continuing to offer them services in the language they understood best.

By September 1966, Lurvey and Lorch formally withdrew from the internship program. They recognized that Schmidt's and Boeckner's gatekeeping attitudes made them poor choices to work in their congregations and formally terminated their students' internships. Schwantes informed Reble that he also considered withdrawing from the program, but he ultimately managed to remain in the program until its conclusion in December. The pastors' and seminary students' generational differences shaped how they approached immigrant integration and ensured that the internship program ended with bitterness. Although the program intended to prepare the students for their subsequent careers as pastors, the internships obscured rather than clarified their future with the Lutheran church.[60] By 1967, Schmidt left the Canada Synod to work as a pastor at an English-language congregation in Erie, Pennsylvania, as a member of the Western Pennsylvania–West Virginia Synod. The other three students remained part of the Canada Synod, but they continued to advance their own perspectives rather than those of their pastors. Vanker returned to his home congregation in Kitchener and questioned whether its pastor worked hard enough to assimilate the church's German DPs, while Holst and Boeckner continued to participate in interfaith efforts with Anglican and United Church congregations.[61] The internships did prepare the students for their future careers in the church, but perhaps not in the ways that Reble had intended.

Conclusion

During the early months of the internship program, Wayne Holst identified how ethnicity, theology, and generation all contributed to the conflict between the seminary students, pastors, and DPs. In a report to Reble, Holst observed that Schwantes's reputation as "'herr [*sic*] pastor' has a connotation for the German-speaking members at Martin Luther that it does not have in American English Lutheranism . . . he seems bound by the traditional. . . . This is especially true among the young people. What the older people see as deserving respect, the young see as shallow and even hypocritical."[62] Although he did not share Holst's negative assessments of Schwantes's German ethnicity, Reble also blamed ethnicity and generation for the internship program's failure. The issues of language maintenance as well as the traditional religious practices of the pastors and the "more modern approach" of the students ensured that the two sides would not agree on how to best serve the DPs.[63]

The conflict over immigrant integration that occurred in Toronto's Lutheran churches opens new avenues for research on postwar immigration history. Although both pastors and students sought to regulate the church's ethnic identity, their generational identities, both in terms of age and time of migration, ensured that they approached this issue differently. As middle-aged first- and second-generation immigrants, pastors and synod officials continued to perform their roles as ethnic elites and fought to maintain the ethnic traditions of the Canada Synod. Their students, however, tried to regulate and diminish the church's ethnic identity. This generational tension within the Lutheran church should urge historians to continue to rethink and examine who constituted a "gatekeeper" in postwar Canadian society. Although the gatekeeper model has thus far been applied to middle-class Anglo

Canadians, the case of the seminary students demonstrates that Canadians who belonged to ethnic and religious groups also functioned as gatekeepers inside of their communities. The seminary students were not motivated by broader fears surrounding citizenship and the Cold War. Instead, they employed gatekeeper strategies to facilitate DP integration into their churches in an effort to grow the size of their congregations and make them more appealing to unchurched Canadians. While their motivations for downplaying the ethnic identities of DPs differed, the students placed the same emphasis on immigrant integration as did Anglo-Canadian gatekeepers in the 1960s. Examining other ethnic and religious communities through the lens of generation may reveal similar young third-, fourth-, and later-generation descendants of immigrants who acted as gatekeepers in the postwar period. Indeed, as Patzelt makes clear in Chapter 6, the German immigrants that migrated to Canada after 1990 did not feel the same pull towards ethnic clubs or German-speaking churches as their forebears. As "modern immigrants" living in a globalized and technologically advanced world, these more recent arrivals had few emotional or practical needs to attend exclusive German-speaking institutions. In this sense, the post-1990 wave of bilingual and affluent German immigrants may have had more in common with the generation of the 1960s seminary students than with the early twentieth-century pastors or first-generation DPs.

Despite the debate surrounding immigrant integration in 1960s Toronto, the pastors' conception of Lutheranism ultimately prevailed in the congregations with large DP populations. Martin Luther and Agricola both remained active and still offered German and Finnish language services to Lutherans in the Toronto area in 2017. Although a new generation of young Lutheran pastors threatened this tradition in the 1960s, the ability of pastors such as Schwantes and Lurvey to draw upon their own immigrant identities allowed them to successfully bridge the divide between themselves and the new generation of postwar immigrants. In cultivating this generational alliance, they ensured that their Lutheran churches would continue to function as sites of ethnic maintenance.

Notes

1 Franca Iacovetta, *Gatekeepers: Reshaping Immigrant Lives in Cold War Canada* (Toronto: Between the Lines, 2006), 6–7.

2 The Canada Synod changed its name to the Eastern Canada Synod when it joined the Lutheran Church in America in 1962. Despite these changes, the name "Canada Synod" remained in popular colloquial use. Although "displaced person" refers to a specific legal category, Canadians often used terms such as refugee, displaced person, immigrant, and new Canadian interchangeably. I have elected to use the term DP for the sake of consistency. For a discussion of these legal categories and how the DPs defined themselves, see Pascal Maeder, *Forging a New Heimat: Expellees in Post-War West Germany and Canada* (Göttingen: V&R unipress, 2011), 23.

3 Carl Raymond Cronmiller, *A History of the Lutheran Church in Canada* (Toronto: Evangelical Lutheran Synod of Canada, 1961), 242.

4 On postwar German immigrant interactions with Canadians, see Hans Werner, *Imagined Homes: Soviet German Immigrants in Two Cities* (Winnipeg: University of Manitoba Press, 2007); Alexander Freund, "Contesting the Meaning of Migration: German Women's Immigration to Canada in the 1950s," *Canadian Ethnic Studies* 41–42, no. 3/1 (2009–2010): 1–26; and Maeder, *Forging a New Heimat*.

5 Iacovetta, *Gatekeepers*, xii.

6 Ibid., xii, 10–12, 19. For other discussions of gatekeeping in Canadian and American immigrant history, see Erika Lee, "The Chinese Exclusion Example: Race, Immigration, and American Gatekeeping, 1882–1924," *Journal of American Ethnic History* 21, no. 3 (2002): 37–38; and Vic Satzewich, *Points of Entry: How Canada's Immigration Officers Decide Who Gets In* (Vancouver: UBC Press, 2015).

7 Karl Mannheim, "The Problem of Generations," in *Essays on the Sociology of Knowledge*, ed. Paul Kecskemeti (London: Routledge and Kegan Paul, 1959), 297–98, 310.

8 On postwar trends in North American Lutheranism, see Mark Granquist, *Lutherans in America: A New History* (Minneapolis: Fortress Press, 2015), 262–63, 268–69.

9 Laurier Archives (hereafter LA), Eastern Synod of the Evangelical Lutheran Church in Canada fonds (hereafter ESF), 11 Lutheran Church in America, Folder 11.6.1.2., "Preserve and Extend . . . Through Home Missions: An Address by the Appeal Director, the Rev. Norman Berner," 1955.

10 Granquist, *Lutherans in America*, 209.

11 LA, ESF, Folder 50.10.1.3, Unnamed to Otto Reble, 3 March 1965.

12 LA, ESF, Folder 50.10.1.3, Reble to Delton Glebe, 4 July 1965.

13 LA, ESF, Folder 50.10.1.3, Internship—Pilot Project, n.d.

14 Holst, for instance, identified as a sixth-generation German Canadian. For biographical information, see LA, ESF, Folder 5.0.6; Wayne Holst, "Are We Still a People of Compassion?" *Anglican Journal* (21 September 2015), http://www.anglicanjournal.com/articles/-are-we-still-people-of-compassion (accessed 23 June 2016).

15 For biographical information on the aforementioned pastors, see material in LA, ESF, Folder 5.0.6 and 3.68.11.1. See also E. Clifford Nelson, *The Lutherans in North America* (Philadelphia: Fortress Press, 1975), 272–76.

16 LA, ESF, Folder 50.10.1.3, Wayne Holst to Reble, 5 January 1966.

17 LA, ESF, Folder 50.10.1.3, Holst to Reble, 5 January 1966.

18 LA, ESF, Folder 50.10.1.3, Glebe to Reble, 28 October 1965.

19 LA, ESF, Folder 50.10.1.3, Barry Boeckner's Monthly Intern Report, 8–30 May 1966.

20 LA, ESF, Folder 50.10.1.3, Wayne Holst's Evaluation of the Toronto Internship, 7 June 1966; Gordon Schmidt's Report, May 1966.

21 LA, ESF, Folder 50.10.1.3, Holst's Evaluation, 7 June 1966.

22 LA, ESF, Folder 50.10.1.3, Schmidt's Report, May 1966.

23 LA, ESF, Folder 50.10.1.3, Schmidt's Report, June–July 1966.

24 LA, ESF, Folder 50.10.1.3, Schmidt's Report, May 1966; Schmidt's Report, June–July 1966.

25 LA, ESF, Folder 50.10.1.3, Holst's Evaluation, 31 October 1966.

26 LA, ESF, Folder 50.10.1.3, Holst's Final Evaluation, January 1967.

27 Maeder, *Forging a New Heimat*, 222–23; Alexander Freund, "Troubling Memories in Nation-building: World War II Memories and Germans' Inter-ethnic Encounters in Canada after 1945," *Histoire sociale/Social History* 39, no. 77 (2006): 145–47.

28 LA, ESF, Folder 50.10.1.3, Holst's Final Evaluation, January 1967.

29 LA, ESF, Folder 50.10.1.3, Boeckner's Report, 8–30 May 1966.

30 Iacovetta, *Gatekeepers*, 53–54, 76, 85–90.

31 LA, ESF, Folder 50.10.1.3, A Personal Evaluation of the Vacation Church School at Martin Luther Church, Mimico, October 1966.

32 Ibid.

33 Iacovetta, *Gatekeepers,* 90–92.

34 LA, ESF, Folder 50.10.1.3, Holst to Reble, 29 August 1966.

35 LA, ESF, Folder 50.10.1.3, Schmidt's Report, May 1966.

36 LA, ESF, Folder 50.1.2.6.7.1, Leslie Lurvey to Otto Olson Jr., 29 December 1966.

37 LA, ESF, Folder 50.10.1.3, Lurvey's Report, August 1966.

38 LA, ESF, Folder 50.10.1.3, Eberhard Schwantes's Evaluation, August 1966.

39 Ibid.

40 Ibid.

41 LA, ESF, Folder 50.10.1.3, Albert Lorch's Report, n.d.

42 LA, ESF, Folder 50.10.1.3, Internship Program, May 1966.

43 Mannheim, "The Problem of Generations," 309–10.

44 Bryan Palmer, *Canada's 1960s: The Ironies of Identity in a Rebellious Era* (Toronto: University of Toronto Press, 2009), 23.

45 LA, ESF, Folder 50.10.1.3, Schwantes's Evaluation, August 1966; Lutheran Internship, 11 August 1966.

46 Mary Louise Adams, *The Trouble with Normal: Postwar Youth and the Making of Heterosexuality* (Toronto: University of Toronto Press, 1997), 30; and Mona Gleason, *Normalizing the Ideal: Psychology, Schooling, and the Family in Postwar Canada* (Toronto: University of Toronto Press, 1999), 110.

47 LA, ESF, Folder 50.10.1.3, Schwantes's Evaluation, August 1966.

48 LA, ESF, Folder 50.10.1.3, Reble's Memorandum, 9 September 1966.

49 LA, ESF, Folder 50.10.1.3, Boeckner's Report, 8–30 May 1966.

50 LA, ESF, Folder 50.10.1.3, Holst's Final Evaluation, January 1967.

51 LA, ESF, Folder 50.10.1.3, Boeckner's Report, August 1966.
52 LA, ESF, Folder 50.10.1.3, Boeckner's Final Evaluation, n.d.
53 LA, ESF, Folder 50.10.1.3, Lutheran Internship, 23 June 1966.
54 LA, ESF, Folder 50.10.1.3, Holst's Final Evaluation, January 1967.
55 LA, ESF, Folder 50.10.1.3, Schmidt's Evaluation, 17 January 1967.
56 LA, ESF, Folder 50.10.1.3, Schwantes's Evaluation, August 1966; Lutheran Internship, 28 November 1966.
57 LA, ESF, Folder 50.10.1.3, Holst's Evaluation, 7 June 1966.
58 LA, ESF, Folder 50.10.1.3, Schwantes's Evaluation, August 1966; Lutheran Internship, 28 November 1966.
59 LA, ESF, Folder 50.1.2.6.7.1, Lurvey to Olson, 29 December 1966.
60 LA, ESF, Folder 50.10.1.3, Holst's Evaluation, 31 August 1966.
61 See LA, ESF, LSP12, Minutes of the 106th Annual Convention of the Evangelical Lutheran Synod of Canada, 1968, 42. For Vanker's gatekeeping efforts after his internship, see LA, ESF, LM10 Kitchener St. Peter's Evangelical Lutheran Church, reel 18, Annual Congregational Meeting Minutes, 29 January 1967. Holst continues to comment regularly in a column in *The Anglican Journal*.
62 LA, ESF, Folder 50.10.1.3, Holst's Evaluation, July 1966.
63 LA, ESF, Folder 50.10.1.3, Reble's Memorandum, 9 September 1966.

CHAPTER 6

Migration Trajectories and the Construction of Generational Discourses among Contemporary German Immigrants in Ottawa in the 2000s

ANKE PATZELT

After the British and the French, Germans form one of the largest ethnic groups of European origin in Canada, and their migration to Canada has a long tradition, dating back to the beginning of the sixteenth century.[1] They can thus look upon an eventful history, which has been influenced by world (political) events as well as by the complex history of the German nation-state and its changing territories.[2] Especially after the Second World War, large numbers of Germans came to Canada in search of a new home.[3] A total of about 200,000 Germans entered Canada between 1951 and 1957.[4] Even today, Canada is still among the top eleven destination countries, attracting between 2,000 and 3,000 German immigrants each year.[5] However, research on these more recent, post-1990 waves of German immigrants in Canada is lacking. Most studies thus far have focused on Germans who arrived in the 1950s or up until the beginning of the 1990s.[6] Yet, exploring the experiences of recent German immigrants to Canada is important because—compared to previous generations—Germans immigrating to Canada today face completely different circumstances. First, with the processes of democratization and liberalization taking place after the Second World War, West Germany transformed from a totalitarian dictatorship to a stable democracy. After the student protests of the late 1960s and attendant claims of coming to terms with the past (*Vergangenheitsbewältigung*), former structures of authority and discipline were abandoned, profoundly altering the country's social environment.[7] Second, the fall of the Berlin Wall in 1989 and German reunification in 1990 constituted a significant change to German society, which deeply impacted the understanding and the image people had of Germany's national identity and international role. Third, in the 1990s and 2000s in Germany, as well as elsewhere, globalization introduced new forms of communication and transportation that made it easier to maintain close ties with family and one's home country's society, culture, economy, and politics.[8] Thus, the migration process and the effects of time-space compressions resulting from globalization have influenced the understandings these migrants have of themselves.[9] Accordingly, the 1950s and 1960s political, cultural, and social circumstances that shaped postwar immigrants were significantly different from those of more recent migrants. Several scholars have claimed that recent German migration experiences, the migrants' construction of ethnic identity, and the ways in which they relate to Germany and Canada differ from those of previous generations.[10] So far, however, no empirical research has been undertaken to investigate these differences.

This chapter addresses this research gap by examining contemporary (post-1990) German immigrants in Ottawa. By drawing on in-depth interviews with nine recent German immigrants (arriving between 1990 and 2007) as well as participant observation in Ottawa's German-speaking community, I investigate the circumstances of and reasons for the interviewees' migration trajectories, their ways of maintaining ties to Germany, their involvement in German clubs and organizations in Canada, and the ways in which they relate to Germany as their country of origin and Canada as their current country of residence. A special focus in this analysis is placed on the interviewees' explicit and implicit differentiation between themselves and previous generations of German immigrants, especially those who had arrived in the postwar years. Previous studies demonstrate the importance of examining immigrant generations (e.g., the first generation of foreign-born immigrants, and the second and third generation of native-born children and grandchildren) defined along genealogical lines.[11] Other studies show that immigrant generations (e.g., different cohorts of first-generation immigrants which migrated at different points in time) are also shaped by "specific socio-historical contexts."[12]

Such an approach applies Karl Mannheim's[13] notion of generation—as a group that is shaped by the specific historical and social context in which its individuals are socialized—to the study of immigrant generations. Mannheim's idea allows us to capture and understand the different migration and integration experiences of various cohorts of first-generation immigrants from the same country of origin "that extant theoretical approaches leave undocumented and unexplained."[14] Such a framework is particularly useful when analyzing the experiences of different first-generation immigrant cohorts coming from countries that have undergone significant historical and socio-political changes, like Germany. In order to capture these differences within the first generation and thus obtain a better understanding of the migration experiences of my interviewees, as well as their perceptions of how they differ from previous German immigrant cohorts, this chapter focuses on the construction of generational discourses among my interviewees.

More specifically, my approach is informed by the concept of social generations, defined by the Portuguese sociologists Sofia Aboim and Pedro Vasconcelos.[15] Drawing on Mannheim's work, they acknowledge that generations are shaped by their shared historical locations, but they also argue that "generations are better conceived as discourses with which individuals relate in order to build self-identification."[16] The main focus of their concept of social generations is, therefore, on the discourses and labels which are not only created by external influences, such as social institutions, but also, and more importantly, are mobilized by individuals themselves. This can occur, for example, through processes of self-identification, by which beings differentiate themselves from other people. According to Aboim and Vasconcelos, "Generations only exist if, sitting in a given structural location, discourses about one's own time are mobilized for self-identification."[17] Thus, even if individuals do not necessarily actively produce generational discourses in the first place, it is only through people's use of these discourses as a means of self-identification that these generational discourses become relevant and establish themselves in society. By examining the ways in which the interviewees differentiated between themselves and German immigrants who arrived in Canada during the 1950s and 1960s, it is possible to identify some of the generational discourses, which were mobilized by the more recent immigrants, and gain a better understanding of this generation of migrants.

The Circumstances of and Reasons for Migrating to Canada

My interviewees came from different parts of Germany and were highly qualified; with one exception, they all had obtained a university degree.[18] At the time of their interviews, they were between the ages of forty and fifty-four, and while the earliest project particpant had moved to Canada in 1990, the latest had arrived in 2007. Most of them had had a secure and well-paid job in Germany before leaving the country, and they had been, generally speaking, living a comfortable life. Thus, there were no apparent political or economic triggers for them to leave Germany and move to Canada.[19] This was reflected in the experiences of the interviewees, many of whom said that they had not necessarily had any previous plans of moving to Canada but somehow "got stuck" there, as Klaus A. (41) put it. Often, they were rather curious about exploring the world and experiencing life in another country and then ended up in Canada, either because they received a job offer from a Canadian employer or because they had met a Canadian partner. Moving and living abroad was not a new experience for them because most had lived abroad before, at least for shorter periods in connection with, for example, university exchanges or work experiences. Canada appeared to be just one of many options for them. Klaus A. followed his French-Canadian wife to Canada. He explained:

> I have always felt that I got stuck here somehow; I mean I could just as well be somewhere else. Some people might have a "dream": "I want to come to Canada at some point, like this is my 'dream.'" For me it wasn't like that. I always wanted to get out, but theoretically it could have been somewhere else as well. But I mean Anne [his wife] is Canadian . . . I have talked to people and they told me: "Ah well, you immigrated here." And then I always thought: "Yes, well I did that, but more, well let's say unconsciously." I mean, I actually feel that I am a German and that I am more on a transit or something. That's how I feel. So, I could be somewhere else as well.[20]

Thus, by differentiating himself from other Germans who might have moved to Canada to fulfill their dreams, as well as by stating that he was not a "typical immigrant" who moved to another country for economic reasons, Klaus A. created an image of himself as a "mobile" individual, who was, contrary to the image he was creating of "typical immigrants," not permanently settled in one place, but flexible to move and live anywhere. These feelings were also reflected in the accounts of other interviewees.

Sara L. (54) highlighted that after she finished her university studies she just wanted to "go out and explore the world" and "do something different." She had never expected to end up in Canada, but "this was just how things turned out" and so she "just went along with that situation."[21] Likewise, Heinz W. (45) said that he did not have any initial plans of moving to Canada. Originally, he went to the United States for an exchange year during his studies and then somehow "got stuck there." After his exchange year, he decided to continue pursuing his master's and PhD studies in the United States and during this time met his wife, whose family lived in Ottawa. After both finished their degrees, they joined his wife's family because it seemed easier to start a life together in Canada than in Germany or the United States.[22] Thus, although the interviewees shared a desire for exploring the world, they were relatively flexible in their decision of where to settle and live. Most of them did not necessarily wish to move to Canada initially but rather ended up there through external circumstances.

These experiences also resulted in the fact that most of the interviewees drew clear boundaries between themselves and previous generations of German immigrants to Canada. They perceived themselves as being unlike postwar Germans. Some interviewees believed that this was the result of the different social conditions in which the two generations had grown up. My interviewees believed that the previous generation came with the hopes and expectations for a better life, escaping hunger, homelessness, and unemployment in Germany. In contrast, they highlighted that they had come to Canada because of a lust for adventure or because they were in a relationship with a Canadian citizen. These differences were quite well reflected in the expressions "Kofferdeutsche" (suitcase Germans) and "Kontainerdeutsche" (container Germans), which I encountered on numerous occasions. These terms refer to the supposition that older immigrants often came to Canada with only a suitcase and little money, having to start their new lives from scratch, whereas more recent waves of German immigrants were able to ship all of their belongings in a container and had their lives perfectly organized upon arrival. Frida B. (46) emphasized this idea: "Well, back then [in the period after the Second World War] you fled from something, or you were seeking something better or something along those lines. I don't have this feeling at all. I just moved and that's all."[23] She continued to state that she only moved abroad because her Canadian husband, who had lived in Germany with her for some years, wanted to return home. Thus, the decision had nothing to do with her wanting to leave Germany but was rather made on a family level. Accordingly, she did not perceive herself as an immigrant to Canada, and, additionally, she saw her move to Canada just as any other move she might as well have made within Germany or Europe.

Frida B. used the term "modern immigrant" to describe her situation, as she thought it best characterized her. She stated, "I feel myself as . . . I would rather describe it as modern immigrants . . . I mean, we're here now, but maybe in the future, we'll be somewhere else." She added, "People today move from A to B. I mean, already students go elsewhere and stuff like that. Thus, these things [moving to another country] are no longer particularly difficult. And I mean, it's not as if you leave with a ship and then you will not be able to see people again for years and years to come." Thus, for Frida B., as for others, there were clear differences between herself and previous generations of emigrants from Germany, and she had distinct ideas of what the emigration process of previous generations looked like compared to her own. Whereas previous generations left with hopes for a better life and often had to turn their backs on their home country, either forever or at least for a long time, having only limited possibilities to maintain ties, for her and other individuals of her generation, international mobility was a normal part of their lives.[24]

Moving across national borders was, more or less, given the same significance as moving within one's own country. The reasons and circumstances for migration described above, and especially the feeling of being "modern immigrants," who can easily move between different places and do not necessarily see themselves spending the rest of their lives in Canada, can be seen as a result of the immigrants perceiving globalization as providing possibilities of relatively free movement across borders. While these perceptions are accurate to a certain extent, it is important to highlight that the notion of being "modern immigrants" is not completely new. In fact, more recent generations of immigrants often tend to classify themselves as "modern" when compared to previous generations to establish boundaries between both groups and stress their distinctive characteristics. The German-Canadian historian Alexander Freund, for example, studied single women from Germany who came to Canada during the 1950s and found that they also saw themselves as "modern adventurers." At least initially, these women went to Canada in search of "freedom, independence, and adventure" and had the hopes of pursuing a successful working career, which often was not possible for them in Germany.[25] This underlines that the stereotype which my interviewees held of the postwar generation of German immigrants to Canada was not always valid. Freund's research also emphasizes that the self-applied label of being "modern" was not unique to my group of interviewees but was used by previous generations and with similar intentions. Thus, while the function of establishing oneself as "modern" remained the same (i.e., the differentiation between two generations of immigrants in order to establish identity continued), the meaning of, or the discourse around, being "modern" changed slightly, depending on the social and historical context. For my interviewees, the notion of being "modern" was predominantly associated with relatively free and easy international movement, which was often seen as a result of globalization. The impact of globalization and new forms of communication and transportation are also reflected in the ways in which my interviewees maintained contact with German culture and people.

Maintaining Contact with Germany

Contact with Germany was maintained virtually in all spheres of my interviewees' life. They stayed in contact with family and friends back in Germany and visited the country regularly. They also kept themselves—at least to some extent—informed about the social, political, and economic situation in Germany, and for their entertainment, they accessed German television shows, movies, and magazines online.

Most of the interviewees had the opportunity to visit Germany at least once per year to meet with their family and friends. Understandably, the regularity of visits varied among individuals depending on their social and financial situation. Eva P. (43), for example, recalled that at the beginning of her stay in Canada, after her children were born, her parents once covered the costs of the flights for the whole family to Germany. After this initial visit, however, she and her family could not afford to return to Germany for ten years. Being in a more stable financial situation today, she reported that her family now went to Germany every two or three years.[26] Most other interviewees reported that they visited Germany at least once per year or more often. Imke M. (40) said: "Well, during the first two years, we went back twice a year, during summer and for Christmas.... But now it has become common to go there [Germany] once a year, namely for six weeks in summer."[27] Heinz W. (45) also visited Germany at least once a year. He said that during these visits he usually stayed with his family for a while and also met with a group of six to seven good friends, with whom he maintained close and regular contact. On a more regular basis, Peter J. (47) visited Germany because of his work. At the beginning of his stay in Canada, he could not find a job and therefore decided to do some freelancing work for German information technology (IT) companies. Today, he is the joint owner of a German company, and this makes it necessary for him to travel to Germany five to six times per year.[28]

Apart from regular visits, contact with family and friends in Germany was also maintained through other forms of communication. Some of my interviewees, especially those who arrived in Canada at the beginning of the 1990s, highlighted how much easier communication with Germany had become in recent years. While at the beginning of their stay in Canada they mainly wrote letters and talked to their family and friends via telephone, which was still expensive at the time, by the mid-2000s, calls became much cheaper and new forms of communication, such as email, Facebook, and Skype, made it easier to maintain close and regular contact. Eva P., who came to Canada in 1991, explained how she initially communicated: "Well, by letter. And then at some point it got cheaper to phone, so then I started to talk on the phone more often." Peter J. emphasized the importance of new forms of communication and especially the role of the internet. At the time of the interview, he stated that he and his family were using "all types of media" to stay in contact with friends and family in Germany and that "roughly within the last fifteen years, so many things have changed." Although the internet already existed in 1997 when he and his wife came to Canada for the first time, it was not yet as popular and convenient as today and phone costs were still expensive. Thus, "back then, communication possibilities were still relatively limited, but now, these things don't really matter any longer. That means, today, you can pretty much have contact at any time." This new connectivity and the possibility of actively taking part in the everyday life of other people even if they were living thousands of kilometres away was also underlined by Beate K. (48). She said that both her parents in Germany and her children in Canada had an iPad and, thus, could talk to each other while walking through their respective homes, connecting in ways that had not been possible when she first arrived in Canada in 1994.[29]

The impact of these new possibilities, which arose with the development of the internet, was also reflected in other spheres of the interviewees' lives. The internet was not only used to keep themselves, at least to some extent, informed about the social, political, and economic situation in Germany (e.g., by accessing the online versions of different German newspapers or watching German news online) but also to access other German television shows, movies, or magazines and, thus, maintain everyday habits from back in Germany. For example, Frida B. said: "I read the *Brigitte* [a German women's magazine] on my iPad; that makes me really happy." Heinz W. mentioned: "I watch the *Lindenstraße* [German soap opera] regularly every week, every episode." Others continued to read German books on a regular basis, by downloading them on their e-reader or, as Klaus A. did, by ordering them online from Germany. These experiences highlight that in the multimedia world of the early twenty-first century, the number of ways to maintain ties to the country of origin, as well as the intensity and speed at which this was possible, had increased significantly compared with the situation faced by earlier generations of migrants. While Germans immigrating to Canada in the 1950s and 1960s also could maintain ties and keep themselves informed about German politics and culture (e.g., by listening to German radio stations, ordering books from Germany, or subscribing to German magazines), the pace at which this contact was possible was slower and the costs were higher. Even for my interviewees, the tremendous changes in communication technologies and access to online media during the 1990s and 2000s, which, today, allow for instantaneous access to these means, have transformed their lives in significant ways as compared to when they first arrived in Canada.

Some of my interviewees assumed that these changes in communication and transportation also had an impact on the willingness of more recent German immigrants to join established German organizations in Canada. Klaus A., for example, stated that he thought that people of his generation did not have the same need to "cluster up" as older generations of German immigrants because they had arrived under distinct circumstances and had different means of maintaining ties abroad. He explained that a lot of Germans had emigrated to Canada after the Second World War because their home country was in ruins or because they had been displaced from their home towns or regions. Taking the example of his uncle who was originally from East Prussia and a prisoner of war in England for some years after the war, Klaus A. explained that his uncle back then either had the option of moving to West Germany, where he did not feel at home, nor had ever lived before the war, or to Australia or Canada. In the end, his uncle decided to move to Canada because he knew that a lot of ethnic Germans had settled there in lively communities with German shops, clubs, and organizations. Klaus A. assumed that such German communities developed in part because his uncle and other people of his uncle's generation were not able to go back to the Germany they lost and thus were searching for contact with other Germans and for a sense of familiarity in Canada. This was not at all the case for individuals of his own generation, however, because, as Klaus A. explained, "today you can be in Canada, but you can watch German TV, you can Skype, you can fly home once a year or more often. Yeah, today, you can be anywhere, so you do not need to rebuild your home." Frida B. expressed similar ideas; she indicated that the need for German organizations might not be as strong for herself and others of her generation. She stated, "And then it's a question of whether there is a need for this because the German church [Martin Luther Church in Ottawa] was certainly founded by people who missed Germany, who were homesick, who wanted to build up a small, I don't know.... And I mean it's nice, when you go there, everyone is speaking German, and you're singing German songs that you know. But on the other hand, it is very different today with the internet, and in today's information society you can get a lot of these things in other ways." While it is true that compared to today's migrants the postwar generation of Germans immigrating to Canada did not have the same communication and transportation avenues at their disposal, it is important to acknowledge that over time, they too made use of these new resources. Thus, while initially this generation did not have the possibility to regularly visit Germany and to stay in

Figure 6.1. Building of the German Martin Luther Church, Ottawa, Ontario, 2013. Credit: Anke Patzelt.

contact on a daily basis with their friends and families, over time, they too took advantage of more affordable air fares, cheaper phone costs, and the internet to re-establish their ties to Germany.[30] Despite this, however, many of my interviewees had the impression that because the postwar generation did not have access to these possibilities (i.e., international connectivity and mobility) at the beginning of their stay in Canada, they were more prone to found German organizations and/or become members of already existing groups and organizations as well as to take part in a German community life so that they would be able to maintain their German heritage.

Participation in German Organizations

While there was a lively community of German-speaking organizations, associations, and clubs (i.e., the German Benevolent Society,[31] the Maple Leaf–Almrausch Club, the Concordia Choir, and the German Language School) as well as two German churches (Martin Luther Gemeinde and St. Albertus Pfarrgemeinde) already well-established in Ottawa upon the arrival of my interviewees,[32] their interest in joining these organizations and churches was low. Several reasons were mentioned for abstaining from German organizations. Frida B., for example, said that she could not identify with the older members, who formed the majority of these facilities. This was a feeling that was shared by several other interviewees and seemed to be the most salient factor. In particular, she emphasized that the image these older German immigrants had of Germany, which they envisioned during the 1940s and 1950s, "has absolutely nothing to do" with the Germany that she knew and in which she had grown up.[33] She gave the example of a fundraising event that was organized by a German club in Ottawa to which she and her husband went when they arrived in Canada. She explained that this was one of the "most German events" she had ever attended and that she had never experienced anything like it in Germany. She thought that it was particularly problematic when people tried to "make events, such as this, especially German" by, for example, emphasizing characteristics such as "old German oak and frilled curtains" because, in her view, this was no longer a true reflection of contemporary Germany. In fact, she thought that events like that "were rather dissuasive." Imke M. felt similarly: "There are some very bizarre things, right! For example, there is a Sauerkraut dinner. . . . But I think it's more [for] people who are like twenty to thirty years older than I am, and who arrived twenty to thirty years before me, and who really have a completely bizarre image of Germany, which has absolutely nothing to do with what I associate with Germany. And, thus, I feel completely out of place at such events and, therefore, don't go there."

Moreover, Imke M. emphasized two other factors, which she thought contributed to the low participation of more recent German immigrants to Canada in these organizations and clubs. First was the fact that Germany's different regions have diverse traditions and cultural practices, which makes it hard to define what it means to be German because "what is perceived as being typically German by some is not at all typically German for others." Secondly, she had the impression that people of her own generation were not that interested in formal clubs or organizations but were rather looking for informal gatherings or get-togethers. These experiences and feelings were largely shared by the other interviewees; only one of them was actively involved in one of the German churches and regularly attended events there. For others, who taught German culture and literature, attending events of different German organizations or clubs was part of their job; yet, they would not otherwise have participated in such activities.

Despite this low interest in German clubs and organizations, which were founded by and, thus, targeted the older generations of German immigrants in Canada, it was fairly common among the interviewees to participate in more informal events, such as movie screenings organized by the Goethe-Institut, a German association that promotes cultural exchange and language education. The regularity with which these events were attended, however, varied among the informants, depending on time and personal interest. Peter J. pointed out that he hardly ever visited such events due to a lack of interest and time, whereas his wife, Anja J. (47), attended German movie screenings on a regular basis because she enjoyed them a lot.[34] Moreover, choosing to participate in certain German organizations or events was often connected to a desire to teach the German language to their children or impart knowledge about German culture and traditions to them. Hence, interviewees' participation in such activities was limited to a certain period when their children were young. It was common that the informants joined a German playgroup when their children were younger and sent them to the German language school (at least for some time) when they got older. Several others participated in events such as the annual St. Martin's procession and St. Nicholas Day celebrations, organized by the German Martin Luther Church. These activities, nonetheless, did not result in any further involvement in the German churches or other German organizations.

Feelings of Attachment to Germany and Canada

While different authors have examined the—at times hostile—encounters which German immigrants in Canada had to face in regard to their German ethnicity and past during and after the two world wars, my interviewees did not report any such incidents.[35] In fact, most of them felt that Germany's history was no longer a dominant issue in the perception of Germans by others and that they were no longer judged upon it. Rather, some mentioned that as Germans they were "appreciated migrants" compared to other immigrant groups in Canada.[36] Despite this, the awareness of what had happened during the Nazi regime still seemed to be present among the informants, and the legacy of the Second World War still seemed to have an influence on the ways some interviewees were behaving or feeling toward certain events or habits in Canada. Having been socialized in a Germany in which *Vergangenheitsbewältigung* was a central part of the public discourse and the educational system, they had learned that patriotism was not something to be focused upon. Thus, they were skeptical about national pride and patriotism. Frida B., for example, was shocked when she first found out that her son had to sing the Canadian national anthem at school every morning. Although she said that things had gotten a bit more relaxed in Germany in regard to national pride, for her, being part of the Sixties generation, this was "very strange." Frida B. continued to say that she came home that day and told her husband: "It's terrible, they [the children] have to sing the national anthem every day." She further explained that in Germany "you don't deck yourself with the German colours" and that this was why she was so critical of her son having to sing the national anthem. Consequently, she had a hard time understanding the "glorification" of the Canadian soldiers who died for their country on Remembrance Day. She, as a German, was critical of such activities. Sara L. also mentioned her displeasure with the "glorification" of the doings of Canadian soldiers, especially during the Second World War. Moreover, she saw it as her duty as a teacher of the German language to inform her students about the Nazi era and explain how it was possible that such a thing could happen. Although this awareness of Germany's past did influence the ways in which some of my interviewees felt toward certain habits and events in Canada, it did not influence their identification with either country in any significant way. While changes to the outward identification as German were reported by some of my interviewees, these were not related to Germany's past. Both Frida B. and Imke M. had similar experiences concerning this matter. Both of them felt a need to tell people that they were from Germany at the beginning of their stay in Canada, while over time it became less important for them to share this information when interacting with people. Imke M. assumed that this decrease of externally identifying as being German also led to the fact that she and her family today, after six years of living in Canada, were no longer perceived as "the Germans" by other Canadians. She also highlighted, however, that the decrease of others' external identification of her as German did not impact her internal feelings of being German: "Well, actually in these situations the identification with this [being German] decreases. That's actually interesting. I mean it seems as if externally the identification decreases, but it continues to exist. I mean, I'm very strongly feeling German, but I no longer feel the need to tell everyone that I'm German."

This strong internal identification with being German was also reflected in the ways my interviewees related to Germany and Canada respectively. Most of my informants continued to feel a close attachment to Germany and viewed it as their home or homeland. This was because Germany was the country in which they had been socialized and, thus, the experiences that they had while growing up in Germany to a large extent impacted the formation of their personalities. Canada, on the other hand, was identified more as their current place of living where they were working and taking care of their families. Frida B. shared that she had already established a strong feeling of home when she first moved away from her hometown of Freiburg. She said: "I had already developed such a feeling back then: Yes, that's where I come from, from the Black Forest. And the landscape and everything, that feels like, when you stand somewhere in that area, and the panorama and the base slope, well, yes, that's where I like to be and that's where I belong." Whereas when talking about Canada, she stressed: "That's where I live, that's where I earn my money and where I raise my family, raise my kids . . . I am living here, I think it is a nice place to be, but I don't think that I have a highly emotional attachment to the country." Eva P. felt similarly and said: "Germany definitely still is my home [*Heimat*]. Canada is the place where I am living and where I can find the comfort of a home, where I have my social environment, and of course my family." Thus, while she identified Germany as her homeland, she saw Canada as her present home—as a place of residence, comfort, and growth. When trying to explain these different notions of homeland or *Heimat* in Germany and home in Ottawa, Canada a bit more, she highlighted that she associated the former more with concrete places while the latter was connected to feelings and interpersonal relations:

> Well, *Heimat* refers to the land on which you have walked, the paths, streets, surroundings, flora, fauna, air, noises, neighbourhood, maybe events, memories from school, certain places where you can eat and drink certain things, places which you visited and especially liked, such as a special museum, which cannot be found here [in Canada] or a castle or a particularly beautiful chateau which is part of the *Heimat*. And home is what is learned and what you are used to. It's where you feel comfortable, where you can relax, where you are around people that you can trust and who support, love, and help each other, where you can reach out or look for the things you would like to do. It is the place where you know that the people you are responsible for are taken care of and are provided with everything they need. I do not to any extent connect these things with Germany right now. Germany, rather, is an emotional homeland, in practical terms, so to speak. Well, I think, this is the difference.

In the same respect, other interviewees still viewed Germany as a homeland that had shaped them, but they felt that Canada was offering them a better life and suited their personalities better, or simply made them feel better. Peter J. agreed that Germany was still his homeland, whereas Canada symbolized adventure and was his adopted home. He was happy to visit Germany and valued his German heritage. He did not see either country as being better or worse than the other but rather had the feeling that Canada suited him the best at present. He described a certain "vibe" which Canada and the mentality of Canadians produced in him, which created this feeling.

Overall, the interviewees' perception of Germany and Canada and their identification with the respective country was less influenced by Germany's past than that of the postwar generation who often experienced hostility and sometimes even physical harm due to the events of the Second World War. None of my interviewees reported such incidents, and they did not feel that they were judged because of Nazism and the Holocaust. The fact that the interviewees had grown up in a time in which *Vergangenheitsbewältigung* was emphasized in all spheres of public life, however, resulted in their general understanding that patriotism was something that needed to be handled with caution. Thus, while internally, they strongly identified with Germany as their country of origin and identity formation, openly showing (national) pride was not a behaviour with which any of them felt comfortable.

Conclusion

Germany's social situation during which the interviewees grew up as well as the circumstances under which they immigrated to Canada were significantly different from those of previous waves of German immigrants. This could be explained by, for example, the influence of new transportation and communication resources, which facilitated the ability for contemporary German immigrants to maintain close ties with their country of origin. Because they could move freely between the two countries from the beginning of their time in Canada, many of my informants perceived themselves as "modern immigrants." These global transformations, as well as the social and political changes that had taken place in Germany since the end of the Second World War, resulted in a distinct mobilization of generational discourses by the 1990s and 2000s German migrants to Canada. My interviewees used these discourses to differentiate between themselves as "modern immigrants" and the postwar generation of German immigrants, whose values and images of Germany they did not share. As previous studies demonstrate, however, this identification as "modern" was not unique to the group of my interviewees but rather constituted a pattern that was used by newly arrived groups of migrants alike—irrespective of the date of their arrival—to differentiate between themselves and previous generations of migrants. Thus, it was rather through shaping the discourses around what it meant to be "modern" than by simply using this term that my interviewees constructed their identity and mobilized generational discourses. These discourses were partly based on accurate observations, but partly also on stereotypical assumptions about the older German generation, as with regard to their use of technology, for example. It was by emphasizing these—correctly or incorrectly assumed—differences that the interviewees created a discourse about their own experiences and their own generation. In accordance with the concept of generation by Aboim and Vasconcelos, the internal self-construction of the interviewees seemed to be the most decisive factor for their generational understanding. These observations support the findings of other researchers that there is no single German-Canadian identity. Rather, the identity construction of different generations of German immigrants is impacted by the particular social and cultural situations wherein they grow up, the conditions under which they leave Germany, and, more importantly, their own perception of these circumstances. As such and in alignment with other studies, my work emphasizes the importance of analyzing not only immigrant generations along genealogical lines but also the necessity of studying the differences among distinct cohorts of first-generation immigrants who migrated during different socio-historical periods. However, due to the small sample size in this research as well as its limited geographical focus, the findings presented in this chapter can only be seen as a snapshot of the migration trajectories and the creation of generational discourses among contemporary German immigrants in Ottawa. Further research examining these processes among recent waves of Germans living in other regions of Canada is needed to see if these findings can be generalized.

Notes

1 Gerhard Bassler, "Deutsche Einwanderung und Siedlung in Kanada," in *Adler auf dem Ahornbaum. Studien zur Einwanderung, Siedlung, Kultur- und Literaturgeschichte der Deutschen in Kanada*, ed. Hartmut Froeschle (1983; repr., Toronto: German-Canadian Historical Association, 1997), 1–12.

2 Hartmut Froeschle, *The German-Canadians: A Concise History / Die Deutschkanadier. Geschichtlicher Überblick* (Toronto: Historical Society of Mecklenburg Upper Canada, 1992).

3 Roland E. Schmalz, "Former Enemies Come to Canada: Ottawa and the Postwar German Immigration Boom, 1951–57" (PhD diss., University of Ottawa, 2000); Manuel Meune, *Les Allemands du Québec: Parcours et discours d'une communauté méconnue* (Montreal: Méridien, 2003); John C. Walsh, "Re-thinking Ethnic Boundaries: The Negotiation of German-Canadian Ethnic Identities in Ottawa, 1945–1975" (Master's thesis, University of Ottawa, 1996).

4 Schmalz, "Former Enemies Come to Canada"; and Meune, *Les Allemands du Québec.*

5 Angelika E. Sauer and Matthias Zimmer, *A Chorus of Different Voices: German-Canadian Identities* (New York: Peter Lang, 1998); and Statistisches Bundesamt, *Bevölkerung und Erwerbstätigkeit: Wanderungen* (Wiesbaden: Statistisches Bundesamt, 2020) https://www.destatis.de/DE/Service/Bibliothek/_publikationen-fachserienliste-1.html (accessed 18 September 2020).

6 Gerhard Bassler "Germans in Canada: An Introduction to the Historiography," *Immigration History Newsletter* 20, no. 1 (1988): 1–10; Wsevolod W. Isajiw, "Ethnic

Identity Retention," in *Ethnic Identity and Quality: Varieties of Experiences in a Canadian City*, eds. Raymond Breton et al. (Toronto: University of Toronto Press, 1990), 34–91; Wsevolod W. Isajiw, "Identity and Identity Retention among German Canadians: Individual and Institutional," in ed. Sauer and Zimmer, *A Chorus of Different Voices*, 67–83; Karin Hardt-Dhatt, *Etude socio-lingusitique sur l'intégration de l'immigrant allemand au milieu québécois* (Québec: Université Laval, 1976); Andrea Koch-Kraft, *Deutsche in Kanada: Einwanderung und Adaption* [sic]*: Mit einer Untersuchung zur Situation der Nachkriegsimmigration in Edmonton, Alberta* (Bochum: Brockmeyer, 1990); K.G. O'Bryan, J. G. Reitz, and O. Kuplowska, *Non-official Languages: A Study in Canadian Multiculturalism* (Ottawa: Minister Responsible for Multiculturalism, 1976); Manfred Prokop and Gerhard Bassler, *German Language Maintenance Across Canada: A Handbook* (Edmonton: Manfred Prokop, 2004); Jeffrey G. Reitz, "Language and Ethnic Community Survival," in *Ethnicity and Ethnic Relations in Canada*, eds. Rita A. Bienvenue and Jay E. Goldstein (Toronto: Butterworths, 1985): 105–23; and Beatrice Stadler, *Language Maintenance and Assimilation: The Case of Selected German-Speaking Immigrants in Vancouver, Canada* (Vancouver: CAUTG, 1983).

7 Matthias Zimmer, "Deconstructing German-Canadian Identity," in ed. Sauer and Zimmer, *A Chorus of Different Voices*, 21–39.

8 Michael Kearney, "The Local and the Global: The Anthropology of Globalization and Transnationalism," *Annual Review of Anthropology* 24 (1995): 547–65; Vijay Agnew, "Introduction," in *Diaspora, Memory, and Identity: A Search for Home*, ed. Vijay Agnew (Toronto: University of Toronto Press, 2005), 3–17; and Paul Kennedy and Victor Roudometof, "Transnationalism in a Global Age," in *Communities across Borders: New Immigrants and Transnational Cultures*, eds. Paul Kennedy and Victor Roudometof (London, New York: Routledge, 2002), 1–26.

9 Agnew, "Introduction."

10 Ibid.; Christian Lieb, "German Diaspora Experiences in British Columbia after 1945," in *German Diasporic Experiences: Identity, Migration, and Loss*, eds. Mathias Schulze et al. (Waterloo: Wilfrid Laurier University Press, 2008), 305–15.

11 Ruben G. Rumbaut, "The Agony of Exile: A Study of the Migration and Adaptation of Indochinese Refugee Adults and Children," in *Refugee Children: Theory, Research, and Services*, eds. Frederick L. Ahearn Jr. and Jean L. Athey (Baltimore: Johns Hopkins University Press, 1991), 53–91. The genealogically defined conception of immigrant generations is used in numerous studies within the field of ethnic and migration studies, for example, to examine the outcomes of integration/assimilation across immigrant generations. For studies, see: Alejandro Portes and Ruben Rumbaut, *Legacies: The Story of the Immigrant Second Generation* (Berkeley, CA: University of California Press, 2001); and Philip Kasinitz et al., *Inheriting the City: The Children of Immigrants Come of Age* (Cambridge, MA: Harvard University Press, 2008). For studies specific to Canada, see: John Berry and Feng Hou, "Acculturation, Discrimination and Wellbeing among Second Generation of Immigrants in Canada," *International Journal of Intercultural Relations* 61 (2017): 29–39; and Monica Boyd and Siyue Tian, "Educational and Labor Market Attainments of the 1.5- and Second-Generation Children of East Asian Immigrants in Canada," *American Behavioral Scientist* 60, no. 5–6 (2016): 705–29.

12 Min Zhou, "Changing Generational Dynamics in Chinese America across Time," *Diaspora: A Journal of Transnational Studies* 18, no. 1–2 (2015): 89–116. See also: Susan Eckstein, "The Clash of Cuban Immigrant Cohorts," in *Cuba Today: Continuity and Change since the Periodo Especial*, eds. Mauricio A. Font (New York: Bildner Center

for Western Hemisphere Studies, CUYN Graduate Center, 2004), 129–45; Mette Louise Berg and Susan Eckstein (eds.), "Special Issue: Re-imagining Diasporas and Generations," *Diaspora: A Journal of Transnational Studies* 18, no. 1–2 (2015); and Mette Louise Berg, *Diasporic Generations: Memory, Politics and Nation among Cubans in Spain* (Oxford: Berghahn Books, 2011).

13 Karl Mannheim, "The Problem of Generations," in *Essays on the Sociology of Knowledge*, ed. Paul Kecskemeti (New York: Routledge, 1952), 276–322.

14 Susan Eckstein, *On Deconstructing Immigrant Generations: Cohorts and the Cuban Émigré Experience* (San Diego, CA: Working Paper 97, Center for Comparative Immigration Studies, University of California at San Diego, 2004) https://ccis.ucsd.edu/_files/wp97.pdf (accessed 29 June 2018).

15 Sofia Aboim and Pedro Vasconcelos, "From Political to Social Generations: A Critical Reappraisal of Mannheim's Classical Approach," *European Journal of Social Theory* 17, no. 2 (2014): 165–83.

16 Ibid., 165.

17 Ibid., 176.

18 While many of the Germans who arrived in Canada during the 1990s and 2000s were highly educated and highly skilled migrants who were born and raised in Germany, another large group of approximately 11,300 persons arrived during this period and it was composed of so-called ethnic Germans (i.e. individuals of German descent who had been born in Russia and Kazakhstan and resettled in Germany during the 1980s and 1990s). See Alexander Freund, "Representing 'New Canadians': Competing Narratives about Recent German Immigrants to Manitoba," *Journal of Mennonite Studies* 30 (2012): 339–61.

19 Recent research has highlighted that migration movements of highly skilled individuals between countries of the so-called "global North" can no longer be understood as a means to escape from hunger, political instability, or persecution, and neither can they be understood as a means for improving the economic or social situation of oneself or one's family/household. Rather, these migrations can be seen as a means of self-realization. As such, these movements are often self-initiated, or are the accidental result of one's personal life trajectories. My interviewees' migration experiences can be interpreted along these lines. See Elisabeth Scheibelhofer, "Understanding European Emigration in the Context of Modernization Processes: Contemporary Migration Biographies and Reflexive Modernity," *Current Sociology* 57, no. 1 (2009): 5–25; and Elaine Ho, "Migration Trajectories of 'Highly Skilled' Middling Transnationals: Singaporean Transmigrants in London," *Population, Space and Place* 17, no. 1 (2011): 116–29.

20 Klaus A., interview by Anke Patzelt, Ottawa, 13 March 2013. Translations of all interviews from German into English are mine. The names of all interviewees have been changed in order to secure confidentiality. The number in the brackets refers to the informants' age at the time of the interview. All interviews were conducted in March and April 2013.

21 Sara L., interview by Anke Patzelt, Ottawa, 26 March 2013.

22 Heinz W., interview by Anke Patzelt, Ottawa, 14 March 2013.

23 Frida B., interview by Anke Patzelt, Ottawa, 26 March 2013.

24 The chapters by Farges, Ensslen, and Frie in this collection underline my interviewees' understanding of previous cohorts of German immigrants as individuals who were forced to leave their home country because of social, political, or economic hardships, and/or who were seeking a better life.

25 Alexander Freund, "Contesting the Meanings of Migration: German Women's Immigration to Canada in the 1950s," *Canadian Ethnic Studies* 41, no. 3 (2010): 1–26.

26 Eva P., interview by Anke Patzelt, Ottawa, 8 April 2013.

27 Imke M., interview by Anke Patzelt, Ottawa, 14 April 2013.

28 Peter J., interview by Anke Patzelt, Ottawa, 1 April 2013.

29 Beate K., interview by Anke Patzelt, 9 March 2013.

30 Anke Patzelt, "Notions of Home and Belonging for *Alteinwanderer* and *Neueinwanderer* in the German-Speaking Community in Ottawa," in *Diasporic Constructions of Home and Belonging*, eds. Florian Kläger and Klaus Stierstorfer (Berlin: De Gruyter, 2015), 183–206; and Alexander Freund, *Aufbrüche nach dem Zusammenbruch* (Göttingen: V&R unipress, 2004).

31 While the German Benevolent Society Ottawa was still operating at the time I was conducting my research, it seems to no longer exist today.

32 Barbara Lorenzkowski, "Making Music—Building Bridges: German-Canadian Identities in the Nation's Capital 1958–1999," in *Ottawa: Making of a Capital*, eds. Jeff Keshen and Nicole St-Onge (Ottawa: University of Ottawa Press, 2001), 307–30; Patzelt, "Notions of Home and Belonging"; see, also: Anke Patzel, "Of 'Modern Immigrants' and 'German Bread': A Case Study of Ethnic Identity Construction Amongst Contemporary German Immigrants in the City of Ottawa, Canada" (Master's thesis, Malmö University, 2013).

33 Sara Frankenberger (Chapter 8 in this collection) highlights an important factor that contributed to the different attitudes and images of Germany among my interviewees and those of the immediate postwar generation of German immigrants to Canada, namely the fact that the postwar generation was not confronted to the same extent about coming to terms with their German past because they were not exposed to "normative German societal pressures." This fact is also emphasized in Roger Frie's Afterword in this collection.

34 Anja J., interview by Anke Patzelt, Ottawa, 1 April 2013.

35 Alexander Freund, "A German Post-1945 Diaspora? German Migrants' Encounters with the Nazi Past," in Schulze, *German Diasporic Experiences*, 467–78; Lieb, "German Diaspora Experiences"; and also, see the chapter by Freund in this collection.

36 In the Afterword to this collection Roger Frie also emphasizes this sentiment, stating that the representation of Germans in Canada changed from them being perceived as enemies toward them being perceived as respected partners.

CHAPTER 7

"We Never Really Talked About It": Second- and Third-Generation German Canadians' Family Memories of the Holocaust

SARA FRANKENBERGER

This chapter explores how the descendants of German immigrants in twenty-first-century Canada remembered the stories of their parents' and grandparents' experiences during and after the Second World War. It asks how these wartime and postwar memories affected how the younger generations talked about and remembered the Holocaust. Previous research on postwar German Canadians and their families has focused on immigration experiences, ethnic identity, and three-generational family narratives about grandparents' experiences in Nazi Germany. This chapter, however, focuses on family memories of the Holocaust. How did German-Canadian families talk about the Holocaust and how did members of the second and third generations remember it? Specifically, how did families talk either about their own involvement in Nazi crimes or the knowledge of their relatives' perpetration of atrocities? What kind of information was shared? Did members of the third postwar generation of German Canadians still show similar patterns of silence as those of Germans in Germany?

As a new German Canadian, first-generation Canadian and fourth-generation postwar German, I was curious to understand how the experience of German Canadians in regards to family memories of the war and the Holocaust differed from that of Germans in Germany and if there were any feelings of guilt and shame that participants might report. I wanted to know if there were differences resulting from factors such as a distinct focus in the Canadian history curriculum, the emotional distance to the events in Germany, and fewer opportunities to connect with German family members. In Germany, despite public efforts to increase commemoration of the Holocaust and its victims,[1] a representative research study by Harald Welzer, Sabine Moller, and Karoline Tschuggnall[2] found that family members across generations did not talk about the Holocaust or family involvement in the Holocaust and instead showed a tendency to heroize and absolve their family members of guilt. Also in Germany, similar patterns were found in research by Gabriele Rosenthal and Bettina Völter.[3]

While this chapter focuses specifically on memory transmission and recollection mainly among the second and third generations of West German immigrants to Canada, it is important to note the differences in memory recollection and public perception of involvement in the Nazi agenda in other European nations. Countries that sided with and supported the Nazi regime, like Italy and Austria, were able to avoid the sanctions by the allies as well as questions related to guilt and active participation following the war.[4] Therefore, members of their second and third generations, such as second- and third-generation Italian Canadians and Austrian Canadians, were unlikely to experience the same sense of guilt and shame in relation to their cultural heritage as did German Canadians. Still, it would be interesting to explore how Italian and Austrian Canadian families talked about their family members' involvement in the Second World War and what were their opinions about fascism and the Nazi regime. Austria officially admitted its involvement in the Nazi regime in 1991, following decades of public and official denial of its support of the Nazis during the war.[5] According to German historian Harold Marcuse, Italy's support of the Nazi regime, particularly at the general population level, was less pronounced than in Austria, where the majority of the inhabitants had supported the annexation in March 1938. Similar to Austrians, Italians were able to avoid association with the Nazi ideology; questions of guilt about the Holocaust after the war and the public exploration of Italy's participation in the genocide began only in the early 2000s.

In Poland, the country having fallen under Soviet influence following the war, there was a discrepancy between family memories and the official, public memories of the war. Some argue this inconsistency allowed for anti-Semitism to continue to thrive in Poland until the 1980s. In Britain, there was a coherent story of important battles and events of the war as well as the collaborative efforts of the Allied forces. This allowed Britons to remember their family involvement from the perspective of the victors of the war. Although there has been some criticism related to the extent of the bombings and how much was known about the Holocaust before action was taken, there was little change in the public and private recollections throughout the second half of the twentieth century.[6] According to Marcuse, the Soviet Union's public discourse of the war was focused on the Soviet victory and omitted Stalin's initial support of the Nazi regime. Following the end of the Soviet Union, former Eastern-Bloc countries have begun to reshape these recollections to incorporate their memories and experiences. Similarly, there was a difference between East Germany and West Germany in how the history of the Second World War and the Holocaust was taught in schools and discussed in public life.

In this chapter, I argue that seventy years after the end of the war, second- and third-generation German Canadians continued to struggle in coming to terms with the Nazi past and the Holocaust. These difficulties were confirmed by the silence and avoidance tactics that shaped their family memories. The chapter is based on a qualitative research study consisting of ten interviews with second- and third-generation German Canadians conducted in Vancouver, British Columbia, in 2016. The interviewees were born in Canada between 1950 and 1975; their families had emigrated from Germany in the first two decades after the Second World War. My narrative analysis identified similarities and differences in patterns of talking about the past that were described in previous studies in Germany and Canada. After briefly surveying the relevant literature on memory transmission and research on how German and German-Canadian families talked about the Holocaust, the first part of this chapter discusses three strategies of silence among second- and third-generation German Canadians. The second part provides detailed examples and analysis of research findings. I wrap up the chapter with final conclusions and suggestions for future research.

When speaking with Germans and those of German descent about their heritage, a question that often comes up and causes discomfort is the issue of guilt and shame in relation to the German people as the perpetrators of the Holocaust. Based on the number of party membership cards, the Bundesarchiv (German Federal Archives) estimates that up to 12.7 million Germans were members of the Nazi Party and about 0.9 million were actively involved in its paramilitary organizations.[7] Inevitably, one is faced with questions such as: "What did my family members know about the Holocaust?"; "How extensively were they involved in the war and the genocide?"; and "Did they support the Nazi ideology?" In the context of generations, some may argue that the question of guilt does not apply to the second and third generations as they were far removed from the events and did not actively participate. This position neglects the ongoing effects of the Holocaust and the continued responsibility to remember the suffering it caused.[8] Thus, the question should not be discussed in terms of personal responsibility due to family involvement or feelings of guilt or shame about one's German heritage, but rather from a humanistic perspective, on the basis of a moral and ethical responsibility to not allow the victims of the Holocaust to be forgotten or its events to be distorted due to silence.[9]

Intergenerational Memory and the Transmission of Silence

The theoretical framework underlying this chapter is intergenerational memory transmission, wherein the concept of "generation" takes on a central role as family memories are transmitted between generations by members of different generations, who are each shaped by the collective and cultural memory of their time.[10] The Holocaust defined not only the generations that experienced it but also those who followed.[11] The terms first, second, third, and fourth generation imply continuity among the postwar generations and how memories get passed on from one generation to the next.[12] Such transmission can at times be compared to the children's game of "telephone."[13]

The first generation—or the war generation—is the generation that witnessed or participated in the war, Nazi Germany, and the Holocaust. The term refers to the adults or young adults who were developmentally mature enough to understand the impact and meaning of the Nazi ideology and had to make choices in relation to the Nazi regime.[14] In the context of migration, it is important to ask how German immigrant families in Canada went about the process of dealing with the German past or *Vergangenheitsbewältigung* in the absence of normative German societal pressures.[15] As German-Canadian historian Alexander Freund asked in 2002, "How has the process of migration, intercultural exchange and, increasingly, transnational life shaped [German migrants'] negotiations of memory, history, and identity?"[16] According to the German educational sciences professor Matthias Proske, the current culture around the discussion and education about the Holocaust resulted from the 1968 student revolts.[17] Therefore, families who moved abroad before this time may not have received the kind of information and opportunities to confront and process their German past as did those who stayed in West Germany. Thus, these immigrant families were on their own when dealing with their country's difficult past.[18] Even if, or potentially because, it was never addressed openly, the silence did not cease to have an effect despite the migration. After all, although silence about the Holocaust may not be requested or encouraged explicitly by family members, the lack of discussion of the Nazi past within families did not preclude a transmission of psychological effects of the past.[19]

Consequently, the war generation members' way of dealing with the past exhibited a systematic omission of information about their relationship to the Nazi years and the Holocaust. Their response marked the beginning of the silence, unprocessed experiences, and memories that were passed on to the next generation.[20] The second generation—the "children of the war"— were born in the 1930s and 1940s.[21] This generation often saw their parents engage in silence in response to the past and consequently adopted a similar tradition of silence, which Dan Bar-On has called "the double wall of silence."[22] Although they are sometimes described as the generation that started the conversation about and the confrontation with National Socialism during the 1968 student rebellion,[23] the second generation had nevertheless internalized the trauma from the war as well as feelings of collective guilt, and, at times, shame of their German heritage and the associations with Nazi Germany—without directly witnessing the Nazi regime.[24]

The third generation, consisting of West Germans born in the 1960s and 1970s, was exposed to an increasing amount of school education, public information, and discussion about the Holocaust.[25] Scholars have found that this generation of grandchildren had a more distanced and abstract relationship with the Holocaust and the war period than the previous generations.[26] However, its members did "continue to experience significant adverse emotional effects in relation to Germany's role during WWII."[27]

Germany's first generation dealt with the past by keeping silent about it. Silence, according to the German philosopher Theodor Adorno, was a means of avoidance that allowed postwar Germans to suppress feelings of guilt and shame; at the same time, psychologists have argued that silence was also a result of experiencing these emotions.[28] The later generations, who were not directly involved in the war, continued to show signs and feelings of guilt and shame as a result of intergenerational transmission of memories.[29] Adorno, who returned from exile in the United States after the war, outlined common responses to confrontation with the past, such as resistance through active defensiveness or silence and strong responses that indicated a lack of processing of the past.[30] In some cases, individuals—who were either involved in the Nazi regime or had committed atrocities as part of their involvement with the Nazi party—described perpetrators and their actions with a seeming lack of empathy for the victims. They also failed to acknowledge responsibility, at times claiming to be victims of the Nazi regime themselves rather than reflecting on or admitting their own role in the events.[31] Similar kinds of behaviour were found in recent research on the children of perpetrators and members of the German postwar generations despite their temporal distance to the events and a lack of personal involvement.[32]

For decades and to this day, the topic of the Holocaust has often been met with silence in German families. The literature shows that German families did not talk frequently about the Holocaust and if they did, there was no discussion or admission of family involvement.[33] This silence allowed for predominant narratives of Germans as victims, particularly in the younger generations. Hence, the children and grandchildren of the war generation might not see any reason to feel responsible, since to their knowledge none of their family members had been involved.[34]

At times, families believed that they had talked about the Holocaust, but when probed, it turned out that it was mostly "empty talking." For instance, family members gave vague responses, hinted at involvement, but left the discussion so general that by the next generation the meaning had already changed and the gaps in the stories were filled in with details that absolved family members of guilt.[35] German Canadians, like Germans in postwar Germany, largely responded with silence to questions about the Holocaust. In my interviews, nine of the ten interviewees showed evidence of silence in their responses, either in the form of avoidance or by directly stating that their families had not discussed the Holocaust and German responsibility. In this collection's Afterword, Roger Frie describes this silence as the "door that remains shut" and outlines a number of possible reasons for this phenomenon in German immigrant families, including the desire to assimilate quickly and leave the past behind. Even so, it is important to recognize that German Canadians are a diverse group whose experiences varied greatly depending on where in Germany they came from. Frie offers an important consideration, however, by stating that "to the degree that they identify as 'German,' an identity created by way of family, history, and memory, then they are inevitably obliged to ask the hard questions." Furthermore, part of this German identity is the ethical obligation to know and accurately represent the German history of the Holocaust.

One may wonder how these feelings of guilt and shame were transmitted between generations if the topic was truly met with such considerable silence. According to German social psychologists Gabriele Rosenthal and Harald Welzer, it was specifically through the legacy of silence that the feelings of guilt and shame were carried forward to the next generations. Mechanisms in this silent transmission of negative feelings included distortions such as heroization and reframing.[36] The Norwegian memory scholar Irene Levin quotes other theorists who have described silence as the "elephant in the room." She outlines the transmission of silence's unspoken presence: "Similar to the elephant, the silencing processes are omnipresent. Sometimes they are communicated through small fragments, remarks or even jokes. Other times they come through just by facial expressions. In other times again they are present through the absence and not understandable intervals between stories. Memories, being painful or not, do not cease to exist. They can easily take on a life of their own, beyond the control of the individual. . . . The Holocaust is such an invisible elephant—shaping personal lives, relationships and processes by its very real but also unapproachable presence."[37] The silence is enabled by individuals and their social context, often with the intention of protecting themselves from the negative emotions that come with talking about and acknowledging the difficult stories.[38] Patterns of silence are learned by modelling—children and family members mimic the behaviour of individuals around them and, in the case of memories, within their memory community.[39]

Due to the legacy of silence, when families do confront the memories of the Holocaust, they tend to deal with the Nazi past on an abstract, cultural level rather than take on their own, personal past and family connections. This makes it easier to defer the question of responsibility to the Nazi regime and surrender the process of wrestling with the past to authorities such as schools and public education campaigns.[40]

"Dealing with the Past Abroad": Immigration as Avoidance?

When families settle in a new country, the focus for many years is on assimilating, building a new life, and finding a community. In research on immigrant acculturation, low external pressures to assimilate and the maintenance of an ethnic identity have been found to be important for successful integration into a new culture.[41] As past research on German Canadians has found, German postwar immigrants showed increased efforts to assimilate. The relinquishing of their ethnic identity was often motivated by a desire to leave behind the German past, particularly when faced with discrimination due to the events of the Second World War and the Holocaust.[42] The Canadian psychologist Roger Frie notes that this increased effort to assimilate may have had the effect of decreased "opportunities for self-reflection, memory, and responsibility among and between generations of German immigrants."[43] German Canadians' perceived pressure to assimilate might have led to the loss of ethnic identity and of cultural practices in the second and third generations of German Canadians, who often did not speak German.[44] Loss of language, however, did not necessarily result in a loss of connection with German culture; instead, cultural and ethnic symbols as well as emotional concepts and characteristics of German culture may have persisted without German-Canadian families actively teaching their children the German language.

In the interviews presented in this chapter, evidence of avoidance and silence when speaking about the German perpetrator group and the Holocaust were found in all narratives, particularly when it came to the question of family involvement or bystander status. The accounts contained little mention of perpetrator stories, and if a story suggested involvement of family members in the Holocaust, a statement emphasizing the innocence of the family member followed immediately, particularly among members of the third generation. Most interviewees either stated that they did not ask about the past or suggested they did ask but were told that their parents or grandparents had not known anything. When reading between the lines, it became clear that the interviewees had not asked for more details or failed to challenge inconsistencies in stories, potentially to avoid facing the possibility of learning of family involvement. By denying that family members had known about or been involved in atrocities, relatives could avoid the question of family members' guilt and their responsibility to commemorate the victims of the Holocaust. When interviewees were asked about collective guilt, they challenged its legitimacy by arguing that they were far away in Canada or that they had been born after the war. Despite their insistence on the spatial and temporal distance from the events of the Holocaust, many interviewees exhibited avoidance and patterns of silence on the topic of the Nazi atrocities and reported feelings of guilt and shame in relation to their German heritage. This suggests that temporal distance from the 1930s and 1940s and the geographical distance from Germany did not eliminate the legacy of silence or facilitate a constructive process of dealing with the past among members of the second and third German-Canadian generations. In this chapter's interviews, silence came across through what was not said and through claims that family members did not talk about the Holocaust. It is possible that underlying factors motivating this silence included feelings of guilt and shame because of the association of the informants' German heritage with the Nazi past and the Holocaust.[45]

(Not) Talking about the Holocaust

The following section includes interview excerpts from interviews with second- and third-generation German Canadians interviewed in the Greater Vancouver area between June 2016 and August 2016. These excerpts focus on how German-Canadian families did or did not talk about the Holocaust. Interviewees' names are pseudonyms and were removed along with any identifying details to maintain privacy and confidentiality. Specific information on place of birth and other details that may be of interest for the reader were included where available and needed for context. All interviewees had responded to advertisements placed on Craigslist, a U.S. website that hosts classified notices, and in a German newspaper. These ads asked for "German Canadians" whose families had immigrated from Germany between 1950 and 1975 to be interviewed about their family memories related to the Second World

War. Two interviewees were found through referrals from research participants. Following a brief phone call to confirm their suitability for the project and their identification as "German Canadian," I set up meetings with each participant that lasted on average one hour and were conducted either in the participants' homes or in a quiet public space; except for one interview, all were conducted in English.

My first interviewee for this project was a warm, welcoming, and open-minded woman I shall name Rita, who had an active interest in German culture and history.[46] Rita welcomed me into her home on a sunny June afternoon and, after introducing me to her numerous German-themed collectibles and her Bavarian husband, she proceeded to share her experiences, insights, and concerns as a postwar German Canadian. Rita was born in Prince Rupert, British Columbia, in 1956 to German parents who had grown up in Bremen. She was thus a second-generation German Canadian and second-generation postwar German. Her father had fought for Germany during the war and suffered from what today would be diagnosed as post-traumatic stress disorder (PTSD). This made him difficult to get along with, abusive towards his wife and children, and dependent on alcohol. Rita found herself in a similarly abusive relationship with her first husband and left, a decision she wished her mother, who stayed with her father despite their problems, had been able to make for the sake of Rita and her brother. Rita's second husband had grown up near Augsburg, Bavaria and moved to Canada as an adult; he self-identified as a German Canadian and, according to Rita, was less interested in German culture than she was. Rita maintained her cultural heritage but was not fluent in German and struggled to learn it as an adult. She reported that German music was her strongest point of connection to the culture and language and this was passed on to her by her parents. Rita did not teach German to her own children from her first marriage but they were interested in learning.

During our two-hour conversation, Rita described a strong interest in history and current events, offering her insights and ideas about German Canadians, the Second World War, and her father. When I asked if the topic of the Holocaust had ever come up in family conversations and whether she recalled any specific memories or conversations around the topic, Rita described what her family had told her:

> I know the big question is going to come because everyone in my generation asks this question: "How did you not know about the Holocaust? How did you not know?" I am sure everyone wiggles in their seats. I asked my parents both about this. [My mother] said in Bremen there were Jews throughout the war and she said there was so much commotion and so much hunger near the end that nobody noticed that there. ... And then my dad brought up a good point that during the Second World War when all the Japanese were taken from their homes in Steveston [British Columbia] and their property was sold for next to nothing and their boats were sold, how come nobody noticed? But they all said that they really didn't notice.

Rita's mother said that it was such a tumultuous time that the disappearance of their Jewish neighbours was not noticed. Her father compared Germans' response to Nazi atrocities to Canadians' seeming ignorance of Japanese-Canadian internment during the war. Her father, who was a radio operator during the war and signed up when he was seventeen years old, according to Rita, refused to talk about his wartime experience in detail. When asked about whether her father talked about the Holocaust, she said:

> No, he just drank himself to oblivion. He didn't really talk about it [his wartime experiences], no. All I know is he couldn't stand being around screaming children. All I know is he was on a ship in the North Sea with civilians on it. And the ship had been hit and he survived but he could hear screaming children and after this he could not stand being around children. Even the normal fussing, he had to leave the room. We had a very strange childhood because of my dad's drinking. I'm sure I'm not the only one. In my generation, when you're a child who grew up in the Seventies, a lot of the parents drank heavily. I guess now they take drugs or pop pills.

After stating that her father "didn't really talk about it [the Holocaust]," Rita immediately changed the topic to the psychological damage her father had experienced during the war. Rita's focus on the personally relevant narratives seems to reinforce the notion, put forward by the

American sociologist Daniel Levy and his Israeli colleague Natan Sznaider, that in the context of strong emotions that surround the suffering of family members, such suffering is much closer to the individual than the suffering experienced by the victims of the Holocaust at the hand of the Nazi regime.[47] Despite her difficult relationship with her father, Rita chose to discuss her father's alcoholism rather than the Holocaust. In the end, the Holocaust was a topic that was theoretically more emotionally distant for her than her experiences as the child of an abusive father who turned to alcohol to manage his Second World War experiences.

Similar to Rita, Emma had a strong interest in German history and culture. She had also developed her own theories about the German experience during and after the war. Emma was born in Toronto in 1970. Emma's mother was born in Bessarabia (within modern-day Moldova and Ukraine) and moved to Canada when she was thirteen years old; her father, born in Germany, immigrated at the age of twenty. Emma's maternal grandparents were from Bessarabia and her paternal grandparents from Poland. Her parents met in their church congregation in Toronto. Emma was involved in the German community in Vancouver and taught German for many years. She told the following story about her family members' knowledge of the Holocaust: "Many people I know for years had the pictures of Germany on the old map. My parents didn't participate in the Holocaust, they were children. My grandma, who wasn't in Germany, always cried when the topic came up. She was that traumatized and didn't want to talk about it and others didn't want to talk about it either and I didn't really dare to ask them. I do have a good conscience because they didn't really participate. And besides, many of the camps weren't even in Germany. They were mostly in Poland." Emma realized that she had never really asked her family about the Holocaust because her parents had been children and her grandmother showed such a strong emotional response to the topic of the war that she did not want to upset her further. Emma's statement that she had a good conscience about the topic since her family did not participate implies that because of the silence she concluded that there were no stories.

This use of silence to exonerate the first generation of Holocaust guilt has been found in research conducted with families in Germany.[48] When there is no evidence or active discussion of a family connection, the tendency among relatives seems to be to believe that there was no family involvement in the Nazi regime and the Holocaust. And even when family members did share memories that suggested active involvement, members of the younger generation believed that their family members were innocent or even actively resisted the Nazi regime. These tactics were presumably carried out by the younger relations in an attempt to distance their own identity from the Nazi connection.[49] Emma implied that since most of the concentration camps were in Poland, Germans were somehow not responsible, even though the camps were built by the Nazi regime after the occupation of Poland. It is possible that holding on to the narrative of the "good non-participating Germans" allowed Emma to continue to feel positive about her German identity and to distance herself from Nazi Germany. Her resistance to recognize known historical facts and to question her own family members' knowledge and responses suggests that she preferred to remain in the ambiguous silence that allowed her to avoid the confrontation with her own family's German past.[50]

Just a few years younger than Emma but equally proud of his German heritage, Wolf, a cheerful and lively sports fan, was born in Vancouver in 1975. He had spent some time in Germany as an adolescent, travelling around with his hockey team. Wolf's parents had migrated from Germany to Canada in 1970. He said that he "was raised to be proud of his heritage." He was unaware of any family involvement, but, he said, his mother had made a point of teaching her children a balanced view of the Nazi past, as she was worried about them feeling bad. A balanced view, according to Wolf's mother, was one that discussed the Nazi period from multiple perspectives, those of the Germans, the allies, and the greater historical context. When I asked him, "Has the topic of the Nazi past and the Holocaust ever come up in family discussions? If yes, when is it most likely to come up? Who brings it up and how is it talked about? Can you recall any specific memories or family interactions around this topic?" Wolf said:

> I don't know about the concentration camps. I actually play cards with my dad and a lot of his buddies and the feeling I get is that everything was kept on such a need-to-know basis. Like, unless you were high up in the military, you didn't know. I think they were too scared to challenge anything.

> You couldn't challenge anything. Some may or may not have had an inkling of what was going on but you didn't dare say anything because then you were next. Early on in Hitler's reign, everything was great but then later on, a lot of people disagreed but couldn't really do anything.

Wolf initially stated that he believed only a few military officials knew about the Holocaust and if people did know, they were too scared to challenge what was happening. He then said that even if people knew they didn't say anything because they were worried they would be incriminated and end up in a concentration camp themselves. This statement implies that there were people who did know but deliberately kept quiet and took on a bystander role because they were afraid of the consequences. Wolf then disclosed that many people disagreed but were not able to stand up for what was right because of fear. Wolf's description removes blame from his father's generation and the German civilians by focusing on the fact that they either did not know or if they did know, there was nothing they could have done since it would have meant being targeted themselves.[51] This example highlights how the members of the third generation created their own explanations from the narratives of the first generation. The defence "there was nothing we could have done," often found in interviews with postwar Germans, was a common way of avoiding guilt and responsibility.[52] While historians have been increasingly focusing on the role of the police state in discouraging dissent and coercing the German population into silence, some suggest that Nazi war crimes were not treated with as much secrecy as was often believed and, instead, were even celebrated.[53]

Another perspective on what Germans did and did not talk about was offered by Peter, a liberal and talkative third-generation postwar German and second-generation Canadian whose stories ranged from his father's time in the German army to his family's hardships trying to settle in Canada. Peter's German parents immigrated to Canada in 1956. He was born in 1960. He still spoke German at the time of the interview and frequently visited Germany, particularly after his parents had returned to Germany in the 1980s. Peter's father was a decorated soldier during the war but Peter described him as a liberal, left-wing individual who defied authority. His mother had significant emotional difficulties as a result of the abuse she had experienced at a Catholic boarding school during the war. Peter's stories contained numerous references to the financial and emotional hardships faced by his parents and himself as a young child in Canada. He also shared some colourful stories of his father's heroic acts as a soldier. Peter reflected on how the Holocaust was discussed in Germany: "I can't remember that we ever talked about the Holocaust or the Nazi period. But that was never really a topic in my family. That's not unusual but it's a shame. That was the same in Germany at that time, only since the Seventies. When I go to Germany now, and that's twice a year, there's every night two hours on the Nazi period on TV. Generally Germans are so open but that [i.e., the Holocaust] they don't talk about." Peter's family did not talk about the Holocaust despite his father having been a left-wing, authority-defying Marxist, according to Peter. Peter identified the legacy of silence in Germany and noted that, in his observation, despite the ongoing education and media coverage since the 1970s, people still did not openly talk about the Holocaust. This observation has also been described in the literature and highlights the importance of open discussion about the German Nazi past within families and through educational efforts, since many Germans would prefer to remain silent until the Nazi past and the Holocaust are forgotten.[54] In Peter's experience, while there was dialogue on a societal level and access to televised information, this open discussion did not seem to transfer to the family level, where such conversations needed to happen in order to make the Holocaust personally relevant and salient to Germans and those of German heritage and to allow inroads into processing the family's past.

Another example of the lack of conversation about German family history was offered by Natascha, whose parents had immigrated to Canada in the 1960s. Born in Canada in 1967, she was a second-generation German Canadian and a member of Germany's third generation. While the family initially struggled financially, they were well off later on and became involved in the German cultural community that was alive and well in Vancouver in the 1970s and 1980s. During her childhood, Natascha frequently travelled with her family. Her mother was from Russia but did not teach her children Russian and instead made a point of maintaining her children's paternal German heritage by making German food and enrolling the children in German school. Natascha did not identify as Russian Canadian or Russian German Canadian. Instead, she specifically noted her connection to her German heritage and attempted to foster it more in recent years through relearning the language and food preparation as her daughter was starting to show interest in her mother's cultural heritage. Natascha said her family did not talk about the Holocaust:

> No, I never asked my family. I was nineteen when my dad died. I'm sure that kinda stuff might have come up if I had been older and had my own kids. Had he lived I probably would have gone into business with him. Lots of conversations were probably missed and I have not talked to my mother since the funeral. I have never talked to my aunt about it. It would be interesting to know but, you know, we're so far removed from it here. It doesn't impact our lives, so I've never thought to ask about it. You don't just really ask about that like "Hey, how about that Holocaust?"

Natascha believed that there might have been more opportunities to talk about the Holocaust had her father been still alive but at the same time admitted that she never asked. Her statement that she grew up so far removed from the Holocaust and Germany that it did not impact her life implies that she did not feel any obligation to confront the Holocaust within her own family or as a German Canadian. She reflected that it is a difficult topic to talk about and suggested that the discussion may not have been encouraged in her family. Despite being so far removed from the Holocaust, she still felt as though it was not something one talked about.[55] Without realizing it, Natascha was describing the "double wall of silence" (Bar-On) and cultural notions of acceptable family memories. Natascha's statements reflected the legacy of silence that ran through three generations and was not ameliorated by growing up so far away from Germany.

Consequently, participants were not silent in response to the question of their family memory of the Holocaust by actively skipping the question or denying a response; instead, their silence was apparent in the absence of memories that included direct discussion of the Holocaust or admission of family involvement. In contrast, families talked about the war, reasons why it happened, and even knew who in the family had been affiliated with the Nazi regime. Even within these conversations, however, there was little or no direct recognition of the role of Germans or family members as perpetrators. In its place, there was a focus on theoretical explanations for the Second World War, the Holocaust, and why it all happened—a common form of avoidance of feelings of collective shame as a result of German heritage. Interviewees' focus on logical explanations and external factors allowed them to avoid discussing family members' guilt or that of the German population at large. By describing the reasons from an objective metaperspective and by engaging in retrospective moral rationalization, individuals can emotionally distance themselves from the event.[56]

Explaining Away the Perpetrators: Just a Fellow Traveller

In taking a closer look at how family members discussed the perpetrators and bystanders in their midst, the following excerpts provide examples of how responsibility and acknowledging family involvement were avoided through silence and omission. I met Fritz on a 2016 sunny August afternoon in downtown Vancouver. He was a short, friendly, middle-aged man and the way he dressed reminded me of an American tourist, as he was wearing a colourful shirt, khaki shorts, and a small messenger bag. Sitting on the large communal patio of his downtown Vancouver apartment building which overlooked the city, I was surprised to find that, despite being born in Canada and being financially successful, Fritz would probably have preferred to live in Germany. His statements and theories stood out and reminded me of the literature that I had read to prepare for this project, wherein family members denied relatives' involvement in the Holocaust despite all evidence to the contrary. It turned out that his stories came the closest to an interviewee in my project ever acknowledging family involvement in the Holocaust.

Fritz was born into a German-immigrant family in Toronto in 1965. He described feeling lost between the two cultures and having resented his family for moving to Canada. Fritz had a strong interest in the Nazi past and knew that his father had been a member of the Hitler Youth. Fritz shared reflections on "the German nature" as well as his request that his wife not tell friends about his heritage as it often led to comments about the Nazi period. He said that he had specifically asked his wife not to introduce him as "her German man." He recounted a recent incident with a same-sex couple, friends of his wife whom they had invited over for dinner, which led to comments and an uncomfortable dinner conversation about the crimes the Nazis committed against the LGBTQ community.

Fritz used this example to illustrate that despite him feeling a strong connection to German culture, sometimes it was better not to be known as being of German descent because it could lead to difficult conversations. At the same time, Fritz was quite aware of his family history and, as Fritz shared during the interview, his grandmother, a tax collector and educated vegetarian who made her own moonshine, had uncles who worked in the concentration camp administration. This is how he answered a question on whether his family had ever talked about the Holocaust:

> Yes, on Father's side they were tax collectors. They grew up very Bohemian, didn't go to church, spoke Esperanto, became vegetarians. They made this really strong, illegal alcohol and sold it. Very well-educated as well. She [my grandmother] spoke several languages. Amazing for a woman. Her brothers as well. Their uncles were sea captains and were actually in the concentration camps in South Africa in the First World War. And then during the Second World War worked in the camps, in administration, and they would always tell her that the camps in South Africa were actually worse than the camps in Germany. Not a lot of people know that. I talk to my cousins in Germany about it and there of course you can't say that maybe it wasn't that bad and maybe there were people who were trying to make things better, like Schindler actually trying to get things better. So my family never saw the roundups but they knew about it. It wasn't like the pictures you see though.

The admission that Fritz's great-uncles were concentration camp administrators in Germany was immediately followed by a statement that the camps in Germany were not as bad as the ones in South Africa, suggesting an attempt to minimize his family's involvement by comparing the German and South African concentration camps. Fritz claimed that while his family never saw concentration camp roundups they knew about them and could confirm that it was not like in the pictures. Presumably Fritz is referring to images of concentration camp roundups seen in documentaries and history books but one may wonder how his family members could have compared the scenes when they, as he recalls, had not actually seen them. It is possible that this juxtaposition may have been an attempt to normalize the German perpetrator history.[57] Fritz believed the family narrative that South African concentration camps were worse than Nazi camps. He suggested that his cousins in Germany disagreed with his view not because it was wrong but because it was not acceptable, which is indicated by his statement that "there [in Germany] of course you can't say that." Thus, Fritz focused on the shared stories from his parents rather than what his cousins in Germany believed. He did not question the parts of his family memory that were contradictory or comment on the fact that his relatives had not only seen concentration camps but actually worked in them. Instead, he suggested that it had not been as "bad" as was commonly believed. Fritz's attempts at normalizing are commonly seen in children and grandchildren of perpetrators. For him, this included elements of denial, perhaps in an effort to distance himself from this family history and the potential impact of admitting the severity of such involvement on his own identity as a proud German Canadian.[58] One may wonder if underlying this denial was a deep sense of shame, as Fritz requested not to be introduced as German. As the shame researcher Brené Brown states, "shame thrives in silence," and although Fritz talked about his family history, he did not directly acknowledge the parts that were difficult, nor did he share how they affected him as a third-generation German Canadian.[59]

The final and most striking example of German Canadians talking or not talking about the Holocaust is a fellow traveller story that came up during my conversation with Michael, an educated professional in the legal field who self-identified as a member of the LGBTQ community. The term fellow traveller or *Mitläufer* describes an individual who participated in and was involved in the Nazi regime but did not express strong support for the Nazi ideology in their denazification questionnaire or during their tribunal hearing.[60] They may have been deemed to have "good character" on the basis of testimony from sympathetic colleagues, clergy, and friends during their hearings. *Mitläufer* was one of the five categories identified in the questionnaire (*Fragebogen*) used in the denazification process, conducted by the allies starting March 1946, to identify war criminals and to eliminate the Nazi ideology from the German population.[61] This attempt and process has generally been deemed a failure, particularly by voices from within Germany, as it is believed that many individuals who had significant involvement with the Nazi party and ideology were not held accountable. This belief is illustrated by the fact that out of the 950,126 individuals who were asked to appear before the tribunal, only 23,776 were deemed to be offenders and main offenders.[62]

Michael's descriptions were rich in detail and offered the occasional critical comment and attempt to interpret his family members' reactions and behaviour. Michael was born in 1973 to a German mother and a Danish father who had immigrated to Canada in the early 1960s. Michael's German grandfather, uncle, as well as his mother's cousin were involved in the Nazi regime. His father, who was named Adolf by his Danish parents, was interested in the Holocaust and disappointed to learn of his wife's father's involvement in the Nazi party. Michael's story about his maternal grandfather during the war provides an example of a "follower story":

> My grandmother passed away earlier. He [Grandfather] had a lady he lived with but they weren't married. She was a stepmother essentially. I know a bit more through her. He didn't have to go to the war because he had a farm and he was quite a good equestrian. He also had a good name in the cattle industry. I had read a document from 1947 that my uncle gave me and it was an *Entnazifizierungsfragebogen* [denazification questionnaire]. He claimed on that that because of his interest in horses he had joined the SA [*Sturmabteilung*, paramilitary wing of the Nazi regime] and the party and he was later on in Russia and Ukraine. He was a friendly person and social and not [a] hateful one but certainly at the time I don't know what he knew but I am very convinced that he does not have blood on his hands. My dad was very shocked after he had just married my mom and he saw a photo of him in a SA uniform and he asked a lot of family members and they said "he was a *Mitläufer*." And he was eventually a *Truppenleiter* [troop leader; the correct German term is *Truppenführer*, a lower-ranking officer in the SA] but that's all I know.

Michael described how his father, after he married Michael's mother, was shocked to find out about his wife's father's involvement as troop leader but was assured by family members that his father-in-law was simply a follower. Michael learned more about his grandfather from another relative and insisted that his grandfather had not committed war crimes as he was only a "fellow traveller," albeit one who had been an SA troop leader. Generally, such followers are considered indirect supporters of the Nazi agenda but are not seen as having directly contributed to the Nazi crimes.[63] The family's assessment of Michael's grandfather as a nice, social "fellow traveller" is a common narrative found among members of the postwar generations when describing relatives who were involved in the Nazi party.[64] One may wonder how Michael's mother felt about her father's position as SA troop leader; Michael's story suggests there might have been a considerable wall of silence as she had not told her husband about her father's past. Michael also stated in the interview about his mother that "now [that] she's getting older she is sharing more stories. I have not heard as many from her when I was a child but far too many from my father."

Conclusion

My research shows that the patterns of silence and avoidance—when discussing family knowledge of and involvement in the Holocaust—previously identified in native Germans were also apparent in the stories of second- and third-generation postwar German Canadians, despite immigration and increased historical education. The avoidance behaviours found in German Canadians' family memories of the Holocaust, shared in this project, teach us the challenges of remembering a difficult past when the topic is treated with silence.[65] The behaviour that underlies these recurrent patterns of memory transmission seems to be silence. It encapsulates what is said or what is not said, including the sense that a specific topic cannot be discussed without fear of offending others or that there are repercussions for one's own identity as a member of this cultural group, all suggesting an underlying sense of shame. As Brown argues, shame is the fear of disconnection; therefore, the antidote to shame is empathy, connection, and honest conversation, wherein individuals embrace vulnerability and explore their feelings in relation to their difficult cultural heritage.[66] These studies of patterns of silence and ways to address them could be used to inform programs that support individuals and societies dealing with a difficult cultural past, particularly members of the perpetrator group.[67] This research on German Canadians may prove particularly useful when it comes to finding inroads into the truth and reconciliation process in Canada. It can help non-Indigenous Canadians to understand their need to engage in dialogue and acknowledge their own responsibility in coming to terms with the reality of residential schools and colonialization.

Due to the small sample size, the conclusions drawn from the interviews reflect the subjective experience of the interviewees and do not reflect the diverse experiences and family backgrounds of the larger population of postwar German-Canadian immigrants. These patterns nevertheless provide insight and directions for future research. Potential areas of further research include a comparison of the family memories of ethnic Germans and native Germans, considering that about a third of German-Canadian postwar immigrants were expellees.[68] Furthermore, it would be interesting to conduct multi-generational and longitudinal interviews with several groups of German Canadians.

In conclusion, second- and third-generation postwar German Canadians showed similar patterns of silence in relation to discussing the Holocaust as did postwar Germans in Germany. Across the interviews, there was limited evidence of reflection on the question of responsibility to remember and commemorate the Holocaust, even though families had talked about the Second World War in general. Given that silence enables avoidance, it raises the question of collective guilt and responsibility despite the absence of knowledge or discussion of events, especially among younger generations. The stories of my informants suggest that several generations of German Canadians continued to struggle with family memories of the Nazi past and the Holocaust, not knowing how to talk about and make sense of them. In particular, it may have been challenging for them to make the difficult German past meaningful for themselves as German Canadians and to integrate this heritage into their dual identity.

Notes

1 Jeffrey K. Olick, "What Does It Mean to Normalize the Past? Official Memory in German Politics since 1989," *Social Science History* 22, no. 4 (Special Issue: Memory and the Nation) (Winter 1998): 550.

2 Harald Welzer, Sabine Moller, and Karoline Tschuggnall, *"Opa war kein Nazi": Nationalsozialismus und Holocaust im Familiengedächtnis* (Frankfurt am Main: Fischer, 2002), 124.

3 Gabriele Rosenthal and Bettina Völter, "Three Generations in Jewish and Non-Jewish German Families After the Unification of Germany," in *International Handbook of Multigenerational Legacies of Trauma*, ed. Yael Danieli (New York: Plenum Press, 1998), 305.

4 Harold Marcuse, "Memories of World War II and the Holocaust in Europe," in *A Companion to Europe 1900–1945*, ed. Gordon Martel (New York: Wiley-Blackwell, 2006), 493.

5 Ibid., 494.

6 Ibid., 499.

7 Bundesarchiv (German Federal Archives), "Berlin Document Centre," *Hintergründe zu Geschichte und Hauptbeständen*, 15 June 2013, http://www.bundesarchiv.de/DE/Content/Artikel/Ueber-uns/Aus-unserer-Arbeit/berlin-document-center.html (accessed 31 May 2019).

8 Roger Frie, "Memory and Responsibility: Navigating Identity and Shame in the German-Jewish Experience," *Psychoanalytic Psychology* 29, no. 2 (2012): 212; and Henri Parens, "Aftermath of Genocide—the Fate of Children of Perpetrators," *International Journal of Applied Psychoanalytic Studies* 6, no. 1 (2009): 31–34.

9 Jürgen Habermas, "Keine Normalisierung der Vergangenheit," in Habermas, *Eine Art Schadensabwicklung* (Berlin: Suhrkamp, 1987), 13; and Frie, "Memory and Responsibility," 211.

10 Marie Louise Seeberg, Irene Levin, and Claudia Lenz, *The Holocaust as Active Memory: The Past in the Present* (Abingdon: Routledge, 2013), 2.

11 Rosenthal and Völter, "Three Generations," 5; Ernst van Alphen, "Second-Generation Testimony, Transmission of Trauma, and Postmemory," *Poetics Today* 27, no. 2 (2006): 475; and Sigrid Weigel, "'Generation' as a Symbolic Form: On the Genealogical Discourse of Memory since 1945," *The Germanic Review: Literature, Culture, Theory* 77, no. 4 (2002): 269.

12 van Alphen, "Second-Generation Testimony," 476.

13 Welzer et al., "*Opa war kein Nazi*," 81.

14 Susan Rubin Suleiman, "The 1.5 Generation: Thinking about Child Survivors and the Holocaust," *American Imago* 59, no. 3 (2002): 282.

15 Alexander Freund, "Dealing with the Past Abroad: German Immigrants' *Vergangenheitsbewältigung* and their Relations with Jews in North America since 1945," *Bulletin of the German Historical Institute* 31 (2002): 52.

16 Ibid., 51.

17 Matthias Proske, "'Why Do We Always Have to Say We're Sorry?': A Case Study on Navigating Moral Expectations in Classroom Communication on National Socialism and the Holocaust in Germany," *European Education* 44, no. 3 (2012): 41.

18 Alexander Freund, "Troubling Memories in Nation-building: World War II Memories and Germans' Inter-ethnic Encounters in Canada after 1945," *Histoire sociale/Social History* 39, no. 77 (May 2006): 153.

19 Irene Levin, "Silence, Memory and Migration," *Journal of Comparative Family Studies* 44, no. 6 (2013): 719.

20 Oliver Fuchs, Lou-Marie Krüger, and Pumla Gobodo-Madikizela, "An Exploration of German Subjectivity: Three Generations After the End of World War Two," *The Humanistic Psychologist* 41, no. 2 (2013): 136.

21 Michael Heinlein, "Das Trauma der deutschen Kriegskinder zwischen nationaler und europäischer Erinnerung: Kritische Anmerkungen zum gegenwärtigen Wandel der Erinnerungskultur," *German Monitor* 73, no. 1 (2011): 118.

22 Dan Bar-On, "Holocaust Perpetrators and Their Children: A Paradoxical Morality," *Journal of Humanistic Psychology* 29, no. 4 (1989): 425.

23 Proske, "'Why Do We Always,'" 44.

24 Fuchs et al., "An Exploration of German Subjectivity," 145; Henri Parens, "Aftermath of Genocide," 26.

25 Fuchs et al., "An Exploration of German Subjectivity," 138.

26 Proske, "'Why Do We Always,'" 59; Harald Welzer, "Grandpa Wasn't a Nazi: The Holocaust in German Family Remembrance," American Jewish Committee (2005): 11, online at http://courses.washington.edu/berlin09/Readings/Welzer_Grandpa.pdf (accessed 3 June 2017).

27 Fuchs et al., "An Exploration of German Subjectivity," 155.

28 Theodor W. Adorno, "Education After Auschwitz," in Adorno, *Critical Models: Interventions and Catchwords*, trans. Henry W. Pickford (1966; repr., New York: Columbia University Press, 1998), 191–204; Bar-On, "Holocaust Perpetrators"; Roger Frie, "From Memorials to Bomb Shelters: Navigating the Emotional Landscape of German Memory," *Psychoanalytic Inquiry* 34, no. 7 (2014): 654; and Wulf Kansteiner, "Testing the Limits of Trauma: The Long-term Psychological Effects of the Holocaust on Individuals and Collectives," *History of the Human Sciences* 17, no. 2–3 (2004): 109.

29 Heinlein, "Das Trauma der deutschen Kriegskinder," 114.

30 Theodor W. Adorno, "Einleitung zum Vortrag: 'Was bedeutet Aufarbeitung der Vergangenheit?'" In Adorno, *Gesammelte Schriften* 10 (Frankfurt am Main: Suhrkamp, 1977): 816–17.

31 Katharina von Kellenbach, "Vanishing Acts: Perpetrators in Postwar Germany," *Holocaust and Genocide Studies* 17, no. 2 (2003): 310.

32 Fuchs et al., "An Exploration of German Subjectivity," 155; Welzer et al., "*Opa war kein Nazi*," 126; and Bar-On, "Holocaust Perpetrators," 428.

33 Rosenthal and Völter, "Three Generations," 9.

34 Welzer et al., "*Opa war kein Nazi*," 19.

35 Ibid., 24.

36 Rosenthal and Völter, "Three Generations," 5.

37 Levin, "Silence, Memory and Migration," 719.

38 Frie, "From Memorials to Bomb Shelters," 661; and Levin, "Silence, Memory and Migration," 720.

39 Levin, "Silence, Memory and Migration," 719.

40 Emma Dresler-Hawke, "Reconstructing the Past and Attributing the Responsibility for the Holocaust," *Social Behavior and Personality: An International Journal* 33, no. 2 (2005): 136; and Frie, "Memory and Responsibility," 206.

41 Jean S. Phinney, et al., "Ethnic Identity, Immigration, and Well-being: An Interactional Perspective," *Journal of Social Issues* 57, no. 3 (2001): 495.

42 Freund, "Dealing with the Past," 52; and Evelyne Massa and Morton Weinfeld, "We Needed to Prove We Were Good Canadians: Contrasting Paradigms for Suspect Minorities," *Canadian Issues* (Spring 2009): 21.

43 Frie, "Memory and Responsibility," 211.

44 Manfred Prokop, "The Dynamics of German Language Maintenance in Canada," *Forum Deutsch* 16 (2008): 14.

45 Dresler-Hawke, "Reconstructing the Past," 135.

46 As stated earlier, interviewees' names are pseudonyms and were removed along with any identifying details to maintain privacy and confidentiality.

47 Daniel Levy and Natan Sznaider, "Memories of Universal Victimhood: The Case of Ethnic German Expellees," *German Politics and Society* 23, no. 2 (2005): 19.

48 von Kellenbach, "Vanishing Acts," 313; and Welzer et al., "*Opa war kein Nazi*," 195–210.

49 Welzer et al., "*Opa war kein Nazi*," 13.

50 Ibid., 206.

51 Dresler-Hawke, "Reconstructing the Past," 135; and Frie, "Memorials to Bomb Shelters," 653.

52 Welzer et al., "*Opa war kein Nazi*," 53.

53 Robert Gellately, *Backing Hitler: Consent and Coercion in Nazi Germany* (Oxford: Oxford University Press, 2002), 264.

54 Rosenthal and Völter, "Three Generations," 9; Vered Vinitzky-Seroussi and Chana Teeger, "Unpacking the Unspoken: Silence in Collective Memory and Forgetting," *Social Forces* 88, no. 3 (2010): 1104.

55 Parens, "Aftermath of Genocide," 33.

56 Kristen Renwick Monroe, "Cracking the Code of Genocide: The Moral Psychology of Rescuers, Bystanders, and Nazis During the Holocaust," *Political Psychology* 29, no. 5 (2008): 718.

57 Patrick Finney, "Ethics, Historical Relativism and Holocaust Denial," *Rethinking History* 2, no. 3 (1998): 365.

58 Bar-On, "Holocaust Perpetrators," 45.

59 Brené Brown, *Daring Greatly: How the Courage to Be Vulnerable Transforms the Way We Live, Love, Parent, and Lead* (New York: Penguin, 2015), 62.

60 C.M. Clark, "West Germany Confronts the Nazi Past: Some Recent Debates on the Early Postwar Era, 1945–1960," *The European Legacy* 4, no. 1 (1999): 115.

61 Ibid., 116.

62 Ibid.

63 Monroe, "Cracking the Code of Genocide," 714.

64 Welzer et al., "*Opa war kein Nazi*," 124.

65 Dresler-Hawke, "Reconstructing the Past," 134.

66 Brown, *Daring Greatly*, 74–75.

67 Dresler-Hawke, "Reconstructing the Past," 134.

68 Freund, "Troubling Memories," 135.

CHAPTER 8

Creating Family Legacies: Descendants Memorialize Their German Female Ancestors

CHRISTINE ENSSLEN[1]

In 2008, Celeste Rider, at the time the provincial librarian for the Saskatchewan Genealogical Society, became concerned about lost opportunities to remember and document the lives of female Saskatchewan settlers. Motivated to commemorate these long-dead pioneers, Rider offered individuals the opportunity to publicly memorialize their female ancestors' lives by writing accounts of pioneer women who had lived in Saskatchewan before 1950. Children, grandchildren, great-grandchildren, and great-great-grandchildren of forty women of German origin took this opportunity to create and preserve a record of their valued ancestor's life for inclusion in Rider's edited collection of altogether 413 accounts, which appeared as *Women Pioneers of Saskatchewan*, published by the Saskatchewan Genealogical Society in 2009.

Many of these German pioneer women, frequently either accompanying or following their parents or husbands, immigrated to Canada to leave behind poor economic prospects, political instability, or in some cases familial turmoil. They came to Saskatchewan with hopes of acquiring farmland and finding opportunities to start afresh.[2] Thirty-five of the forty women were born outside of Canada. Eighteen were born in German settlements in Russia, eight in Germany, four each in Poland and the United States, and one in Ukraine. They were born between 1850 and 1925. Most became homesteaders in Saskatchewan.

Using the accounts or biographies in Rider's book, this chapter examines how descendants of German women immigrants commemorated their ancestors in this public memorialization project. These records allow for an understanding of the ways early twenty-first-century Canadian families attempted to preserve history intergenerationally. While this history had been passed down through translating memories into family lore and safe-keeping photographs, family journals, mementos, and important documents, in some cases Rider's fear that memories of women pioneers had been forgotten had indeed come true. Consequently, this chapter also examines how various biographies were constructed when information failed to be transmitted through intergenerational memory. Motivated to provide complete accounts, biographers sought to fill the gaps within the family lore. Some undertook research on their own, others imagined possible histories, and yet others mourned the loss of this information. The biographies illuminate patterns of narrative remembrance by showing which elements of German culture and German immigrant experience the descendants included and how they discussed them when they created accounts intended to commemorate Canadian history.

Rider's collection is part of a larger movement in Saskatchewan to commemorate prairie pioneers. Although Rider's publication may be the most substantial contribution to this genre, similar collections are motivated by the desire to preserve the lives and contributions of immigrant farmers and rural schoolteachers (who taught the children of pioneers and frequently were themselves the children of pioneers).[3] While some of these accounts chose to profile pioneer women exclusively, others accepted submissions that profile men or women. These collections consist of either biographical accounts solicited from family members, as is the case with Rider's collection, or interviews and archival research that someone unrelated to the pioneers has formatted into full or partial biographies. These commemorative compilations stress the importance of remembering and valuing the past and emphasize that the hard work of these pioneers laid the foundation for the province's success. The former Saskatchewan Liberal Party leader, Lynda Haverstock's foreword to *Egg Money* typifies this sentiment. She wrote: "The Canada that we know and appreciate today would certainly be a different place, were it not for bold, resilient, and incredibly hard-working women, [*sic*] we are blessed citizens to have inherited tremendous legacies for the benefit of generations to come."[4]

Much of the academic literature on how German immigrant experience was remembered and represented utilizes oral rather than written histories. The Dakota Memories Oral History Project (DMOHP) was launched in 2005 by bibliographer Michael Miller and American immigration historian Thomas Isern. The project sought to collect oral histories of second- and third-generation ethnic Germans from Russia living on the Northern Plains.[5] In 2006, the DMOHP undertook a special project to collect oral histories preserving the experiences of Germans from Russia living in Saskatchewan.[6] Research published from material collected through the DMOHP has examined the way that second- and third-generation Germans who emigrated from Russia to Dakota remembered their immigrant experiences, strove to maintain their cultural heritage, and remembered their grandparents.[7] The DMOHP also endeavoured to document the distinct ethnic identity and character of German Russians in Saskatchewan.[8] Other research has investigated how anti-German sentiment in the American Midwest was communicated to subsequent generations[9] and what were German Canadians' memories of their experiences during and after the Second World War.[10] This chapter contributes to an examination of how German Canadians' representations of the past were shaped by projects seeking to commemorate Canadian history; it specifically focuses on the unique character of written rather than oral histories.

Collections such *Women Pioneers of Saskatchewan* and the DMOHP allow individuals to participate in public projects of commemoration. These participants have the potential to be "memory makers," positioned to promote their own representations and interpretations of the past.[11] The oral historians involved in collecting material for the DMOHP were acutely aware that participants were in conference with each other and that this played a role in shaping their accounts.[12]

What was unique about Rider's project was that these submissions were written by individuals who were not in conference with the other contributors or Rider. The biographers and their families conceptualized how to commemorate their ancestors not knowing what the other accounts in *Women Pioneers of Saskatchewan* would look like. Despite this, all the accounts in Rider's project of "collected memory"[13] were remarkably similar to each other, both in their biographical format and in the ways that the ancestors were commemorated. This chapter delves into how biographers chose to commemorate their ancestors as well as how issues of German identity and culture organically emerged within this type of a commemorative project.

The first section explores how the nature of being included in Rider's collection shaped what was "remembered" and relayed in these accounts of German immigrants' lives. The second section examines authorship and constraints on the type of story told in terms of multi-generational memory transmission, availability of sources, and the use of speculation. The third section details how German culture was remembered and represented, by specifically examining language, foodways, and religion. The final section addresses the ways in which the biographers navigated the German experience during the world wars. I argue that these accounts can be read as versions of these individuals' lives constructed for a particular purpose and in the context of being a public face of not only an ancestor but also of the entire family line. Descendants took this opportunity to commemorate their ancestors by writing biographies that conveyed deep love for their relatives and appreciation for their work. Additionally, contributors used this emotive history to establish how their ancestors' desirable qualities such as hard work, respectable citizenship, and strength of character had been passed down the family line.

Motivated Biographies: Establishing Pioneer Lineage and Family Success

In 2008, the Saskatchewan Genealogical Society advertised for the public to submit accounts of female pioneers who had lived in either rural or urban parts of the land now called Saskatchewan, any time between 1800 and 1950.[14] This call for submissions was publicized through the genealogical society's members, the society's website, a specially developed brochure, local newspapers, information posted on the RootsWeb mailing list, the Regina public library website, and through a Canadian Broadcasting Corporation (CBC) radio interview as well as other media.[15] Celeste Rider gave few instructions as to the format of these accounts; she did, however, request that submissions be no longer than 2,000 words and stated that one or two photographs could be submitted. Rider ultimately published all 413 submissions that she received.[16]

Other than her request for accounts of female Saskatchewan pioneers, Rider voiced no conditions regarding which aspects of the women's lives should be emphasized. Indeed, Rider did not specifically request "biographies" of these women, but variously called for "stories," "write ups," "records," and, occasionally, "biographies."[17] All contributors nevertheless chose to format and narrate their accounts in the style of a biography: the accounts are linear and outline the women's lives from their birth until their death. In some cases, the pieces ended or grew less detailed after 1950, presumably because Rider had specified an interest in the time up to the 1950s. Rider did not suggest potential topics for biographers to address, but common threads were nevertheless present across these accounts, especially regarding how descendants chose to situate their ancestors as pioneers.

The biographers wrote a particular kind of story to meet the requirements of Rider's project. Submission guidelines specified that the goal of the project was "to produce a record of the women who also played a huge role in the settlement and growth of Saskatchewan."[18] Thus, many of the authors made an effort, either at the beginning or at the end of the biography, to emphasize their ancestor's involvement as a pioneer and contributor to Saskatchewan's heritage. According to the accounts, the pioneer women had led ordinary lives and worked hard. Consequently their accomplishments were not of a grand scale. Biographers explicitly stressed the ways that they felt their ancestor was worthy of inclusion in a project that sought to document women who played a "huge role" settling the province. Karolina Daubert's granddaughter wrote: "As a farm wife and mother, she [Karolina] played a role in the settlement of the province."[19]

Many of these contributors chose to stress their ancestor's pioneer status, presumably to make it clear to both Rider and potential readers why their relative fit the larger aims of the project. For some authors, establishing that their relative was a fit for this book meant defining the term "pioneer" in a way that would apply to their ancestor. When commemorating her great-grandmother, Myrla Birch explained: "It takes a special kind of person to be a pioneer. Are people born that way, or do you learn to how to be one with practice? I suspect it is a combination of some unique characteristics that one innately has—courage, a sense of adventure, positive attitude, acceptance of what is, hope for what can be, faith, caring for others, a sense of humour, all mixed with the right kind of nurturing, that was so special in pioneers."[20]

To ensure inclusion in the collection, biographers also stressed that their ancestor was an exceptionally hard-working woman. Along many others, Elizabeth Schell's granddaughter, Beverly Gutenberg, wrote: "She [Schell] worked very hard all her life; she was made of sturdy fabric, the kind which broke the land, seeded the wheat, reaped the harvest and populated the province of Saskatchewan. She was a pioneer."[21] Stressing the proliferation of the family line was another way of asserting their ancestor's successful contribution to the province. Gutenberg concluded Schell's biography thusly: "[Schell] was survived by eight natural children and two stepchildren, forty-three grandchildren, forty-one great-grandchildren and three great-great-grandchildren. Her descendants have increased considerably since her passing. This immigrant woman has left her mark on the face of Saskatchewan."[22]

The task of translating memories and family lore into a narrative that would be read by the public shaped the way these biographies were written. Whether intended or not, the published accounts had the potential to become part of family tradition as well as a definitive telling of these ancestors' lives for future descendants. Some biographers were aware of this fact; Alethea McLean wrote: "Family history is important for our own self-identification, as the actions of individuals from past generations have a profound impact on future generations, it is beneficial to know the roles these individuals have played within the family structure to discover where families got their start."[23] These biographies functioned as a record of the authors' ancestors' lives that could be easily consulted, shared, and preserved. Contributors felt responsible to present a respectable life story not only to honour their ancestor but also on behalf of all living members and future generations, who might be associated with the documented person.

The biographies were coloured by the fact that they were written by family members rather than historians without attachment to their subject. Descendants were motivated to write about their pioneer ancestors because they wished to share their family history and honour the memory of their female ancestor. Bonnie Meier wrote this of her grandmother, Margaret Dombrowsky: "It is an honour to share the story of my grandmother in celebration of ordinary Saskatchewan pioneer women."[24] The descendants were not neutral biographers. They wrote as ancestors, as family members. Shirley Gadzella wrote as the daughter of a pioneer: "Mom's role in this province's history was simple, yet significant. She was a wife, a mother, a self-taught 'woman of many trades' and a devout Roman Catholic. Her legacy lives on indeed, amongst her children and her grandchildren. Way to go Mom!"[25]

In many ways, the ancestors' past experiences became recast as a result of the nature of Rider's project of commemoration. These written histories functioned much like the oral histories that American oral historian Michael Frisch examined—they too were a means of understanding historical memory, that is, "how people make sense of their past, how they connect individual experience and its social context, how the past becomes part of the present, and how people use it to interpret their lives and the world around them."[26] The biographers similarly linked the past and the present in the way they shaped their ancestors' stories. All authors, for example, expressed great admiration for their ancestors; they desired public acknowledgement that their relatives' sacrifices and hard work had set the stage for the prosperity of future generations. Bertha Klause's biographer wrote: "To quote her son, John, 'She earned her place by the sweat of her brow, and probably never knew the lighter side of life.' We are proud of our grandparents' accomplishments and sacrifices. Their determination, fortitude and exemplary lives served us well as role models. Danke schoen, Grosmutter [*sic*]."[27] Similarly, Audrey Wilson stated her grandmother's farm was still owned by a family member and that "Augusta's descendants have benefitted from her hard work with good lives and opportunities on the prairies and elsewhere."[28]

In addition to deliberately stressing the women's pioneer status and hard work, many authors went further. They used the discussion of their female ancestor's consummate work, determination, and strength of character in order to establish her descendants' moral character and successes. They asserted that their ancestor contributed to the province, and then they transferred her value onto the activities, successes, and moral fibre of her descendants, establishing themselves as hard-working and proud Canadian citizens. Myrla Birch claimed her great-grandmother Lydia Salmond would be "proud to know ... [that her descendants] are strong active community minded citizens. They in turn can appreciate the fine example she provided."[29] Margaret Wagner's granddaughter made similar claims: "Margaret's hard work bore results, her children were well balanced [*sic*] individuals, her grandchildren and great-grandchildren are well educated [*sic*], responsible citizens, every one of which she would be proud."[30]

Authorship, Family Lore, Multi-generational Memory, and Finding Sources

In Rider's collection female relatives primarily adopted the role of family historian: forty-one of the forty-six authors were women.[31] Ten of the biographies were written by the pioneers' children, twenty-three by grandchildren, seven by great-grandchildren, and one by a great-great-grandchild.[32] These authors felt strongly connected to their immigrant ancestors, despite the temporal distance between them and despite the fact that they may never have met the woman they were commemorating. Some descendants remained connected to their homesteading ancestors through continuing to operate the family farm. Sadie Busse's grandchildren continued to farm on her homestead, and the original house was still standing.[33] Bertha Werle's great-granddaughter wrote that the family had received a Century Family Farm Award for continuously farming the original homestead: "The Fieseler farm on SE 22 has the honour of being the second oldest family farm in the rural municipality, having been established in 1889."[34]

Some of the biographers maintained emotional connections to their ancestors through material objects that had been passed down from one generation to the next. According to the Australian oral historian Janis Wilton, even the most utilitarian or everyday material objects can become sites of emotion, remembrance, and commemoration.[35] Rose Schmalz, daughter of Anna Maria Schmalz, wrote that upon her mother's death she ensured that the Christmas cactus that her mother had taken care of for over fifty years ended up in good hands. Though the original plant had died by the time Rose wrote this biography for Rider, she noted that it still lived on as she, her sister, and her nephew all had slips (cuttings from the original plant) of her mother's beloved plant. Furthermore, Rose deliberately preserved other items that had been meaningful to her mother: "Mother treasured the items she inherited from her father, some of which were brought from Russia, and other items, which in those hard times were purchased second-hand (to this day these antiques remain in the family—I made certain of that)."[36] Katherine Vanderlinde died when her granddaughter, Shirley Baker, was five years old. Although sixty-seven years had passed between her grandmother's death and the time Baker wrote her account, she sought out ways to remain connected to her grandmother: "I wear her [Katherine's] wedding ring; it is symbolic of that kindness, gentleness and generosity of my early memories. As her descendants, we feel admiration and gratitude to the memory of this young, vibrant and beautiful bride who chose to be part of our heritage."[37] In this sense, farmland and family heirlooms served as a bridge across the gap of time, tethering descendants to their ancestors.

Though highly motivated to give complete accounts, the biographers were constrained in several ways. As each successive generation was further removed from the woman they were commemorating, they were less likely to have known her or to have been able to consult her about her life. The ten authors who wrote about their mothers had the advantage of knowing their mother, and, furthermore, of being able to remember their parents' farming years, which they had experienced as children. Five of these ten accounts explicitly drew upon the contributors' own memories of the homesteading period. Further removed descendants expressed regret that they had known their grandmother for only a short time (if they had ever met her) and that they also had less access to other older family members who had lived through the pioneer years. June McDonald wrote of her grandmother, Margaret Wagner: "I came to appreciate this plucky woman as the years rolled on but by the time I was mature enough to appreciate her history and strengths she was long gone, very sad for all of us."[38]

None of the biographers had first-hand experience of their ancestor's life prior to immigration. Consequently, only a few authors seemed to have had photographs and other records to draw upon to flesh out their ancestors' everyday realities in Russia, Germany, Ukraine, Poland, or the United States. An organic theme emerged among the biographers of German-identified Russian immigrants. These descendants placed their own family stories into a larger published historical narrative to fill in missing sections of their family histories and to situate their ancestors' lives in a broader world context. For instance, these authors presented variations on a story about an invitation Catherine the Great had issued to attract Germans immigrants to Russia.

Many of the contributors who offered this account seemed to be compensating for the paucity of personal information on an ancestor by choosing to write more broadly about the migration of German-identified men and women to Russian-held territories in the 1800s, upon the promise of religious freedom and economic prosperity.[39] Many of these accounts stated that Germans living in Russia expected peaceful coexistence with Russians, but that these hopes did not materialize in some Russian-based German communities.[40] As the biographers explained, some of the Germans living in Russia moved to Saskatchewan when their autonomy in Russia was being restricted and when policies of Russification were put in place. Karolina Daubert's granddaughter wrote that Karolina and her parents immigrated to Saskatchewan from Russia because Canada was "a nation where people were free from religious persecution, where there was freedom of speech and where families could homestead and make a good life for themselves with hard work and perseverance."[41]

An additional constraint many descendants faced was that their mother or grandmother had not always been willing or able to share a lot of information about the past. Further removed descendants were even more directly hampered by the paucity of information transmitted to and, importantly, remembered by their parents, aunts, and uncles. Few of these early immigrants had written their own personal histories; not all were fully literate in either German or English. Consequently, most of these biographies did not contain the ancestors' own perspectives on their experiences. Three pioneer women, however, had written partial accounts of their lives, which were a rich resource for those commemorating them. Rita Catherine Gadzella's biographer quoted liberally from a forty-one-page account Gadzella had written about her experiences as a teacher's wife; Katharina Epp had kept a journal from 1919 to 1944; and Lydia McCaul crafted a seventy-five-minute presentation of her life story that she presented to a genealogical society, church groups, service clubs, and schools.[42]

In the absence of complete first-hand accounts, family biographers drew on various other sources. In several instances, information about this earlier time had been preserved by efforts from interested family members. Some remained connected to their ancestors through attendance at family reunions and used those gatherings to share family stories. Family reunions held to honour the ancestors were a valued source for several of the contributors. "We [Hegel's family] are all storytellers," Leona Hegel began the biography of her grandmother. She attributed many of the stories she relayed in her account to family reunions.[43] Emma Maria Schepp's descendants began holding reunions in 1973 to honour their immigrant ancestors and preserve their memory.[44] Although Frances Stammen died one year after moving to Saskatchewan, her husband persevered to establish their family's success and to perpetuate her legacy.[45] Their relatives continued to celebrate and honour Stammen despite the fact that none of them ever had the opportunity to know her. In addition to holding a reunion to honour these pioneer ancestors, the granddaughter-in-law who wrote her biography travelled to visit the cemetery where Frances and her husband were buried. Katharina Epp's family created a family register and Elizabeth Schell's, Lydia Salmond's, and Emma Maria Schepp's families made an effort to transmit family lore.[46] Although Schepp's granddaughter had never met her grandparents, she wrote that "memories of their early hardships live on in stories told" and through family photos shared.[47] Euphemia Steinkey's daughter audio-recorded her mother's account of her life over the course of the 1990s and Katherina Wagner's family established contact with descendants in Europe who had survived exile to Siberian labour camps.[48]

As Canadian historians Alexander Freund and Angela Thiessen similarly found in a study of the use of family photographs, to prepare their entries many of these grandchildren and great-grandchildren were liminally positioned as both users and readers of the accessible family documents.[49] As "users," they had knowledge of or heard family lore about the people and moments referenced in the photographs and documents; yet, most biographers had to "read" these documents as outsiders, as many documents were over 100 years old.

Another interesting source of information on pioneer ancestors were documents that had been preserved through the generations. In order to gain insight Katharina Hanrieder's biographer read letters that Hanrieder and her husband had written to relatives back in Germany sharing news of farming successes in the 1920s and crop failures in the 1930s. During the first half of the twentieth century, immigrants relied on written correspondence and German-language newspapers to remain in contact with family members in Russia and Germany.[50] It was through reading one such newspaper that Katerina Gutenberg learned that her brother, who had remained in Russia, had died.[51] Katherina Wagner's granddaughter, June McDonald, read copies of these newspapers to gain a fuller understanding of her ancestors' lives. She wrote:

> Correspondents in the home villages in Russia wrote news to the newspapers reporting births, marriages and deaths, crop yields, weather and anything else of interest. Immigrants in the United States and Canada subscribed to the newspapers and thus found news of the home they had left behind.... They also contributed news of their "new world" for those back home.... The archives of this newspaper are an interesting social history of early settlement and heartbreaking in the extreme when news of a parent who has passed away, for instance, is requested to be passed on to a son or daughter, such as was the case with my own maternal grandfather.[52]

Just as German immigrants read the newspapers to learn of geographically distant family members back at home, so, too, did some descendants read these newspapers to reach back temporally.

Oral historians involved in the Dakota Memories Oral History Project strategized as to which questions to ask to encourage individuals to share nuanced memories and they organized memory prompts such as walks, looking at photo albums, cooking, and music demonstrations.[53] Contributors to *Women Pioneers of Saskatchewan* received no such prompts from Rider, but many nevertheless did memory work on their own. Furthermore, as they were creating written submissions they had the time to undertake research and corroborate with family members. These descendants sifted through old family letters; read the North America-based German newspapers that their grandparents had subscribed to; and consulted ship's logs, censuses, homestead records, books written about the period, old photographs, and presumably other material that they did not mention in the biography. These efforts to preserve family history through the safekeeping of the woman's own account, through intergenerational memory (the passing down of "family lore" or family memories), and through historical and genealogical research allowed the authors the opportunity to access aspects of their female ancestors' lives that they had no personal knowledge of. In some cases these investigations even allowed descendants access to glimpses of female ancestors' feelings, thoughts, and personality.

Many biographers lamented that they did not have information on important life events of their subjects. Consequently, what was remembered or preserved came to the fore in these accounts. Descriptions of these women's characters as well as personalized aspects of the women's lives were absent from many biographies. In some cases, these absences may have been intentional. Many authors, however, stated that they lacked information. Wishing to present thorough biographies, the descendants did not limit themselves to simply sharing family lore. Instead, grandchildren and great-grandchildren speculated about details where they had no concrete information. Some wrote of "imagining" both activities and emotions. They openly speculated about their ancestor's lives with their best guesses as to which year a photograph was taken, what was eaten for breakfast, where their ancestors lived as a newlyweds, or details regarding their family's lineage.

The least grounded speculations concerned ancestors' values, emotions, and feelings. These conjectures functioned as a way of personalizing the biographies and forging an emotional bond between themselves and their grandmother as well as between their grandmother and the reader. For instance, Bev Weston, Katharina Hanrieder's granddaughter, personalized her grandmother's immigration journey by piecing together a story based upon her research, including tracking down ship passenger lists and visiting train cars that were in use during that historical period. Drawing on this groundwork as well as family lore, she speculated about the travel experiences of her grandmother: "I have tried to imagine what it must have been like for Katharina when she stepped off the train. She must have been tired, probably desperately wanting a bath; she had two tired and no doubt cranky children, and a baby not yet one year old."[54] Weston was not the only descendant to attempt to imagine herself in her ancestor's shoes. Bonnie Meier wrote that her grandmother, Margaret Dombrowsky, must have felt terribly isolated on the farm, not only geographically but also because of the language barrier she faced, as many of her neighbours did not speak German.[55] Other cases also contained fictive attempts to breathe life into the story of those who had passed away long ago.

Remembering and Representing German Culture

Rider's collection was framed as a commemoration of pioneer experiences, not as a collection about immigrant lives. Despite this, biographers considered it important to emphasize their ancestors' German immigrant experience. Ancestors' ethnic heritage came to the fore especially since these accounts were constructed as linear biographies. The contributors, therefore, wrote about what they knew about ancestors' lives prior to their immigration. These descendants also found it important to remember and preserve their ancestors' German cultural practices, which they did through their discussion of language, foodways, and religion.

In 1904, the German newspaper *St. Peter's Bote*, published in St. Peter's Colony (forty kilometres out of Regina, Saskatchewan), lamented: "Unfortunately . . . there are many people in our colony who, because of their long stay in the United States, have lost their German heart and spirit, those, who, when they speak with the English try to hide their German nationality."[56] The twenty-three German-identified women who emigrated from Russia, Poland, and Ukraine all spoke German as their first language even though they were born in countries where German was not the mother tongue. According to Katerina Gutenberg's great-great-granddaughter, Katerina's ancestors immigrated to Odessa in the early 1800s and "retained their own language and brought it to the 'new' world when they immigrated here in the early part of the 20th Century."[57] German language in these accounts was remembered in three differing yet overlapping ways: as a means of community, a means of isolation, and a means of assimilation.

Many German-identified individuals homesteaded in German-language communities in Saskatchewan.[58] Ethnic-based settlement patterns, in fact, allowed for the maintenance of culture and language. Consequently, for women such as Russian-born Augusta Welke her rural community was a place where German identity could be maintained through language, religion, and cultural practices.[59] Similarly, Lois Neighbour chose to stress the German language in her accounts of her grandmother, Polish-born Emilie Petrich, and her mother Johanna Walter. Petrich and Walter, according to Neighbour, were so embedded in a German-speaking rural community that the family did not need to become proficient in English until they moved to Saskatoon in 1912.[60]

Other biographers pointed out that while their ancestors' lives were often difficult, the German language was a way of maintaining togetherness. They wrote that rural community members and their relatives gathered together and spoke German, joyously sang in German, and prayed together in German.

Nevertheless, German language was also remembered and represented as a barrier and a means of isolation. Elizabeth Maier's granddaughter wrote that her grandmother "often felt isolated unless she was with people who could speak German."[61] The stories that have been preserved and transmitted in some families stressed the hardships that these women faced because they did not know English. The contributors presented their ancestors' lack of English as a creator of economic and emotional difficulty. The family of the Russian-born Elizabeth Riehl remembered her experiences as such: Riehl immigrated to Canada with her brother in 1926. In order to support herself and raise money to help other family members immigrate, she found herself in the position of looking for work in an English-speaking community. Her biographer highlighted that both the work that she was hired to perform and the language barrier were very hard for her.[62] Similarly, the granddaughter of Ukrainian-born Margaret Dombrowsky, Bonnie Meier, emphasized her ancestor's language struggle and the ways this further compounded her isolation. Meier wrote that her grandmother's homestead was geographically isolated and underscored that the occasional trips away from the farm were generally not opportunities to visit loved ones but rather trips to town to purchase goods in a language she struggled to speak. Meier writes that Margaret Dombrowsky always remained "self conscious [*sic*] about her English," so much so that over twenty years after first immigrating to Canada she formed a close friendship with a Dutch war bride on the basis of their shared struggles with the English language.[63]

Women who were adults when they immigrated to North America or were raised in German-speaking prairie communities had a much harder time learning English than their counterparts who were taught English in school. During the First World War, nationalistic concerns led to the passing of the School Attendance Act in 1917. This act mandated that all children between seven and fourteen were required to attend school. By 1918 this act was amended to forbid the use of languages other than English in the classroom and schoolyard.[64]

The significance of language acquisition is exemplified by Karolina Vogel; she and her family immigrated to Canada in 1908 when she was three years old. Her granddaughter chose to stress that Vogel learned to speak English when she started school at age seven. Her granddaughter, in fact, felt that Vogel's experience of learning English was such an important part of her life that she emphasized that until Vogel left school at age thirteen, she came home at the end of the school day and taught her younger siblings the new English words she had learned.[65] Ninety years after Vogel left school, her family still remembered not only the school's name but also the name of the teacher who taught her English. Not all experiences of learning English were remembered as fondly. Anne Martha Schemenauer was born in 1911 to German parents who had emigrated from Poland in 1906. Her family, like all the other families in the area, exclusively spoke German at home. Schemenauer's granddaughter wrote that upon entering school, her grandmother and her classmates could speak German to each other only in secret, when they were sure that their teacher could not overhear them.[66]

The biographers did not make clear to what extent, if at all, the women's descendants still spoke German. In some cases, language had not been transmitted. Margaret Wagner and her husband spoke and often sang in German while they farmed the Saskatchewan prairies during the 1920s and 1930s, but their grandchildren never learned German. As her granddaughter wrote: "Communication was difficult between Margaret and her grandchildren. Her first language remained German while that of her grandchildren was English."[67] In the face of this anglicization, some of these women were concerned about language maintenance. Anna Maria Hager's daughter wrote: "My mother was most concerned with keeping the German language 'alive' in the home. She pretended that she was unable to speak or understand English. However, one day we discovered she could understand and speak English quite well. She didn't realize any of us kids were in the house."[68] Second-generation German immigrants were much less likely than their parents to use German in their daily lives. Likely, the School Attendance Act, in part, fulfilled its intended purpose of assimilating immigrant children. While these children spoke German at home and often at church, they learned English at school and presumably most of them lived in contexts where they were required to speak English. However, as Frankenberger highlights in

Chapter 7, although many of these descendants did not speak German, they still had strong emotional ties to German culture and identity. In the accounts of the prairie pioneers, connections to German culture came to the fore in the discussion of food. As almost all of the women lived on Saskatchewan farms and worked as farmers' wives, the labour these ancestors put into providing food for their families was stressed across the biographies. Consequently, they helped their husbands farm grain fields, supported the family through selling eggs and dairy products, and laboured to grow and make most of the food the family consumed. The discussion of food in these accounts did not simply detail the domestic labour that was involved in feeding the family. Biographers emphasized that it was specifically German food that was being made and consumed. According to American immigration historians Clark and Isern, "second- and third-generation Germans from Russia are . . . quite dedicated to the preservation of their foodways. As they tell it, German-Russians were people of the plains, and as a result relied on the land for their livelihood."[69] While Clark and Isern specifically focused on Germans who immigrated to Saskatchewan from Russia, the forty biographies in Rider's collection indicated that German-identified immigrants from other countries also fit this pattern.

Food was remembered fondly in these accounts, especially by descendants who had the opportunity to taste the food that the women being commemorated made. Food memories have particular character, as Canadian historian Marlene Epp explains: "The common association of eating and nostalgia reveals 'the symbolic capacity of food to contain the past.'"[70] Foodways are strongly connected to ethnic identity.[71] As such, many of the biographers underlined that their female ancestors made German food such as sauerkraut, dill pickles, pickled whole cabbages, kuchen, and noodle dishes. Casting his mind back over seventy years, Katherine Weber's son Ed related with fondness the dishes his mother made: "She specialized in the preparation of many kinds of noodles with such German names as *kase knepfla, plachenta, dampfnoodle* and many others. Also bread and various kinds of *kuchen* were baked. A soup called *borsch* made of many vegetables, especially beets, became a staple food. At Christmas her special dish was *holuptsi*, a dish baked with a ground meat and rich mixture wrapped in sour cabbage leaves. The family could hardly wait for them."[72] These food memories were important to many contributors. Ed Weber boasted of his mother's bread- and bun-making abilities, the various ways she preserved rhubarb, and her technique for pickling cabbage for cabbage rolls.

Biographers like Ed Weber used their food memories to highlight their mothers' talents. Others used discussions of food to situate their mothers' culinary aptitude as a key element of their success as pioneers. They emphasized that the women's baking, gardening, pickling, and preserving skills were especially important in the 1930s when the Great Depression made money scarce. From 1929 to 1937, Saskatchewan experienced an extreme drought that made it difficult for farm families to grow crops for sale and vegetables to feed themselves.[73] As Margaret Wagner's granddaughter, June McDonald, wrote, potato and noodle dishes featured prominently in Margaret's kitchen as they were "budget stretching" dishes.[74] McDonald additionally submitted a biography for her mother Euphemia "Fanny" Steinkey. For McDonald's relatives, family foodways were so inextricably linked to family heritage that cooking constituted a link to the past and a way of keeping the memory of ancestors alive. She commemorated her mother by stating: "A lasting legacy to her children and grandchildren was the importance of family as well as the preparing and sharing of good food, we are all soup makers."[75] As Canadian historian Royden Loewen has argued, "foodways not only secured a link with the past, they ensured the survival of key words even after Old World languages fell into disuse."[76]

Moreover, contributors wove these women's religious beliefs throughout the biographies. Almost three quarters of the accounts mentioned their ancestor's faith.[77] Twelve of the women were Catholic, one United Church, one Presbyterian, one Apostolic, three Lutheran, and one may have been Mennonite. Ten other accounts mentioned that their ancestors were Christian, but made no mention of their specific denomination. The migration history of many of these Germans to Saskatchewan, in fact, was tied to religious concerns. The Germans who immigrated to Russia had responded to a promise of religious self-determination, land, the right to self-government, and exemption from military service.[78] The German colonies in Russia were culturally cohesive and organized by religion.[79] German immigrants attempted to maintain the same religious cohesiveness when establishing homesteads in Canada.[80] According to the Canadian Germanist Edmund Heier, "the decisive element in establishing a homestead in a farm district was again provided by religious denomination, as in Russia. In this manner many farm districts or settlements were founded by people of the same faith but who had come from different countries."[81] Many of the female ancestors homesteaded in districts where they shared religion with their neighbours. Only two found themselves having to switch denominations, as they were the only Baptist families in their respective communities.

Consequently, it is unsurprising that many of the biographers remembered religion as a source of community. Similarly to Clark and Isern's findings, church services and functions were remembered by contributors to *Women Pioneers of Saskatchewan* as allowing German immigrant farm families the opportunity to practise their faith, socialize with their neighbours, and "maintain ethnic values."[82] Family members chose to stress that many of their pioneer ancestors were actively involved in promoting their religious communities by helping to establish local churches, singing in the choir, participating in religious activities and organizations, and working to transmit their faith to their children. These accounts presented religion as central to these women's identities and daily lives and therefore as something they strove to pass on to their descendants. According to June McDonald, the Saskatchewan district where her ancestors lived was predominantly Catholic. The family of her grandmother, Elisabeta Steinkey, and other local families named their children after Catholic saints and celebrated their name day (the corresponding saint's feast day) rather than birthdays.[83]

Such transmission of religious beliefs was also represented as a connection across generations. As Myrla Birch, Lydia Salmond's great-great-granddaughter, wrote: "Grandma also had a strong religious faith and was committed to having their own Church and cemetery in the community. Her children and grandchildren were instilled with a spiritual faith that would carry them for generations along life's journeys—good and bad."[84] While not all religious values were successfully passed on, these standards were also remembered as something that children had to negotiate. While Bertha Klause's children were involved in the church, part of the family lore recounted to Klause's granddaughter was how they had to hide their "sinful" billiard and card playing from their parents.[85] Regardless of how successfully these women transmitted Christianity to their children, the focus on religion in these accounts shows that the biographers believed religion to be central in the lives of their ancestors.

Freund and Quilici write that immigration stories told by successful American immigrants often reinforce the myth that America was a land of opportunity, omitting the hardships that immigrants faced upon arriving in a new country.[86] The biographers in Rider's collection similarly represented their ancestors' immigration to Canada as affording them prosperity and opportunity. Yet their "successful" immigration stories were complicated by the fact that they were tasked by Rider to write accounts of pioneer life. During the early years of homesteading, many farmers found themselves isolated, living in primitive conditions, and working hard to build a home, break their farmland, and produce enough food to support their families.[87] Farming success also varied from year to year based on weather conditions, blights and pests, the price of grain, and the quality of their homestead soil.[88] The authors acknowledged these difficulties and framed their ancestors' strong religious beliefs as being of invaluable assistance for them to overcome the difficult times they encountered as pioneers. Katherine "Katie" Vanderlinde's biographer wrote: "The Catholic Church remained an important part of Katie's life; it was both a place of refuge and a place to give thanks. The colony had been founded in faith and the pioneers needed that faith to cope with the hardships and disappointments as they occurred."[89]

Biographers such as Bertha Klause's granddaughter, Eunice Romanowick, characterized religion as a source of resilience in the face of hardships. Romanowick wrote that Bertha and her husband found it difficult to support themselves as homesteaders. Consequently, every winter her husband walked 200 miles to Estevan to work in a coal mine while Bertha stayed behind to care for their growing family. She and her thirteen-year-old son had to walk eighteen miles to town to trade eggs and butter for other necessities in order to survive the harsh winters. Faith and determination were themes Bertha's biographer underscored in this account. Her granddaughter wrote: "Their [Bertha and her children's] existence would depend on her tenacity to persist, relying on her firm belief that her God would guide their destiny."[90] A decade later, Bertha's husband was blinded in a farm accident. From that point on Bertha and her sons ran the farm and she continued to operate it through her sixties during the Great Depression. According to Romanowick, "Our grandmother persisted, undaunted by the wraths of nature, the relentless wind and dust, again relying on her Christian belief that 'we shall overcome.'"[91]

Bertha Klause was not the only woman whose biography included stories of unforeseen hardships and heartbreak; others' family members were severely injured, died from illness or in freak accidents, and even experienced fires ravaging their farms. The contributors stressed their ancestors' faith and cast their religion as something that allowed them to surmount difficulty. The women's biographers stated variously that her faith "sustained her and gave her peace,"[92] "kept [her] going,"[93] and that the church "was a place of refuge."[94] Sister Christina Schell, the only nun out of the forty women, was even more so memorialized in this way: "Overcoming extreme adversity, Sister Christina Schell credited God with saving and enriching her life as a refugee, immigrant and Sister of Charity of the Immaculate Conception."[95]

The Germans who immigrated to Saskatchewan identified with the dominant religious practice of the region—Christianity.[96] Practising a faith that was valued by all levels of government and directly observed within both the Catholic and public school systems meant these women and their families could practise their faith without discrimination.[97] Presumably their biographers felt they could write about this element of their ancestors' culture comfortably as it fit within the larger Saskatchewan immigrant narrative.

World Wars: Loss and Silences

Sacrifice and loss are woven throughout these immigration stories. Biographers expressed that while their ancestors immigrated with the hopes of a prosperous future, they grieved the sacrifice of leaving family behind. Intergenerational memories of the world wars were shaped around this mourning. The authors emphasized that these women were already saddened by the separation and the knowledge that they might never again see the family members they had left behind. Their only methods of contact were through German newspapers and letters.

Katharina Hanrieder's biography exemplified this story of loss. Hanrieder emigrated from Germany in 1913. Her granddaughter, Bev Weston, recounted an intergenerational memory of Hanrieder's sorrow over leaving her family behind. Weston's mother's memory of seeing Hanrieder cry in 1933 upon receiving a letter with a family photograph was a memory that stayed with her for seventy-five years. Weston wrote that even this bittersweet communication through letters and photographs eventually came to an end. Hanrieder could not stay in touch with her family in Germany during the Second World War because, according to Weston, communication with enemy countries was cut off. When Hanrieder resumed communication with her family after the war, she learned that some of her relatives had died. She then visited her remaining family in Germany, but sadly her sister passed away before she finalized her travel plans.[98] Memories of loss and sadness during the war years were not unique to Katharina Hanrieder. Hedwig Marienfeld's biographer wrote that she lost her father, mother, and sister between 1937 and the end of the 1940s.[99] Her father died in an accident just prior to the war and according to her granddaughter, "[Hedwig's] mother was found dead on the roadside in the Russian zone by some neighbours. The family had wanted her to flee with them but she said 'they won't harm an old lady.' [Additionally] Hedwig never heard again from her sister. No one knows what happened to her.... During their trials and hardships just trying to survive in this harsh new land Hedwig also had to deal with never seeing her family again."[100] Adelgunda Miller, born in Russia but residing in Germany during the 1910s, experienced a similar tragedy. In the opinion of the author of her account, she was lucky to be in Germany during the Russian Revolution as seven of her siblings in Russia starved to death.[101]

While these biographers were motivated to provide complete narratives of their female ancestor's life, discussing the German immigrant experience of the war years was particularly complicated as Rider's project sought to commemorate the Canadian pioneer experience. None of the accounts included memories of how these individuals were treated as Germans in the prairies during the wars. As Alexander Freund writes in Chapter 1, general hostility toward German Canadians mounted during this period. The Wartime Elections Act of 1917 disenfranchised Canadians who were born on enemy soil after 1902. Furthermore, according to German-Canadian historian Rudolf Helling, "private individuals and groups of people menaced the well-being of persons of German background and ancestry."[102] German-Canadian women's experiences during the war years constituted a noticeable gap in these collective biographies. In fact, twenty-nine of the accounts failed to mention either war, let alone the impact it had on their ancestors. This absence seems to have been a choice on the part of the biographers. Many of the contributors who were writing about their own mothers would have had some memories of the Second World War and could have written about their own memories. Furthermore, grandchildren and great-grandchildren could have consulted other living family members who remembered the wars. However, German Canadians found themselves outside of the national master narrative regarding Canada's righteousness of participating in the Second World War.[103] Consequently, German Canadians "searched for ways to integrate painful memories into their lives. As we know from memory research, memories are not fixed but rather continually challenged by and adapted to changing social situations."[104] As Freund demonstrates, these women's silences about the world wars were characteristic of the larger German-Canadian silence regarding this time.[105]

Not only did these biographies mourn the loss of relatives who died during the world wars, but they further mourned the loss of family history. It seems that many of the female pioneers were also reluctant to discuss their experiences in their homelands. Elizabeth Riehl's account was the only one to mention that she and her husband enjoyed relating stories of the "old country" during interwar years, although interestingly none of these stories were included in the biography.[106] The author of Katherina Wagner's piece explicitly discussed Wagner's reluctance to share memories about the past. June McDonald wrote: "After a century of fleeing revolutions, it is no wonder this family lived quietly in Canada, not talking much of the 'Old Country.' They just wanted to integrate and not be noticed. Sadly, for descendants, that means much of our family history has been lost."[107]

These biographies were shaped into pioneer stories celebrating the hard work of ancestors and their contribution to Saskatchewan's history. Absent from these stories were accounts of the discrimination that Germans faced during these years. The only references to this are oblique, in that these ancestors could not speak German at school or in the schoolyard.[108] Either those years and the difficulties faced did not translate into family lore to be preserved and remembered, or the authors chose to omit them while writing a biography that was intended to celebrate Saskatchewan's "pioneer" status. It is possible that the nature of Rider's project did not lend itself to voicing and preserving these difficult memories. Memories that were critical of other pioneers would have seemed out of place in a commemorative collection such as this one.

Conclusion

Rider's goal was to preserve the memory of women pioneers in Saskatchewan. Whether intended or not, her commemorative project also created the opportunity for individuals to undertake memory projects suited to their own interests and goals. As "memory makers" these biographers were positioned to promote their own interpretations of the past as well as the present and the future. The authors could not only craft and publicly share celebratory accounts of their ancestors, but also, through linking these pioneer women's successes to their own lives, they could attempt to ensure the creation of future memories of themselves and their family line as successful. While Freund aptly argues that "memories are not fixed," this commemorative project was an attempt to create a lasting version of these women's and their family members' lives.[109]

Rider did not actively solicit stories of pioneers' ethnicity, but elements of the women's German experience were actively preserved through intergenerational memories and were included in these biographies. Language, foodways, and religion were all specifically linked to their German ethnic identity. However, these aspects of German identity were remembered and represented in these accounts in complicated and, in some cases, conflicting ways, as means of community and isolation, as well as of assimilation and of lasting traditions still practised today. Much of the academic research using oral histories examines German immigrant experience of second- and third-generation Russian-German immigrants or German immigrants more broadly. What is unique and interesting about Rider's collection is that the biographers themselves chose to include a discussion of German culture and German identity. Furthermore, what elements of German culture these authors chose to include, how they remembered them, and how they chose to frame these memories is important because the contributors made these decisions without guidance or prompting.

Women Pioneers of Saskatchewan allowed descendants the opportunity to publicly memorialize their ancestors. Unlike with oral histories, these biographer-descendants could thoughtfully, and perhaps even strategically, gather material and shape the accounts to fit Rider's call for worthy "pioneers" as well as their own determinations as to what was appropriate to include. Moreover, they could share drafts among family members and revise until they were satisfied. Consequently, these contributions became highly constructed accounts of German "pioneer" women. In order to better understand how descendants assemble commemorative accounts such as these, future research should be directed to understand how family biographers strategically structure public memory projects of which they are a part. Further research into other commemorative projects would allow for a rich understanding of the ways commemorative accounts are shaped.

Notes

1 The author would like to thank both June Corman and Alexander Freund for their thoughtful commentary.

2 The reasons these women immigrated to Canada fit larger immigration patterns of German-identified people to North America and more specifically Saskatchewan. See Jessica Clark and Thomas Isern, "Germans from Russia in Saskatchewan: An Oral History," *American Review of Canadian Studies* 40, no. 1 (2010): 71–85; and Ute Schmidt, *Bessarabia: German Colonists on the Black Sea*, trans. J. Gessele (Fargo, ND: Germans from Russia Heritage Collection, 2011).

3 For examples of collections of pioneer biographies, see Eileen Comstock, *Sunny Side Up: Fond Memories of Prairie Life in the 1930s* (Markham, ON: Fifth House Publishers, 2001); Deana Driver, ed., *Egg Money: A Tribute to Saskatchewan Pioneer Women* (Regina, SK: DriverWorks Ink, 2012); Mennonite Historical Society of Saskatchewan, "Saskatchewan Valley Pioneers," 28 May 2014, https://mhss.sk.ca/pioneers/index.shtml (accessed 18 May 2019). For examples of collections of rural teacher biographies, see John Charyk, *Syrup Pails and Gopher Tails: Memories of the One-Room School* (Saskatoon, SK: Western Producer Prairie Books, 1983); Elizabeth McLachlan, *With Unshakeable Persistence: Rural Teachers of the Depression Era* (Edmonton, AB: NeWest Press, 1999); and Elizabeth McLachlan, *With Unfailing Dedication: Rural Teachers in the War Years* (Edmonton, AB: NeWest Press, 2001).

4 Lynda Haverstock, "Foreword," in Driver, *Egg Money*, 8.

5 Jessica Clark, "'Work Makes Life Sweet': Germans from Russia Remember Their Childhood," *The Historian* 72, no. 4 (2010): 809–30.

6 Clark and Isern, "Germans from Russia in Saskatchewan."

7 Clark, "'Work Makes Life Sweet'"; and Jessica Clark, "More than a Photo: Germans from Russia Remember Their Familial Relationships," *Journal of Family History* 36, no. 3 (2011): 333–49.

8 Clark and Isern, "Germans from Russia in Saskatchewan."

9 Maris Thompson, "'It Always Kinda' Frightened Them That They'd Be Sent Back': German American Origin Stories from Southwestern Illinois," *Oral History Forum d'histoire orale* 32 (2012): 1–21.

10 Alexander Freund, "Troubling Memories in Nation-building: World War II Memories and Germans' Inter-ethnic Encounters in Canada after 1945," *Histoire sociale/ Social History* 39, no. 77 (2006): 129–55; and Alexander Freund, "German Immigrants and the Nazi Past: How Memory Has Shaped Intercultural Relations," *Inroads: A Journal of Public Opinion* 15 (Summer/Fall 2004): 106–17.

11 Joan Tumblety, "Introduction: working with memory as source and subject," in *Memory and History: Understanding Memory as Source and Subject*, ed. Joan Tumblety (New York: Routledge, 2013), 1–16.

12 Clark, "'Work Makes Life Sweet.'"

13 Jeffery Olick defines collected memory as "the aggregated individual memories of members of a group." Jeffrey K. Olick, "Collective Memory: The Two Cultures," *Sociological Theory* 17, no. 3 (1999): 338.

14 Celeste Rider, "Introduction," in *Women Pioneers of Saskatchewan*, ed. Celeste Rider (Regina: Saskatchewan Genealogical Society, 2009), v.

15 Ibid.; and Prairie History Blog, "Women Pioneers of Saskatchewan Book Project," 17 June 2008 http://www.reginalibrary.ca/blogs/index.php?blog=7&m=2008 (accessed 10 February 2017).

16 Joan Miller, "Women Pioneers of Saskatchewan Book 2," *Luxegen Genealogy and Family History*, 9 December 2009, http://www.luxegen.ca/canada/women-pioneers-of-saskatchewan-book-2/ (accessed 15 February 2017).

17 Rider, "Introduction," v; Prairie History Blog, "Women Pioneers of Saskatchewan Book Project;" and Joan Miller, "Women Pioneers of Saskatchewan," *Luxegen Genealogy and Family History*, 19 November 2008 http://www.luxegen.ca/genealogy/women-pioneers-of-saskatchewan/ (accessed 17 February 2017).

18 Prairie History Blog, "Women Pioneers of Saskatchewan Book Project."

19 Denise Daubert, "Daubert, Karolina (née Vogel)," in Rider, *Women Pioneers of Saskatchewan*, 101.

20 Myrla Birch, "Salmond, Lydia (née Hennegar)," in Rider, *Women Pioneers of Saskatchewan*, 425.

21 Beverley Gutenberg, "Schell, Elizabeth (née Rieger) (Meier, Brotzel)," in Rider, *Women Pioneers of Saskatchewan*, 433.

22 Ibid., 434.

23 Alethea McLean, "McCaul, Lydia (née Meier) (Miller)," in Rider, *Women Pioneers of Saskatchewan*, 303.

24 Bonnie Meier, "Dombrowsky, Margaret (née Rempel)," in Rider, *Women Pioneers of Saskatchewan*, 110.

25 Shirley Bridget Gadzella, "Gadzella, Rita Catherine (née Novakowski)," in Rider, *Women Pioneers of Saskatchewan*, 161.

26 Michael Frisch, *A Shared Authority: Essays on Craft and Meaning of Oral and Public History* (Albany: State University of New York Press, 1990), 188.

27 Eunice Romanowick, "Klause, Bertha (née Schultz)," in Rider, *Women Pioneers of Saskatchewan*, 247.

28 Audrey Wilson, "Schobert, Augusta Wilhelmine (née Loeffler)," in Rider, *Women Pioneers of Saskatchewan*, 441.

29 Birch, "Salmond," 427.

30 June McDonald, "Wagner, Margaret (née Wagner)," in Rider, *Women Pioneers of Saskatchewan*, 506.

31 Rider did not ask biographers to provide information about themselves. All contributors provided their name, including in some cases their maiden name, and relation to the woman being profiled. Some authors chose to include information about themselves within the biographies.

32 One biography was written by multiple descendants; unfortunately, they did not clarify their relation to their ancestor. There are a total of thirty-nine different contributors to the thirty-nine biographies written by family members; some accounts were co-authored and four contributors wrote multiple biographies. The Catholic nun Sister Christina Schell was the only individual to have her account written by someone outside of her family. No information was provided about the Catholic nuns who wrote her biography. Her account is not included in the discussion of biographers.

33 Donald F. Smith and Carol Stevenson-Seller, "Busse, Sadie (née Rickbeil)," in Rider, *Women Pioneers of Saskatchewan*, 64–65.

34 Leona Hegel, "Werle, Bertha Sophie Henriette (née Sott) (Fieseler)," in Rider, *Women Pioneers of Saskatchewan*, 526.

35 Janis Wilton, "Imaging Family Memories: My Mum, Her Photographs, Our Memories," in *Oral History and Photography*, eds. Alexander Freund and Alistair Thomson (New York: Palgrave Macmillan, 2012), 61–76.

36 Schmalz did not extrapolate as to what these cherished family heirlooms were. Rose Schmalz, "Schmalz, Anna Maria Adelia (née Berger)," in Rider, *Women Pioneers of Saskatchewan*, 439.

37 Shirley Baker, "Vanderlinde, Katherine (née Boll)," in Rider, *Women Pioneers of Saskatchewan*, 500.

38 McDonald, "Wagner, Margaret," 506.

39 Rider did not request that biographers provide sources for their accounts. Most did not state whether the information they included was gleaned from family members or history books.

40 These accounts are corroborated by texts on the German experience in Russia. See Schmidt, *Bessarabia*.

41 Daubert, "Daubert," 101.

42 Gadzella, "Gadzella," 160–61; Marie Spencer, "Epp, Katharina (née Jantzen)," in Rider, *Women Pioneers of Saskatchewan*, 133–35; and McLean, "McCaul," 303–5.

43 Hegel, "Werle," 524.

44 Shirley Erskine, "Schepp, Emma Maria (nee Schultz)," in Rider, *Women Pioneers of Saskatchewan*, 437–38.

45 Shirley Baker, "Stammen, Frances (née Heine)," in Rider, *Women Pioneers of Saskatchewan*, 471–72.

46 Spencer does not explain what the family register consisted of. Family registers typically consist of information regarding births and deaths of family members. Spencer, "Epp," 133–35; Gutenberg, "Schell," 433–34; Birch, "Salmond," 425–27; and Erskine, "Schepp," 437–38.

47 Erskine, "Schepp," 438.

48 June McDonald, "Steinkey, Euphemia (née Wagner)," in Rider, *Women Pioneers of Saskatchewan*, 475–77; and June McDonald, "Wagner, Katherina (née Kowis) (Bengert)," in Rider, *Women Pioneers of Saskatchewan*, 502–3.

49 Alexander Freund and Angela Thiessen, "Mary Brockmeyer's Wedding Picture: Exploring the Intersection of Photographs and Oral History Interviews," in Freund and Thomson, *Oral History and Photography*, 27–44.

50 Karl Peter and Franziska Peter, "The Kurtenbach Letters: An Autobiographical Description of Pioneer Life in Saskatchewan Around the Turn of the Century," *Canadian Ethnic Studies* 11, no. 2 (1979): 89–96; and Schmidt, *Bessarabia*.

51 Beverley Gutenberg, "Gutenberg, Katerina (née Schweitzer)," in Rider, *Women Pioneers of Saskatchewan*, 184–85.

52 McDonald, "Wagner, Katherina," 503.

53 Clark, "'Work Makes Life Sweet.'"

54 Bev Weston, "Hanrieder, Katharina (née Dirscherl) (Roth)," in Rider, *Women Pioneers of Saskatchewan*, 191.

55 Meier, "Dombrowsky," 110–11.

56 Quoted in Clinton White, "Education Among German Catholic Settlers in Saskatchewan, 1903–1918: A Reinterpretation," *Canadian Ethnic Studies* 16, no. 1 (1984): 90.

57 Gutenberg, "Gutenberg," 184.

58 Bill Waiser, *Saskatchewan: A New History* (Calgary: Fifth House, 2005).

59 Laura Higgs, "Welke, Augusta (née Paul) (Schindel)," in Rider, *Women Pioneers of Saskatchewan*, 523–24.

60 Lois Neighbour, "Petrich, Emilie (née Stephan)," in Rider, *Women Pioneers of Saskatchewan*, 380–82; and Lois Neighbour, "Walter, Johanna (née Petrich)," in Rider, *Women Pioneers of Saskatchewan*, 510–11.

61 Lori Milligan, "Maier, Elizabeth (née Selinger)," in Rider, *Women Pioneers of Saskatchewan*, 293.

62 Kasper Riehl, Marie Pighin, Joseph Riehl, John Riehl, David Riehl, Liz Polard, and Carol Leavitt, "Riehl, Elizabeth (née Moldenhauer)," in Rider, *Women Pioneers of Saskatchewan*, 421–23.

63 Meier, "Dombrowsky," 111.

64 Waiser, *Saskatchewan*.

65 Daubert, "Daubert," 101–2.

66 Carrie Ann Schemenauer, "Schemenauer, Anne Martha (née Klashinsky)," in Rider, *Women Pioneers of Saskatchewan*, 435–37.

67 McDonald, "Wagner, Margaret," 506.

68 Theresia Hager, "Hager, Anna Maria (née Hirsch)," in Rider, *Women Pioneers of Saskatchewan*, 186.

69 Clark and Isern, "Germans from Russia in Saskatchewan," 77.

70 Marlene Epp, "'The Dumpling in My Soup Was Lonely Just Like Me': Food in the Memories of Mennonite Women Refugees," *Women's History Review* 25, no. 3 (2016): 369.

71 Jon Holtzman, "Food and Memory," *Annual Review of Anthropology* 35 (2006): 361–78; and Monica Janowski, "Introduction: Consuming Memories of Home in Constructing the Present and Imagining the Future," *Food and Foodways* 20, no. 3–4 (2012): 175–86.

72 Ed Weber, "Weber, Katherine (née Degenstein)," in Rider, *Women Pioneers of Saskatchewan*, 517.

73 Elizabeth Mooney, "Great Depression," Canadian Plains Research Center, University of Regina, 2006, https://esask.uregina.ca/entry/great_depression.jsp (accessed 10 February 2017); and Iain Stewart, "Drought," Canadian Plains Research Center, University of Regina, 2006, https://esask.uregina.ca/entry/drought.jsp (accessed 10 February 2017).

74 McDonald, "Wagner, Margaret," 505.

75 McDonald, "Steinkey, Euphemia," 477.

76 Royden Loewen, *Ethnic Farm Culture in Western Canada* (Ottawa: Canadian Historical Association, 2002), 23.

77 This is not to say that the rest of the women were not religious; some of the authors had little information on their ancestors' lives and others may have chosen not to include it.

78 Schmidt, *Bessarabia.*

79 Bradley Baltensperger, "Agricultural Change among Great Plains Russian Germans," *Annals of the Association of American Geographers* 73, no. 1 (1983): 78.

80 Rudolf Helling et al., *A Socio-Economic History of German-Canadians: They, Too, Founded Canada: A Research Report* (Wiesbaden: F. Steiner, 1984).

81 Edmund Heier, "The Immigration of the Russo-German Catholics and Lutherans Into Canada," *Canadian Slavonic Papers* 4, no. 1 (1959): 165.

82 Clark and Isern, "Germans from Russia in Saskatchewan," 78.

83 June McDonald, "Steinkey, Elisabeta (née Kuntz)," in Rider, *Women Pioneers of Saskatchewan*, 473–75.

84 Birch, "Salmond," 426.

85 Romanowick, "Klause," 246–47.

86 Alexander Freund and Laura Quilici, "Exploring Myths in Women's Narratives: Italian and German Immigrant Women in Vancouver, 1947–1961," *Oral History Review* 23, no. 2 (Winter 1996): 19–43.

87 Waiser, *Saskatchewan.*

88 Ibid.

89 Baker, "Vanderlinde," 500.

90 Romanowick, "Klause," 246.

91 Ibid., 247.

92 McDonald, "Steinkey, Euphemia," 477.

93 Birch, "Salmond," 427

94 Baker, "Vanderlinde," 500

95 Sisters of Charity, "Schell, Sister Christina," in Rider, *Women Pioneers of Saskatchewan*, 432.

96 For a summary of the relationship between religion and homestead patterns on the prairies, see A. Becker, "The Germans in Western Canada: A Vanishing People," *CCHA Study Sessions* 42 (1975): 29–49.

97 Waiser, *Saskatchewan.*

98 Weston, "Hanrieder," 190–92.

99 MaryAnne Suek, "Marienfeld, Hedwig (née Packmohr)," in Rider, *Women Pioneers of Saskatchewan*, 297–98

100 Ibid., 298.

101 Leona French, "Miller, Adelgunda (née Jobs)," in Rider, *Women Pioneers of Saskatchewan*, 326.

102 Helling et. al., *A Socio-Economic History of German-Canadians*, 50.

103 Alexander Freund, "Multicultural Memories? Germans in Canada Since the Second World War," Immigration, Minorities and Multiculturalism in Democracies Conference (Conference paper, Queen's University, Montreal, 25–27 October 2007).

104 Ibid., 3.

105 Ibid.

106 Riehl et al., "Riehl," 421–23.

107 McDonald, "Wagner, Katherina," 503; for more discussion of German-Canadian pioneers' silences about experiences during the First World War, see Alexander Freund, Chapter 1 in this collection.

108 Presumably, German-speaking immigrants would have experienced less discrimination if they were embedded in German-speaking communities; however, the school language ban would still be in place in these communities and they likely would have encountered negative representations of Germans in the media. See Freund, "German Immigrants and the Nazi Past," 106–17.

109 Freund, "Multicultural Memories?" 3.

AFTERWORD

What Does It Mean to be "German Canadian"? The Challenge of History and the Obligation of Memory[1]

ROGER FRIE

In the cultural mosaic of contemporary Canada, German Canadians garner little attention. This was not always the case, and what it means to be "German Canadian" has changed over time. In the decades after the Second World War, a large wave of German immigrants arrived in Canada seeking refuge from economic and political hardships wrought by the long years of conflict. But Germany's defining role as "the enemy" in two world wars, and its perpetration of the Holocaust, meant that being German carried a stigma. Many German immigrants sought to "blend in" within their new cultural surroundings as quickly as possible, and this resulted in a rapid process of assimilation. In the years that followed, the shifting global politics of the postwar world meant that Germany went from being "the enemy" to becoming an essential European partner. Once the "economic miracle" in West Germany took hold, immigration to Canada lessened, as did the stigma of being identified as German. By the end of the twentieth century, the term "German Canadian" had been transformed from a label—conferred on a minority group by the majority—to a means of self-identification. Identifying as German Canadian has allowed recent immigrants and the descendants of former immigrants to acknowledge their family's heritage, language, and nationality.

How we understand the term "German Canadian" is therefore related to the historical period in which immigration occurred. Its meaning also depends upon who is using the term. Is it the actual German immigrant, or the child, grandchild, or great-grandchild of immigrants who identifies as German Canadian? In the same sense, the notion of being "German" has undergone a significant change. In contrast to West Germany of the 1950s and 1960s, contemporary Germany is an increasingly multi-ethnic nation that has learned through trial and error to confront the darkest chapter of its collective history. There is no simple definition of what it means to be culturally German today, just as there is no single way of identifying as German Canadian. There are, at best, cultural communalities, norms, and outlooks linked to language and tradition and sustained through the transmission of history and memory from one immigrant generation to the next.[2]

Given the importance of history and memory for maintaining our cultural identities, it is important to consider how German Canadians relate to their own German past. Modern German history is indelibly linked to the period of National Socialism and the genocide of Jewish communities throughout Europe. To what extent has this history been remembered and acknowledged by German immigrants and their descendants in Canada? The question I am posing is not merely academic. The theme of historical responsibility is at the heart of what it means to be Canadian. In present-day Canada there is a concerted effort to remember and address the country's subjugation of the First Nations over several centuries. In 2015 the Truth and Reconciliation Commission issued its final report that referred to Canada's gross mistreatment of the First Nations as a "cultural genocide." While the atrocities committed by Germans under National Socialism and the cultural genocide carried out through the policies of the Canadian government are fundamentally different in scope and context, they both obligate us to remember and acknowledge the crimes that took place. Seen from this perspective, German Canadians carry a set of cultural identities associated with multiple histories of perpetration.

The moral obligations of memory can seem distant from the concerns of everyday life. Yet, despite the passage of time, historical injustices have implications for the descendants of victims and perpetrators alike. Their effects linger on. The ethical demand to know and remember historical injustice has come to play a central role in educating Canadians.

In a similar sense, seven decades after the Second World War, the moral obligations of remembering the Holocaust remain a central aspect of the German nation's identity and a key aspect of the German federal education system. How does this responsibility relate to German Canadians today? Has the obligation to remember Germany's crimes crossed the distance of place and time? Or did German immigrants arriving in Canada effectively relinquish their obligation? And what about the descendants of postwar German immigrants? What has been remembered and, more crucially, what has been forgotten in the course of constructing and maintaining a German-Canadian identity?

Drawing from my German family history and using autobiographical illustrations of what it was like growing up as the son of German postwar immigrants to Canada, I consider how German Canadians responded to the dark history of the Third Reich. I begin by describing what it meant for me to have a German identity as a child in Canada during the late 1960s and 1970s. I suggest that the way in which German families assimilated into Canadian society created a context wherein it became possible to forget the Nazi past and the Holocaust. But the process of dissociation and denial in many postwar German-Canadian families had an effect on the self-understanding of these families' children and grandchildren, making it harder for them to confront the past and often resulting in feelings of confusion and shame related to their family heritage. I end by considering the possibilities for a German-Canadian cultural identity that is grounded in engagement with history and the obligation to remember.

Identifying as German Canadian

My childhood was immersed in German-immigrant communities whose members emigrated during the 1950s and 1960s and hailed chiefly from West Germany. My early years were spent in the regions of Toronto and Kitchener, known for their high concentration of German immigrants. My parents were born in the city of Hanover in 1935 and experienced the emotional challenges and physical destruction of the war as children. They met in the mid-1950s at a time when Hanover was recovering from the heavy bomb damage it had sustained in the Allied bombing raids. Much of the city still lay in ruins as my parents made their plan to leave for Canada. Both of them left family behind, and most of my relatives continue to live in Hanover to this day.

When my parents arrived in Canada in 1958, the German community provided a base of support that helped them begin the long process of acculturation. My childhood memories are of a German-speaking home filled with members of the community who, like us, were immigrants from Northern Germany. These memories are associated with a sense of belonging and identity, bound up in my mother tongue. German was the preferred means of communication at home, and I spoke German before I spoke English. Like many immigrant children, the narration of my life is a story of two languages and different cultural identities. By the time I entered school, I was able to speak English without an accent, but I struggled with the language and was sensitive to being culturally different. The school environment in which I found myself emphasized cultural assimilation and discouraged bilingualism. At times I felt "German" and at other times I felt "Canadian." But on the whole, it seemed to me that I existed somewhere in the hyphenated space between German and Canadian, waiting to be called out through the use of one language or the other.

Being culturally German in English-speaking Canada of the 1960s and 1970s also meant being part of the Caucasian majority. Canada was a less diverse country than it is today and racial prejudice was more pronounced. But as a child of German postwar immigrants, I was sensitive to other dynamics. It is hard for me to know exactly when or how this sensitivity began, but I remember learning at a young age that there was a stigma attached to being German. My family moved to Vancouver when I was six years old, and growing up there meant that most of my friends were the children or grandchildren of British and Canadian soldiers who had fought the Germans in the Second World War. After school, play in the neighbourhood often consisted of re-enacting the stories or scenes of movies and television shows that portrayed the Allied defeat of Germany. Inevitably, I ended up playing the role of the bad German. My family's cultural background meant that any protestations I had fell on deaf ears. I couldn't escape the historical reality of my past. I didn't want to play the bad German, but I had little choice in the matter. Ethnic taunts were often directed at me.

The experience of being different in my everyday interactions with friends and schoolmates was especially pronounced during Canada's annual Remembrance Day celebration. The bravery of Canadian soldiers was recounted and moving stories of their war against the

Germans were shared. These narratives were engrossing. Yet, at some point, I would become aware that the enemy being described was a German soldier, someone who could easily have been my grandfather or one of my great-uncles. Both my grandfathers and all of my great-uncles were drafted into the German military. My paternal grandfather was a soldier in the Wehrmacht and died in battle on the Russian front soon after Germany invaded the Soviet Union. My maternal grandfather survived the war. He worked first as a civilian in the production of military aircraft and late in the war became a member of the Luftwaffe, involved in the design of the V-2 rocket.

I learned of my grandfathers' histories early on and as a Canadian child I was always conscious of belonging to a culture that was associated with the "Nazis." In moments like our school's annual Remembrance Day celebrations, I fell into a shameful and fearful silence, lest my cultural heritage become obvious to those around me. I wanted to share the pride that other schoolchildren felt in the courage of their grandfathers. It made me realize how much I hoped for a German relative that I could feel good about, someone who stood up against the Nazis. Instead, I learned to hide my background. What did it mean that my grandfathers and great-uncles fought on the side of the Nazis?

The wish for a "good past" and for "good relatives" is part of a collective longing shared by many Germans and their descendants who experience guilt and shame for the actions of the German generation that perpetrated the Holocaust and fought a war of naked aggression throughout Europe. However, many first-generation Germans felt neither guilt nor shame about their support for the Nazis. The interconnection of family means that the younger generations are left to make sense of their parents' or grandparents' actions. The desire for family members to have been "good Germans" can lead to the creation of unfocused and idealized images of relatives. Family narratives that bear little relation to actual facts are constructed and sustained in the hope of warding off the Nazi past. This process appears to have been especially true for postwar German immigrants who were confronted with the history of the Nazi past in a way that Germans living in Germany in the decades directly after the war were typically not.

My sense of what being German meant in the Canada of my childhood was gleaned from my interactions with others. But my true sense of discomfort was communicated to me at home. It was my parents who first told me about the horrors perpetrated by the Germans during the Holocaust. I no longer remember the details of what they said or whether I asked any questions in response. Indeed, what I recall today is the sombre look on their faces, their hushed tone, and the overwhelming sense of foreboding I felt. For many years thereafter, the Holocaust remained for me an amorphous event, marked by a gruesome factual history and beyond articulation. It was a subject surrounded by a fearful emotional weight that made it difficult if not impossible for me to ask questions. Looking back, I think part of this had to do with my fear-laden confusion at hearing about the connection between my loving grandparents and the unimaginable history of genocide. This was also, I believe, a reflection my parents' own struggle to acknowledge the role their parents played. How do you comprehend the love you have for your parents in the knowledge that they belonged to the generation that made the Holocaust possible?

While my family spoke about the Holocaust and the importance of remembering, other aspects of the past were simply not talked about. In particular, I have no memory of engaging in discussions about the beliefs or actions of my grandparents in relation to the Third Reich. It seems that while one door to our German history was opened, the other remained shut. What happened in my family was repeated over and over again in German families throughout the postwar decades. It was a kind of learned cultural response to the Nazi past in which the perpetrators of the war and the Holocaust were cleanly separated from ordinary Germans, loving family members like my grandparents. It was a reflection of what it was like for my parents growing up in Germany after the war. The silence they experienced about all things related to the Third Reich, especially their parents' beliefs and actions during that time, was passed down to me. The lack of an oral narrative meant not knowing what questions to ask nor what answers to look for.

Struggling with Memory

When postwar Germans arrived in Canada during the 1950s and early 1960s, many marvelled that the country seemed untouched by the war. While there was little visible evidence and certainly no physical destruction, many lives had been damaged or lost in the fight against the Germans. In Vancouver the reality of the war and of Germany's perpetration of the Holocaust was perhaps nowhere more apparent than in the close geographical proximity between the small community of Holocaust survivors and the expanding community of postwar Germans. Whether simply by circumstance or cruel irony, these two communities each found their way to the relatively small and distinctly Anglo-Saxon city located on the edge of the Pacific Ocean and ended up living in the same area. The two groups were halfway around the world from the conflict zones and concentration camps of Europe, yet in their new home they lived out inevitable encounters. One of these interactions has been described in a study of Vancouver Holocaust survivors: "When my son was 7, we had German neighbours. They had a son. My son said, 'I'm not going to play with him, he's German.' I said, 'No, he's an innocent child like you.' That really scared me when he said that. We didn't want to bring him up like that . . . I was afraid he was going to hate Germans. I didn't want this to happen to them, to live with this, to hate somebody. I don't hate them [Germans], but I don't know how to love them either."[3]

In the interaction of these two families the vast physical and cultural distance from central Europe and the Holocaust had been reduced to a mere fence between two houses. The encounter between the two boys, one of European Jewish background and the other of German background, raises important questions about how the past was addressed in the German immigrant community and whether, or to what extent, the past was communicated to the German children. Would the young German boy have understood why his neighbour did not want to play with him? While the son of the Holocaust survivors, presumably aware of his parents' history, clearly understood Germany's role as a perpetrator nation, was the German-Canadian child aware of the legacy of perpetration he had inherited? And if not, when would he learn about the Holocaust, about German guilt and responsibility, and from whom? This points to how our understanding of history is shaped in our interactions with other people and is transmitted across generations.

After a public talk I gave on German memory and the Holocaust in Canada, an audience member approached me to share his personal experience. Like me, he was a so-called third-generation German, a grandchild of the generation of perpetrators and bystanders. He grew up in Canada, the son of German immigrants who belonged to the second generation. He recounted the shame he felt when he first learned about the Holocaust at school and recalled going home that same day to confront his parents about why they had never said anything about this terrible and damning history. His parents shrugged off his concern and told him that knowing about this long-ago history was unnecessary. Thereby, they shut down any possibility of further communication about the past or the shame this man clearly felt as a child in being identified with Germany's dark history. As this illustration suggests, descendants of German immigrants to Canada still carry the weight of German history despite their physical, chronological, and cultural distance from the Holocaust. Being fully integrated into their parents' adopted country and culture, descendants often struggle to make sense of their conflicting cultural identities and the feelings that emerge when confronted with the history of National Socialism and the Holocaust. The silence about the past can also give rise to fearful fantasies about how their own family members may have been involved in the Holocaust and what they might have done.

The reasons that families remain silent about the Nazi past and the Holocaust can vary greatly. Some German Canadians see it simply as a history that had been left behind. They choose instead to focus on their own memories of struggle, whether it was the suffering endured during the Allied bombing raids, the hardship of mass migration after the war, or the challenges of integrating into a foreign culture and language. Some families feel the need to hide the shameful history of National Socialism and the Holocaust from their children, perhaps a reflection of personal fears and concerns about the degree to which their relatives were directly or indirectly involved in the Nazi past. In such cases, dissociation often takes the place of dialogue. And then there are other families who see this history as lacking in relevance and would rather not be bothered with these "inconvenient" historical facts. Members of this group are particularly susceptible to racial and anti-Semitic hatreds that are directed against the very victims who endured unimaginable suffering at the hands of the Germans.

A concerted discourse about the importance of remembering the past is only possible when a community has a shared history. But what if this shared history is itself denied and ignored? West German immigrants who left for Canada in the 1950s and early 1960s lived in a defeated country that lacked any narrative about the collective crimes of the Nazi past. Because blame was apportioned to the leaders of National Socialism who were tried at Nuremberg in the late 1940s, the majority of the German population remained silent about their part in the Holocaust, thus reinforcing the accepted view that guilt was not collective. During the 1950s and 1960s the West German education system did not address the Holocaust, let alone admit guilt and responsibility for it. Many teachers were participants in National Socialism and had not disavowed their own backgrounds. It took until the early 1960s, with the Frankfurt Auschwitz Trials, that an understanding of the Holocaust began to filter into German public awareness. Beginning with the student uprisings of 1968, the deeply conservative process of forgetting in West Germany was challenged. Institutions were questioned for the way in which they seamlessly transitioned from Nazism into postwar democracy and this cultural transformation eventually led to the emergence of mandatory Holocaust education in the 1970s.

Most postwar German immigrants had already arrived in Canada by the time these important changes took place and missed the opportunity to participate in West Germany's emerging culture of remembrance. Once in Canada, many of these immigrants experienced a sense of contrition when confronted with the crimes committed by the Germans under National Socialism. But without a meaningful understanding of the importance of Holocaust remembrance, or the conviction that guilt was collective and not simply the purview of a few Nazi leaders and henchmen, there was no sustained engagement with the nature and meaning of these crimes. Above all, questions about the involvement of family members in the Third Reich went unasked. Without an active process of collective remembering the Nazi past became a historical remnant. There were also many German immigrants who neglected or altogether ignored their history, and their rapid integration into Canadian society allowed the past to slip further and further away.

For the children of German immigrants, the need to integrate into Canadian society often meant leaving German history and language behind. They embraced the dominant symbols of their cultural heritage but joined their families in turning a blind eye to uncomfortable reminders of National Socialism. Yet the discrepancy between the symbolic markers of German immigrant culture in Canada and an open accounting of the Nazi past could hardly be more graphic: Christmas markets, Oktoberfests, and concentration camps are all the products of the same German cultural life world. While the former are remembered annually and identified and celebrated as the most "German" of events, the cultural and familial associations with the horrors of the Holocaust are neglected, dissociated, or altogether denied. In the process, a certain German-Canadian identity is constructed and sustained, one that is free of the obligations of memory and historical understanding.

Unless the German boy in the encounter described above was explicitly told about Germany's perpetration of the Holocaust, he likely did not understand the reasons for his Jewish neighbour's reaction. Like many children of German immigrants, the boy probably felt a stigma attached to being culturally German. But did he grasp the concept of historical responsibility? In the decades after the war, the lack of concerted intergenerational dialogue about the history of National Socialism had serious consequences. Possibilities for reflection, understanding, and a moral accounting were lost. In contrast to Germany, where collective remembering and responsibility would become a kind of national touchstone, a silence ensued among many German Canadians. Immigration to Canada not only provided new possibilities, it also became a means to leave the past behind, and in many cases, it actually reinforced the process of forgetting and denial that had begun prior to leaving Germany.

The Ethical Demands of History

I am not suggesting that the path toward open dialogue about the Nazi past and the Holocaust is easy or straightforward. Canada's silence about its role in its 200-year "cultural genocide"[4] of the First Nations has only very recently been openly addressed. Being Canadian today involves the recognition of this shameful past. There is a wide contemporary consensus that knowing this history and confronting it is quite possibly the only way for Canadian society to begin healing historical wounds that have been carried into the present. Being Canadian thus means acknowledging the wrongs that were committed and understanding the importance of this act of remembering. The reflective stance of remembrance and acknowledgement has become an ethical demand.

Contemplating this important shift in Canada's historical understanding of itself must give pause. Does being German Canadian involve any such corresponding demand to know and remember the atrocities of the Holocaust? Identifying as German, even if only as

"German Canadian," is to be associated with a nation of former perpetrators whose atrocities, carried out against European Jews, constitute one of the darkest chapters in modern human history. Indeed, the sense of unease and shame still felt by many German Canadians in relation to the Holocaust suggests that there is much about this history that has remained in the shadows. Many German Canadians may no longer carry German passports, speak German, or even visit Germany. But they are collectively joined together by their cultural history and the memories they carry. To the degree that they identify as "German," an identity created by way of family, history, and memory, they are inevitably obliged to ask the hard questions. How was my family connected to the period of National Socialism? What is my responsibility for knowing and remembering? Was the Nazi past talked about in my family, and if not, why? And perhaps, most fearfully, what were the beliefs and actions of my own relatives during that time?

Indeed, to the extent that German Canadians of the postwar era identify as "German," I would suggest that the obligation to know and remember is little different for them than it is for contemporary Germans. Almost all are linked by their family histories to the period of the Third Reich: to relatives who belonged to the German generation that stood by, supported, and carried out the Holocaust. As we know today, there were sadly very few Germans who actually opposed the regime; an overwhelming majority supported the Nazis and their policies of racial hatred. Despite their physical and cultural distance from present-day Germany, German Canadians are thus faced with the same kind of ethical obligations. They carry the burden of their forebears' collective guilt and responsibility. To be sure, each new generation of Germans, or of German Canadians, is increasingly distant from the Nazi past and, as such, bears no direct responsibility for what happened in the Holocaust. But the obligation to know and remember the massive crimes of the Shoah has not correspondingly lessened with time. Historical injustices do not simply fade away. Their traumatic impact on future generations remains long after they first occur.

Notes

1 The arguments developed in this essay expand on ideas presented in two recent books: Roger Frie, ed., *History Flows Through Us: Germany, the Holocaust, and the Importance of Empathy* (New York: Routledge, 2017); and Roger Frie, *Not in My Family: German Memory and Responsibility After the Holocaust* (New York: Oxford University Press, 2017). A fuller discussion of the issues, particularly as they relate to Germany's frequently ambiguous and difficult relationship with its past, can be found in these books.

2 Distinctions within the broader German-Canadian community, be they language, (high German or a regional dialect), geographical region (the north, south, or the eastern territories populated by Germans until the end of the Second World War), or historical period (West vs. East Germany, for example) all play a role in how German-Canadian identity is defined. Given the important role played by religious institutions in helping new immigrants and in sustaining cultural communities, religious differences also need to be accounted for. Do I identify as Protestant or Catholic, for example, or do I trace my history to the persecuted German-Jewish minority, and if so, would I even want to identify as German Canadian more broadly?

3 Cited in Jean Miriam Gerber, "Immigration and Integration in Post-war Canada: A Case Study of Holocaust Survivors in Vancouver, 1947–1970" (Master's thesis, University of British Columbia, 1989), 55.

4 The Truth and Reconciliation Commission of Canada, "Honouring the Truth, Reconciling for the Future: Summary of the Final Report of the Truth and Reconciliation Commission of Canada" (Winnipeg: The Truth and Reconciliation Commission of Canada, 2015) http://www.trc.ca/websites/trcinstitution/File/2015/Findings/Exec_Summary_2015_05_31_web_o.pdf (accessed 30 July 2017).

BIBLIOGRAPHY

Abella, Irving A. *Coat of Many Colours: Two Centuries of Jewish Life in Canada.* Toronto: Lester and Orpen Dennys, 1990.

Abella, Irving, and Harold Troper. *None Is Too Many: Canada and the Jews of Europe, 1933–1948.* Toronto: Lester and Orpen Dennys, 1982.

Aboim, Sofia, and Pedro Vasconcelos. "From Political to Social Generations: A Critical Reappraisal of Mannheim's Classical Approach." *European Journal of Social Theory* 17, no. 2 (2014): 165–83.

Adams, Mary Louise. *The Trouble with Normal: Postwar Youth and the Making of Heterosexuality.* Toronto: University of Toronto Press, 1997.

Adorno, Theodor W. *Critical Models: Interventions and Catchwords.* Translated by Henry W. Pickford. 1966. Reprint, New York: Columbia University Press, 1998.

———. "Einleitung zum Vortrag: 'Was bedeutet Aufarbeitung der Vergangenheit?'" In *Gesammelte Schriften* 10, 816–17. Frankfurt am Main: Suhrkamp, 1977.

Agnew, Vijay. "Introduction." In *Diaspora, Memory, and Identity: A Search for Home,* edited by Vijay Agnew, 3–17. Toronto: University of Toronto Press, 2005.

Alba, Richard. *Ethnic Identity: The Transformation of White America.* New Haven: Yale University Press, 1990.

Aly, Götz, and Susanne Heim. *Architects of Destruction: Auschwitz and the Logic of Destruction.* Princeton: Princeton University Press, 2002.

Anderson, Christopher G. *Canadian Liberalism and the Politics of Border Control, 1867–1967.* Toronto: University of Toronto Press, 2013.

Arendt, Hannah. "We Refugees." *Menorah Journal* (January 1943): 69–77. Reprinted in *The Jew as Pariah,* edited by Ron H. Feldman, 55–66. New York: Grove, 1978.

Ascher, Abraham. *Was Hitler a Riddle? Western Democracies and National Socialism.* Stanford: Stanford University Press, 2012.

Avery, Donald. *"Dangerous Foreigners": European Immigrant Workers and Labour Radicalism in Canada, 1896–1932.* Toronto: McClelland and Stewart, 1979.

———. "Ethnic and Class Relations in Western Canada During the First World War: A Case Study of European Immigrants and Anglo-Canadian Nativism." In *Canada and the First World War: Essays in Honour of Robert Craig Brown,* edited by David MacKenzie, 272–99. Toronto: University of Toronto Press, 2005.

———. *Reluctant Host: Canada's Response to Immigrant Workers, 1896–1994.* Toronto: McClelland and Stewart, 1995.

Azzi, Stephen, and Norman Hillmer. "Ranking Canada's Best and Worst Prime Ministers." *Maclean's*, 7 October 2016.

Backhouse, Constance. *Colour-Coded: A Legal History of Racism in Canada, 1900–1950*. Toronto: Osgoode Society for Canadian Legal History/University of Toronto Press, 2001.

Bader, Alfred. *Adventures of a Chemist Collector*. London: Weidenfeld and Nicolson, 1995.

Baltensperger, Bradley. "Agricultural Change among Great Plains Russian Germans." *Annals of the Association of American Geographers* 73, no. 1 (1983): 75–88.

Barkai, Avraham. "Deutsch-jüdische Forschungsinseln. Die Leo Baeck Institute in Jerusalem, London und New York." In *Die Jeckes. Jüdischer Almanach des Leo Baeck Instituts*, edited by Gisela Dachs, 13–27. Frankfurt: Jüdischer Verlag im Suhrkamp Verlag, 2005.

Bar-On, Dan. *Fear and Hope: Three Generations of the Holocaust*. Cambridge, MA: Harvard University Press, 1998.

———. "Holocaust Perpetrators and Their Children: A Paradoxical Morality." *Journal of Humanistic Psychology* 29, no. 4 (1989): 424–43.

———. *Legacy of Silence: Encounters with Children of the Third Reich*. Cambridge, MA: Harvard University Press, 1989.

Bartlett, Frederic C. *Remembering: A Study in Experimental and Social Psychology*, 2nd ed. 1932. Reprint,Cambridge: Cambridge University Press, 1995.

Barzel, Neima. "The Attitude of Jews of German Origin in Israel and Germans after the Holocaust, 1945–1952." *Leo Baeck Institute Year Book* 39 (1994): 271–301.

Bassler, Gerhard. "Deutsche Einwanderung und Siedlung in Kanada." In *Adler auf dem Ahornbaum. Studien zur Einwanderung, Siedlung, Kultur- und Literaturgeschichte der Deutschen in Kanada*, edited by Hartmut Froeschle, 1–12. Toronto: German-Canadian Historical Association, 1997.

———. *Escape Hatch: Newfoundland's Quest for German Industry and Immigration, 1950–1970*. St. John's, NL: Flanker Press, 2017.

———. *The German Canadian Mosaic Today and Yesterday: Identities, Roots, and Heritage*. Ottawa: German-Canadian Congress, 1991.

———. "Germans in Canada: An Introduction to the Historiography." *Immigration History Newsletter* 20, no. 1 (1988): 1–10.

———. "Silent or Silenced Co-Founders of Canada? Reflections on the History of German Canadians." *Canadian Ethnic Studies* 22, no. 1 (1990): 38–46.

Bayor, Ronald H, ed. *The Oxford Handbook of American Immigration and Ethnicity*. Oxford: Oxford University Press, 2013.

Becker, A. "The Germans in Western Canada: A Vanishing People." *CCHA Study Sessions* 42 (1975): 29–49.

Beloff, Max. *Imperial Sunset: Dream of Commonwealth, 1921–42*. London: Palgrave Macmillan, 1989.

Benz, Wolfgang. *Das Exil der kleinen Leute: Alltagserfahrung deutscher Juden in der Emigration*. Munich: C.H. Beck, 1991.

———, ed. *Die Juden in Deutschland 1933–1945: Leben unter nationalsozialistischer Herrschaft*. Munich: Beck, 1988.

Berg, Mette Louise. *Diasporic Generations: Memory, Politics and Nation among Cubans in Spain*. Oxford: Berghahn Books, 2011.

Berg, Mette Louise, and Susan Eckstein, eds. "Re-imagining Diasporas and Generations." Special Issue. *Diaspora: A Journal of Transnational Studies* 18 no. 1–2 (2015).

Bergen, Doris L. "Tenuousness and Tenacity: The *Volksdeutschen* of Eastern Europe, World War II, and the Holocaust." In *The Heimat Abroad: The Boundaries of Germanness*, edited by Krista O'Donnell, Renate Bridenthal, and Nancy Reagin, 267–86. Ann Arbor: The University of Michigan Press, 2005.

Berry, John, and Feng Hou. "Acculturation, Discrimination and Wellbeing among Second Generation of Immigrants in Canada." *International Journal of Intercultural Relations* 61 (2017): 29–39.

Berton, Pierre. *The Great Depression, 1929–1939*. Toronto: McClelland and Stewart, 1990.

Bertram, Laurie K. "New Icelandic Ethnoscapes: Material, Visual, and Oral Terrains of Cultural Expression in Icelandic-Canadian History, 1875–Present." PhD diss., University of Toronto, 2010.

Betten, Anne. "Familiales Gedächtnis und individuelle Erinnerung." In *Emotionsausdruck und Erzählstrategien in narrativen Interviews: Analysen zu Gesprächsaufnahmen mit jüdischen Emigranten*, edited by Simona Leonardi, Eva-Maria Thüne, and Anne Betten, 85–121. Würzburg: Königshausen and Neumann, 2016.

Bialas, Wolfgang, and Anson Rabinbach. *Nazi Germany and the Humanities: How German Academics Embraced Nazism*. London: Oneworld, 2007.

Bialystok, Franklin. *Delayed Impact: The Holocaust and the Canadian Jewish Community*. Montreal and Kingston: McGill–Queen's University Press, 2000.

Bigley, Elise. "Creativity, Community, and Memory Building: Interned Jewish Refugees in Canada During and After World War II." Master's thesis, Carleton University Ottawa, 2017.

Bissell, Claude. *The Imperial Canadian: Vincent Massey in Office*. Toronto: University of Toronto Press, 1986.

Blanchard, Jim. *Winnipeg's Great War: A City Comes of Age*. Winnipeg: University of Manitoba Press, 2010.

Bothwell, Robert, Ian Drummond, and John English. *Canada 1900–1945*. Toronto: University of Toronto Press, 1987.

Boyd, Monica, and Siyue Tian. "Educational and Labor Market Attainments of the 1.5- and Second-Generation Children of East Asian Immigrants in Canada." *American Behavioral Scientist* 60, no. 5–6 (2016): 705–29.

Brebner, J.B. *Canada, a Modern History*. Rev. ed. Ann Arbor: University of Michigan Press, 1970.

Brglez, Karen. "Canada at the End of the Cold War: The Influence of a Transatlantic 'Middle Power' on German Unification." Master's thesis, University of Manitoba, 2014.

Bridenthal, Renate. "Germans from Russia: The Political Network of a Double Diaspora." In *The Heimat Abroad: The Boundaries of Germanness*, edited by Krista O'Donnell, Renate Bridenthal, and Nancy Reagin, 187–218. Ann Arbor: The University of Michigan Press, 2005.

Brown, Brené. *Daring Greatly: How the Courage to Be Vulnerable Transforms the Way We Live, Love, Parent, and Lead.* New York: Penguin, 2015.

Brown, Kate. *A Biography of No Place: From Ethnic Borderland to Soviet Heartland.* Cambridge: Harvard University Press, 2004.

Bryce, Benjamin. "Making Ethnic Space: Education, Religion, and the German Language in Argentina and Canada, 1880–1930." PhD diss., York University, 2013.

Bryce, Benjamin, and Alexander Freund, eds. *Entangling Migration History: Borderlands and Transnationalism in the United States and Canada.* Gainesville, FL: University Press of Florida, 2015.

Burleigh, Michael. *Germany Turns Eastwards: A Study of "Ostforschung" in the Third Reich.* New York: Cambridge University Press, 1988.

Casteel, James. "The Politics of Diaspora: Russian German Émigré Activists in Interwar Germany." In *German Diasporic Experiences: Identity, Migration, and Loss,* edited by Mathias Schulze, James M. Skidmore, David G. John, Grit Liebscher, and Sebastian Siebel-Achenbach, 117–30. Waterloo: Wilfrid Laurier University Press, 2008.

Chaktsiris, Mary G. "The Enemy At Home: Defining Enemy Aliens in Ontario During the Great War," In *The Great War: From Memory to History,* edited by Kellen Kurschinski, Steve Marti, Alicia Robinet, Matt Symes, and Jonathan F. Vance, 287–302. Waterloo: Wilfrid Laurier University Press, 2015.

Charyk, John. *Syrup Pails and Gopher Tails: Memories of the One-Room School.* Saskatoon, SK: Western Producer Prairie Books, 1983.

Clark, C.M. "West Germany Confronts the Nazi Past: Some Recent Debates on the Early Postwar Era, 1945–1960," *The European Legacy* 4, no. 1 (1999): 113–30.

Clark, Jessica. "More than a Photo: Germans from Russia Remember Their Familial Relationships." *Journal of Family History* 36, no. 3 (2011): 333–49.

———. "'Work Makes Life Sweet': Germans from Russia Remember Their Childhood." *The Historian* 72, no. 4 (2010): 809–30.

Clark, Jessica, and Thomas Isern. "Germans from Russia in Saskatchewan: An Oral History." *American Review of Canadian Studies* 40, no. 1 (2010): 71–85.

Comstock, Eileen. *Sunny Side Up: Fond Memories of Prairie Life in the 1930s.* Markham, ON: Fifth House Publishers, 2001.

Conforti, Yitzhak. "The 'New Jew' in the Zionist Movement: Ideology and Historiography." *The Australian Journal of Jewish Studies* 25 (2011): 87–118.

Cook, Tim. *Clio's Warriors: Canadian Historians and the Writing of the World Wars.* Vancouver: UBC Press, 2006.

———. *Vimy: The Battle and the Legend.* Toronto: Allen Lane, 2017.

———. *Warlords: Borden, Mackenzie King, and Canada's World Wars.* Toronto: Allen Lane, 2012.

Cronmiller, Carl Raymond. *A History of the Lutheran Church in Canada.* Toronto: Evangelical Lutheran Synod of Canada, 1961.

Cubitt, Geoffrey. *History and Memory.* Manchester: Manchester University Press, 2007.

Detienne, Marcel. *Comparing the Incomparable.* Translated by Janet Lloyd. Stanford: Stanford University Press, 2008.

Douglas, W.A.B., and Brereton Greenhous. *Out of the Shadows: Canada in the Second World War*, 2nd ed. Toronto: Dundurn, 1996.

Draper, Paula Jean. "The Accidental Immigrants: Canada and the Interned Refugees." PhD diss., University of Toronto, 1983.

Dresler-Hawke, Emma. "Reconstructing the Past and Attributing the Responsibility for the Holocaust." *Social Behavior and Personality: An International Journal* 33, no. 2 (2005): 133–48.

Driver, Deana, ed. *Egg Money: A Tribute to Saskatchewan Pioneer Women*. Regina, SK: DriverWorks Ink, 2012.

Dummitt, Christopher. "The Importance of Not Being Earnest: Postwar Canadians Rethink Mackenzie King's Christian Manhood." In *Canadian Men and Masculinities: Historical and Contemporary Perspectives*, edited by Christopher J. Greig and Wayne Martino, 61–75. Toronto: Canadian Scholars' Press, 2012.

Dutil, Patrice A. "Against Isolationism: Napoléon Belcourt, French Canada, and 'La grande guerre.'" In *Canada and the First World War: Essays in Honour of Robert Craig Brown*, edited by David MacKenzie, 96–137. Toronto: University of Toronto Press, 2005.

Eckstein, Susan. "The Clash of Cuban Immigrant Cohorts." In *Cuba Today: Continuity and Change since the Periodo Especial*, edited by Mauricio A. Font, 129–45. New York: Bildner Center for Western Hemisphere Studies, CUYN Graduate Center, 2004.

———. *On Deconstructing Immigrant Generations: Cohorts and the Cuban Émigré Experience*. Working Paper 97, Center for Comparative Immigration Studies, University of California at San Diego, 2004.

Epp, Marlene. "'The Dumpling in My Soup Was Lonely Just Like Me': Food in the Memories of Mennonite Women Refugees." *Women's History Review* 25, no. 3 (2016): 365–81.

Epp, Marlene, and Franca Iacovetta. *Sisters or Strangers?: Immigrant, Ethnic, and Racialized Women in Canadian History*, 2nd ed. Toronto: University of Toronto Press, 2016.

Eric Koch. *Deemed Suspect: A Wartime Blunder*. Toronto: Methuen, 1980.

Esberey, Joy E. *Knight of the Holy Spirit: A Study of William Lyon Mackenzie King*. Toronto: University of Toronto Press, 1980.

Farges, Patrick. *Bindestrich-Kanadier?: Sudetendeutsche Sozialdemokraten und deutsche Juden als Exilanten in Kanada*. Bremen: Edition Lumière, 2015.

———. "'Diese meine Sprache, die so männlich geworden ist.' Jeckes in Palästina/Israel im Spannungsverhältnis zwischen Sprachen und Geschlecht." *L'Homme. Zeitschrift für feministische Geschichtswissenschaft* 26, no. 1 (2015): 63–78.

———. *Le Muscle et l'Espirit. Masculinités germano-juives dans la post-migration*. Brussels: PIE Peter Lang, 2020.

———. "Masculinity and Confinement: German-Speaking Refugees in Canadian Internment Camps (1940–1943)." *Culture, Society and Masculinities* 4, no. 1 (2012): 33–47.

———. "'What Church Do You Go To?' The Difficult Acculturation of German-Jewish Refugees in Canada, 1933–2004." In *Beyond the Nation? Immigrants' Local*

Lives in Transnational Cultures, edited by Alexander Freund, 187–210. Toronto: University of Toronto Press, 2012.

Farney, James, and Bohdan S. Kordan. "The Predicament of Belonging: The Status of Enemy Aliens in Canada, 1914." *Journal of Canadian Studies* 39, no. 1 (Winter 2005): 74–89.

Finlay, J.F., and D.N. Sprague. *The Structure of Canadian History*, 6th ed. Scarborough: Prentice Hall Canada Inc., 2000.

Finney, Patrick. "Ethics, Historical Relativism and Holocaust Denial." *Rethinking History* 2, no. 3 (1998): 359–69.

Freund, Alexander. *Aufbrüche nach dem Zusammenbruch: Die deutsche Nordamerika-Auswanderung nach dem Zweiten Weltkrieg*. Göttingen: V&R Unipress, 2004.

———, ed. *Beyond the Nation? Immigrants' Local Lives in Transnational Cultures*. Toronto: University of Toronto Press, 2012.

———. "A Canadian Family Talks About Oma's Life in Nazi Germany: Three-Generational Interviews and Communicative Memory." In "Remembering Family, Analyzing Home: Oral History and the Family." Special Issue, *Oral History Forum d'histoire orale* 29 (2009): 1–26.

———. "Contesting the Meaning of Migration: German Women's Immigration to Canada in the 1950s." *Canadian Ethnic Studies* 41–42, no. 3/1 (2009–2010): 1–26.

———. "Dealing with the Past Abroad: German Immigrants' *Vergangenheitsbewältigung* and their Relations with Jews in North America since 1945." *Bulletin of the German Historical Institute* 31 (2002): 51–63.

———. "German Immigrants and the Nazi Past: How Memory Has Shaped Intercultural Relations." *Inroads: A Journal of Public Opinion* 15 (Summer/Fall 2004): 106–17.

———. "A German Post-1945 Diaspora? German Migrants' Encounters with the Nazi Past." In *German Diasporic Experiences: Identity, Migration, and Loss*, edited by Mathias Schulze et al., 467–78. Waterloo, ON: Wilfrid Laurier University Press, 2008.

———. "'How Come They're Nice to Me?' Deutsche und Juden nach dem Holocaust in Nordamerika." In *Migration und Erinnerung. Reflexionen über Wanderungserfahrungen in Europa und Nordamerika*, edited by Christiane Harzig, 143–56. Göttingen: V&R unipress 2006.

———. *Oral History and Ethnic History*. Ottawa: Canadian Historical Association, 2014.

———. "Representing 'New Canadians': Competing Narratives about Recent German Immigrants to Manitoba." *Journal of Mennonite Studies* 30 (2012): 339–61.

———. "Toward an Ethics of Silence? Negotiating Off-the-record Events and Identity in Oral History." In *Oral History Off the Record: Toward an Ethnography of Practice*, edited by Anna Sheftel and Stacey Zembrzycki, 223–38. New York: Palgrave, 2013.

———. "Transnationalizing Home in Winnipeg: Refugees' Stories of the Places Between the 'Here-and-There.'" In "Transforming Citizenship: Ethnicity, Transnationalism, and Belonging in Canada." Special Issue. *Canadian Ethnic Studies* 47, no. 1 (2015): 61–86.

———. "Troubling Memories in Nation-building: World War II Memories and Germans' Interethnic Encounters in Canada after 1945." *Histoire sociale/Social History* 39, no. 77 (2006): 129–55.

———. "'Where were you während des Kriegs?' Kriegserzählungen deutscher Migranten in Nordamerika seit 1945." In *Zeichen des Krieges in Literatur, Film und den Medien, Vol. 1: Nordamerika und Europa*, edited by Christer Petersen, 31–67. Kiel: Verlag Ludwig, 2004.

Freund, Alexander, and Laura Quilici. "Exploring Myths in Women's Narratives: Italian and German Immigrant Women in Vancouver, 1947–1961." *Oral History Review* 23, no. 2 (Winter 1996): 19–43.

Freund, Alexander, Nolan Reilly, and Kristina Llewellyn, eds. *The Canadian Oral History Reader*. Montreal: McGill Queen's University Press, 2015.

Freund, Alexander, and Angela Thiessen. "Mary Brockmeyer's Wedding Picture: Exploring the Intersection of Photographs and Oral History Interviews." In *Oral History and Photography*, edited by Alexander Freund and Alistair Thomson, 27–44. New York: Palgrave Macmillan, 2012.

Frie, Roger. "From Memorials to Bomb Shelters: Navigating the Emotional Landscape of German Memory." *Psychoanalytic Inquiry* 34, no. 7 (2014): 649–62.

———, ed. *History Flows Through Us: Germany, the Holocaust, and the Importance of Empathy*. New York: Routledge, 2017.

———. "Memory and Responsibility: Navigating Identity and Shame in the German-Jewish Experience." *Psychoanalytic Psychology* 29, no. 2 (2012): 206–25.

———. *Not in My Family: German Memory and Responsibility After the Holocaust*. Oxford: Oxford University Press, 2017.

Frisch, Michael. *A Shared Authority: Essays on Craft and Meaning of Oral and Public History*. Albany: State University of New York Press, 1990.

Frisse, Ulrich. "The Missing Link: Mackenzie King and Canada's 'German Capital.'" In *Mackenzie King: Citizenship and Community*, edited by John English, Kenneth McLaughlin, and P. Whitney Lackenbauer, 18–34. Toronto: Robin Brass Studio, 2002.

Froeschle, Hartmut. *The German-Canadians: A Concise History / Die Deutschkanadier. Geschichtlicher Überblick*. Toronto: Historical Society of Mecklenburg Upper Canada, 1992.

Fuchs, Oliver, Lou-Marie Krüger, and Pumla Gobodo-Madikizela. "An Exploration of German Subjectivity: Three Generations After the End of World War Two." *The Humanistic Psychologist* 41, no. 2 (2013): 13–158.

Gans, Herbert. "Symbolic Ethnicity: The Future of Ethnic Groups and Cultures in America." *Ethnic and Racial Studies* 2, no. 1 (1979): 1–20.

———. "Toward a Reconciliation of 'Assimilation' and 'Pluralism': The Interplay of Acculturation and Ethnic Retention." *International Migration Review* 31, no. 4 (1997): 875–92.

Gelber, Yoav. "The Historical Role of the Central European Immigration to Israel." *Leo Baeck Institute Year Book* 38 (1993): 323–39.

Gellately, Robert. *Backing Hitler: Consent and Coercion in Nazi Germany*. Oxford: Oxford University Press, 2002.

Geller, Jay Howard, and Leslie Morris, eds. *Three-Way Street: Jews, Germans, and the Transnational.* Ann Arbor: University of Michigan Press, 2016.

Georgi, Viola B. *Entliehene Erinnerung: Geschichtsbilder junger Migranten in Deutschland.* Hamburg: Hamburger Edition, 2003.

Gerber, David A. "Immigration Historiography at the Crossroads." *Reviews in American History* 39, no. 1 (March 2011): 74–86.

Gerber, Jean Miriam. "Immigration and Integration in Post-war Canada: A Case Study of Holocaust Survivors in Vancouver, 1947–1970." Master's thesis, University of British Columbia, 1989.

Gerlach, Christian. *Extremely Violent Societies: Mass Violence in the Twentieth-Century World.* Cambridge: Cambridge University Press, 2010.

Giles, Geoffrey J. *Students and National Socialism in Germany.* Princeton: Princeton University Press, 1985.

Gleason, Mona. *Normalizing the Ideal: Psychology, Schooling, and the Family in Postwar Canada.* Toronto: University of Toronto Press, 1999.

Goldberg, Adara. *Holocaust Survivors in Canada: Exclusion, Inclusion, Transformation, 1947–1955.* Winnipeg, University of Manitoba Press, 2015.

Gordon, Hugh Avi. "Cheers and Tears: Relations Between Canadian Soldiers and German Civilians, 1944–46." PhD diss., University of Victoria, 2010.

Grams, Grant. *German Emigration to Canada and the Support of its Deutschtum during the Weimar Republic: The Role of the Deutsches Ausland-Institut, Verein fuer das Deutschtum im Ausland and German-Canadian Organisations.* Frankfurt am Main: Peter Lang, 2001.

———. "Heim ins Reich: Return Migration from the United States and Canada to the Third Reich, 1933–1941." Forthcoming monograph.

Granatstein, J.L. *Mackenzie King: His Life and World.* Toronto: McGraw-Hill Ryerson, 1977.

Granatstein, J.L., Irving M. Abella, David J. Bercuson, R. Craig Brown, and H. Blair Neatby. *Twentieth Century Canada.* Toronto: McGraw-Hill Ryerson, 1983.

Granquist, Mark. *Lutherans in America: A New History.* Minneapolis: Fortress Press, 2015.

Green, Nancy L. "The Comparative Method and Poststructural Structuralism: New Perspectives for Migration Studies." In *Migration, Migration History, History: Old Paradigms and New Perspectives,* edited by Jan Lucassen and Leo Lucassen, 57–72. New York: Peter Lang, 1999.

Grenke, Arthur. "The Archival Record of German-Language Groups in Canada: A Survey." *Archivaria* 35 (Spring 1993): 214–31.

———. "The Formation and Early Development of An Urban Ethnic Community: A Case Study of the Germans in Winnipeg, 1872–1919." PhD diss., University of Manitoba, 1975/1978.

———. *The German Community in Winnipeg, 1872 to 1919.* New York: AMS Press, 1991.

———. "The German Community of Winnipeg and the English-Canadian Response to World War I." *Canadian Ethnic Studies* 20, no. 1 (1988): 21–44.

Grzyb, Amanda. "From Kristallnacht to the MS *St Louis* Tragedy: Canadian Press Coverage of Nazi Persecution of Jews and the Jewish Refugee Crisis, September 1938 to August 1939." In *Nazi Germany, Canadian Responses: Confronting Antisemitism in the Shadow of War,* edited by L. Ruth Klein, 78–113. Montreal-Kingston: McGill-Queen's University Press, 2012.

Haag, John. "The Spann Circle and the Jewish Question." *The Leo Baeck Institute Year Book* 18 no. 1 (1973): 93–126.

Haar, Ingo, and Michael Fahlbusch. *German Scholars and Ethnic Cleansing, 1919–1945.* New York: Berghahn Books, 2005.

Habermas, Jürgen. "Keine Normalisierung der Vergangenheit." In *Eine Art Schadensabwicklung,* 11–17. Berlin: Suhrkamp, 1987.

Halbwachs, Maurice. *On Collective Memory.* 1925. Reprint, Chicago: University of Chicago Press, 1992.

Hardt-Dhatt, Karin. *Etude socio-lingusitique sur l'intégration de l'immigrant allemand au milieu québécois.* Québec: Université Laval, 1976.

Hardy, Henry Reginald. *Mackenzie King of Canada: A Biography.* Toronto: Greenwood Press, 1970.

Heier, Edmund. "The Immigration of the Russo-German Catholics and Lutherans Into Canada." *Canadian Slavonic Papers* 4, no. 1 (1959): 160–75.

Heinlein, Michael. "Das Trauma der deutschen Kriegskinder zwischen nationaler und europäischer Erinnerung: Kritische Anmerkungen zum gegenwärtigen Wandel der Erinnerungskultur." *German Monitor* 73, no. 1 (2011): 108–25.

Helling, Rudolf A., and Bernd Hamm. *A Socio-Economic History of German-Canadians: They, Too, Founded Canada: A Research Report.* Wiesbaden: F. Steiner, 1984.

Henderson, Jarett, and Jeff Keshen. "Introduction: Canadian Perspectives on the First World War." *Histoire sociale/Social History* 47, no. 94 (June 2014): 283–90.

Herzstein, Robert Edwin. *The War that Hitler Won: The Most Infamous Propaganda Campaign in History.* New York: G.P. Putnam, 1978.

High, Steven. *Oral History at the Crossroads: Sharing Life Stories of Survival and Displacement.* Vancouver: UBC Press, 2014.

High, Steven, Edward Little, and Thi Ry Duong, eds. *Remembering Mass Violence: Oral History, New Media, and Performance.* Toronto: University of Toronto Press, 2014.

Hirsch, Marianne. *Family Frames: Photography, Narrative, and Postmemory.* Cambridge, MA: Harvard University Press, 1997.

———. *The Generation of Postmemory: Writing and Visual Culture After the Holocaust.* New York: Columbia University Press, 2012.

Ho, Elaine. "Migration Trajectories of 'Highly Skilled' Middling Transnationals: Singaporean Transmigrants in London." *Population, Space and Place* 17, no.1 (2011): 116–29.

Hoerder, Dirk. "German-Speaking Immigrants: Co-Founders or Mosaic?" *Zeitschrift für Kanada-Studien* 14, no. 2 (1994): 51–65.

Hoerder, Dirk, and Nora Faires, eds. *Migrants and Migration in Modern North America: Cross-Border Lives, Labor Markets, and Politics.* Durham, NC: Duke University Press, 2011.

Hoffmann, Christhard, ed. *Preserving the Legacy of German Jewry: A History of the Leo Baeck Institute, 1955–2005.* Tübingen: Mohr Siebeck, 2008.

Holtzman, Jon. "Food and Memory." *Annual Review of Anthropology* 35 (2006): 361–78.

Hutchison, Bruce. *The Incredible Canadian: A Candid Portrait of Mackenzie King.* Toronto: Longmans, Green and Company, 1952.

Iacovetta, Franca. *Gatekeepers: Reshaping Immigrant Lives in Cold War Canada.* Toronto: Between the Lines, 2006.

———. "Manly Militants, Cohesive Communities, and Defiant Domestics: Writing about Immigrants in Canadian Historical Scholarship." *Labour/Le Travail* 36 (1995): 217–52.

———. *The Writing of English Canadian Immigrant History.* Canada's Ethnic Group Series 22. Ottawa: Canadian Historical Association, 1997.

Iacovetta, Franca, Roberto Perin, and Angelo Principe, eds. *Enemies Within: Italian and Other Internees in Canada and Abroad.* Toronto: University of Toronto Press, 2000.

Isajiw, Wsevolod W. "Ethnic Identity Retention." In *Ethnic Identity and Quality. Varieties of Experiences in a Canadian City*, edited by Raymond Breton, Wsevolod W. Isajiw, Warren E. Kalbach, and Jeffrey G. Reitz, 34–91. Toronto: University of Toronto Press, 1990.

———. "Identity and Identity Retention among German Canadians: Individual and Institutional." In *A Chorus of Different Voices: German-Canadian Identities*, edited by Angelika E. Sauer and Matthias Zimmer, 67–83. New York: Peter Lang, 1998.

Janowski, Monica. "Introduction: Consuming Memories of Home in Constructing the Present and Imagining the Future." *Food and Foodways* 20, no. 3–4 (2012): 175–86.

Kansteiner, Wulf. "Testing the Limits of Trauma: The Long-term Psychological Effects of the Holocaust on Individuals and Collectives." *History of the Human Sciences* 17, no. 2–3 (2004): 97–123.

Kasinitz, Philip, John H. Mollenkopf, Mary C. Waters, and Jennifer Holdaway. *Inheriting the City: The Children of Immigrants Come of Age.* Cambridge, MA: Harvard University Press, 2008.

Kay, Alex J. *Exploitation, Resettlement, Mass Murder: Political and Economic Planning for German Occupation Policy in the Soviet Union, 1940–1941.* New York: Berghahn Books, 2006.

Kearney, Michael. "The Local and the Global: The Anthropology of Globalization and Transnationalism." *Annual Review of Anthropology* 24 (1995): 547–65.

Keelan, Geoff. "The Forgotten Few: Quebec and the Memory of the First World War." In *The Great War: From Memory to History*, edited by Kellen Kurschinski, Steve Marti, Alicia Robinet, Matt Symes, and Jonathan F. Vance, 235–59. Waterloo: Wilfrid Laurier University Press, 2015.

Kelley, Ninette, and Michael J. Trebilcock. *The Making of the Mosaic: A History of Canadian Immigration Policy*, 2nd ed. Toronto: University of Toronto Press, 2010.

Kelz, Rosine. *The Non-Sovereign Self, Responsibility, and Otherness: Hannah Arendt, Judith Butler, and Stanley Cavell on Moral Philosophy and Political Agency.* New York: Palgrave Macmillan, 2016.

Kennedy, Paul, and Victor Roudometof. "Transnationalism in a Global Age." In *Communities across Borders: New Immigrants and Transnational Cultures*, edited by Paul Kennedy and Victor Roudometof, 1–26. London, New York: Routledge, 2002.

Kershaw, Ian. *Making Friends with Hitler: Lord Londonderry, the Nazis and the Road to World War II.* New York: Penguin, 2004.

Keshen, Jeff. "The Great War Soldier as Nation Builder in Canada and Australia." In *Canada and the Great War: Western Front Association Papers*, edited by Briton Busch, 3–26. Montreal: McGill-Queen's University Press, 2003.

———. *Saints, Sinners, and Soldiers: Canada's Second World War.* Vancouver: UBC Press, 2004.

Klein, L. Ruth, ed. *Nazi Germany, Canadian Responses: Confronting Antisemitism in the Shadow of War.* Montreal-Kingston: McGill-Queen's University Press, 2012.

Knight, Amy. *How the Cold War Began: The Gouzenko Affair and the Hunt for Soviet Spies.* Toronto: McClelland and Stewart, 2005.

Knowles, Valerie. *Strangers at Our Gates: Canadian Immigration and Immigration Policy, 1540–2006.* Toronto: Dundurn, 2007.

Koch-Kraft, Andrea. *Deutsche in Kanada: Einwanderung und Adaption. Mit einer Untersuchung zur Situation der Nachkriegsmigration in Edmonton, Alberta.* Bochum: Brockmeyer, 1990.

Koehl, Robert L. *RKFDV: German Resettlement and Population Policy, 1939–1945: A History of the Reich Commission for the Strengthening of Germandom.* Cambridge: Harvard University Press, 1957.

Koonz, Claudia. *The Nazi Conscience.* Cambridge: Belknap Press, 2003.

Kordan, Bohdan S. *No Free Man: Canada, the Great War, and the Enemy Alien Experience.* Montreal: McGill-Queen's University Press, 2016.

Kotowski, Elke-Vera, ed. *Das Kulturerbe deutschsprachiger Juden: Eine Spurensuche in den Ursprungs-, Transit- und Emigrationsländern.* Berlin-Munich: De Gruyter/Oldenbourg, 2014.

Kottman, Richard. *Reciprocity and the North Atlantic Triangle, 1932–1938.* Ithaca: Cornell University Press, 1968.

Kranz, Dani. "Being a Yekke Is a Really Big Deal for My Mum! On the Intergenerational Transmission of Germanness amongst German Jews in Israel." *Austausch* 2, no. 1 (2013): 43–66.

Kushner, Tony, and David Cesarani, eds. *The Internment of Aliens in Twentieth Century Britain.* London: Frank Cass, 1993.

Laqueur, Walter. *Russia and Germany: A Century of Conflict.* Boston: Little, Brown and Company, 1965.

Lauridsen, John. *Nazism and the Radical Right in Austria, 1918–1934.* Copenhagen: Museum Tusculanum Press, 2007.

Lavsky, Hagit. *Before Catastrophe: The Distinctive Path of German Zionism.* Detroit: Wayne State University Press, 1996.

———. *The Creation of the German-Jewish Diaspora: Interwar German-Jewish Immigration to Palestine, the USA, and England.* Berlin-Boston/Jerusalem: De Gruyter/Magnes Press, 2017.

Lee, Erika. "The Chinese Exclusion Example: Race, Immigration, and American Gatekeeping, 1882–1924." *Journal of American Ethnic History* 21, no. 3 (2002): 36–62.

Lehmann, Heinz. *The German Canadians, 1750–1937: Immigration, Settlement and Culture.* Edited by Gerhard Bassler. St. John's: Jesperson Press, 1986.

Leibbrandt, Gottlieb. "Canadian German Society." *German-Canadian Yearbook* 1 (1973): 255–62.

———. "Deutsche Ortsgründungen und Ortsnamen in der Grafschaft Waterloo." *German-Canadian Yearbook* 1 (1973): 119–30.

———. *Jubiläums Ausgabe: Centennial Issue.* Kitchener: Concordia Club, 1973.

———. *Little Paradise: The Saga of the German Canadians of Waterloo County, Ontario, 1800–1975.* Kitchener: Allprint Company, 1980.

———. "100 Jahre Concordia in Kitchener." *German-Canadian Yearbook* 1 (1973): 263–74.

———. *25 Jahre caritative und kulturelle Arbeit des Hilsfwerkes der Deutsch-Kanadier; Festschrift zum 25 jährigen Bestehen der Canadian Society for German Relief.* Waterloo: Waterloo Print, 1972.

Leochko, Crystal. "Acknowledgement or Avoidance? German-Canadian Immigrant Women's Memories of National Socialism." Master's thesis, University of Manitoba, 2009.

Levin, Irene. "Silence, Memory and Migration." *Journal of Comparative Family Studies* 44, no. 6 (2013): 715–23.

Levine, Allan. *King: William Lyon Mackenzie King, A Life Guided by the Hand of Destiny.* Vancouver and Toronto: Douglas and McIntyre, 2011.

Levitt, Peggy, and Nina Glick-Schiller. "Conceptualizing Simultaneity: A Transnational Social Field Perspective on Society." *International Migration Review* 38, no. 3 (2004): 1002–39.

Levitt, Peggy, and B. Nadya Jaworsky. "Transnational Migration Studies: Past Developments and Future Trends." *Annual Review of Sociology* 33 (2007): 129–56.

Levy, Daniel, and Natan Sznaider. "Memories of Universal Victimhood: The Case of Ethnic German Expellees." *German Politics and Society* 23, no. 2 (2005): 1–27.

Lieb, Christian. "German Diaspora Experiences in British Columbia after 1945." In *German Diasporic Experiences: Identity, Migration, and Loss*, edited by Mathias Schulze, James M. Skidmore, David G. John, Grit Liebscher, and Sebastian Siebel-Achenbach, 305–15. Waterloo: Wilfrid Laurier University Press, 2008.

———. "Moving West: German-Speaking Immigration to British Columbia, 1945–1961." PhD diss., University of Victoria, 2008.

Limor, Micha. "Was ich noch sagen wollte: Wer ist Jecke?." *MB Yakinton. Mitteilungsblatt der Vereinigung der Israelis mitteleuropäischer Herkunft* 79, no. 246 (2011): 2.

Loewen, Royden. *Ethnic Farm Culture in Western Canada.* Ottawa: Canadian Historical Association, 2002.

Lorenzkowski, Barbara. "Making Music—Building Bridges: German-Canadian Identities in the Nation's Capital 1958–1999." In *Ottawa: Making of a Capital*, edited by Jeff Keshen and Nicole St-Onge, 307–30. Ottawa: University of Ottawa Press, 2001.

———. *Sounds of Ethnicity: Listening to German North America, 1850–1914.* Winnipeg: University of Manitoba Press, 2010.

Lowenstein, Steven M. *Frankfurt on the Hudson: The German Jewish Community of Washington Heights, 1933–1983, Its Structure and Culture.* Detroit: Wayne State University Press, 1989.

Lumans, Valdis O. *Himmler's Auxiliaries: The Volksdeutsche Mittelstelle and the German National Minorities of Europe, 1933–1945.* Chapel Hill: The University of North Carolina Press, 1993.

Lüthke, Folkert. *Psychologie der Auswanderung.* Weinheim: Deutscher Studienverlag, 1989.

MacFarlane, John. *Ernest Lapointe and Quebec's Influence on Canadian Foreign Policy.* Toronto: University of Toronto Press, 1999.

Maeder, Pascal. *Forging a New Heimat: Expellees in Post-War West Germany and Canada.* Göttingen: V&R Unipress, 2011.

Mannheim, Karl. "Das Problem der Generationen." *Kölner Vierteljahrshefte für Soziologie* 7 (1928): 157–85, 309–30.

———. *Essays on the Sociology of Knowledge: Collected Works, Volume 5.* Edited by Paul Kecskemeti. 1952. Republished; New York: Routledge and Paul, 1972.

Mansergh, Nicholas. *The Commonwealth Experience, Volume II: From British to Multiracial Commonwealth.* London: Palgrave Macmillan, 1982.

Marcuse, Harold. "Memories of World War II and the Holocaust in Europe." In *A Companion to Europe 1900–1945*, edited by Gordon Martel, 487–503. New York: Wiley-Blackwell, 2007.

Margolian, Howard. *Unauthorized Entry: The Truth about Nazi War Criminals in Canada, 1946–1956.* Toronto: University of Toronto Press, 2000.

Massa, Evelyne, and Morton Weinfeld. "We Needed to Prove We Were Good Canadians: Contrasting Paradigms for Suspect Minorities." *Canadian Issues* (Spring 2009): 15–28.

McInnis, Edgar. *Canada: A Political and Social History.* Toronto: Clarke, Irwin, and Company, 1959.

McKay, Ian, and Jamie Swift. *The Vimy Trap: Or, How We Learned to Stop Worrying and Love the Great War.* Toronto: Between the Lines, 2016.

McLachlan, Elizabeth. *With Unfailing Dedication: Rural Teachers in the War Years.* Edmonton: NeWest Press, 2001.

———. *With Unshakeable Persistence: Rural Teachers of the Depression Era.* Edmonton: NeWest Press, 1999.

Menkis, Richard, and Harold Troper. "Racial Laws vs. Olympic Aspirations in the Anglo-Canadian Press of Fall 1935." In *Nazi Germany, Canadian Responses: Confronting Antisemitism in the Shadow of War,* edited by L. Ruth Klein, 46–77. Montreal-Kingston: McGill-Queen's University Press, 2012.

Meune, Manuel. *Les Allemands du Québec : Parcours et discours d'une communauté méconnue.* Montreal: Éditions du Méridien, 2003.

Moogk, Peter. "Uncovering the Enemy Within: British Columbians and the German Menace." *BC Studies* 182 (Summer 2014): 45–72.

Morton, Desmond. *A Short History of Canada*, 6th ed. Toronto: McClelland and Stewart, 2006.

Mount, Graeme. *Canada's Enemies: Spies and Spying in the Peaceable Kingdom*. Toronto: Dundurn, 1993.

Munke, Martin. "Georg Leibbrandt, Reich Ministry for the Occupied Eastern Territories: An Academic Radical." In *The Participants: The Men of the Wannsee Conference*, edited by Hans-Christian Jasch and Christoph Kreutzmüller, 224–44. New York: Berghahn Books, 2017.

Neatby, H. Blair. *The Politics of Chaos: Canada in the Thirties*. Toronto: Macmillan, 1972.

———. *William Lyon Mackenzie King Volume III, 1932–1939: Prism of Unity*. Toronto: University of Toronto Press, 1976.

Nelson, E. Clifford. *The Lutherans in North America*. Philadelphia: Fortress Press, 1975.

Nolan, Brian. *King's War: Mackenzie King and the Politics of War, 1939–1945*. Toronto: Random House, 1988.

Oberlander, Wendy. "Once It Was Written: The Story After *Nothing To Be Written Here*." Vancouver Holocaust Education Centre's publication. *Zachor*. (Spring 2013): 7–10.

O'Bryan, K.G., J.G. Reitz, and O. Kuplowska. Non-official Languages: A Study in Canadian Multiculturalism. Ottawa: Minister Responsible for Multiculturalism, 1976.

Olick, Jeffrey K. "Collective Memory: The Two Cultures." *Sociological Theory* 17, no. 3 (1999): 333–48.

———. "What Does It Mean to Normalize the Past? Official Memory in German Politics since 1989." In "Memory and the Nation." Special Issue. *Social Science History* 22, no. 4 (Winter 1998): 547–71.

Palmer, Bryan. *Canada's 1960s: The Ironies of Identity in a Rebellious Era*. Toronto: University of Toronto Press, 2009.

Palmer, Howard. *Patterns of Prejudice: A History of Nativism in Alberta*. Toronto: McClelland and Stewart, 1982.

Parens, Henri. "Aftermath of Genocide—the Fate of Children of Perpetrators." *International Journal of Applied Psychoanalytic Studies* 6, no. 1 (2009): 25–42.

Patzel, Anke. "Of 'Modern Immigrants' and 'German Bread': A Case Study of Ethnic Identity Construction Amongst Contemporary German Immigrants in the City of Ottawa, Canada." Master's thesis, Malmö University, 2013.

———. "Notions of Home and Belonging for *Alteinwanderer* and *Neueinwanderer* in the German-Speaking Community in Ottawa." In *Diasporic Constructions of Home and Belonging*, edited by Florian Kläger and Klaus Stierstorfer, 183–206. Berlin: De Gruyter, 2015.

Perin, Roberto. "Clio as an Ethnic: The Third Force in Canadian Historiography." *Canadian Historical Review* 64, no. 4 (1983): 441–67.

Peter, Karl, and Franziska Peter. "The Kurtenbach Letters: An Autobiographical Description of Pioneer Life in Saskatchewan Around the Turn of the Century." *Canadian Ethnic Studies* 11, no. 2 (1979): 89–96.

Phinney, Jean S., Gabriel Horenczyk, Karmela Liebkind, and Paul Vedder. "Ethnic Identity, Immigration, and Well-being: An Interactional Perspective." *Journal of Social Issues* 57, no. 3 (2001): 493–510.

Pinder, Wilhelm. *Das Problem der Generation in der Kunstgeschichte Europas.* Berlin, 1926.

Plaut, W. Gunther. *Unfinished Business: An Autobiography.* Toronto: Lester and Orpen Dennys, 1981.

Poole, Ross. "Enacting Oblivion." *International Journal of Politics, Culture, and Society* 22, no. 2 (June 2009): 149–57.

Portes, Alejandro, and Ruben Rumbaut. *Legacies: The Story of the Immigrant Second Generation.* Berkeley, CA: University of California Press, 2001.

Prokop, Manfred. "The Dynamics of German Language Maintenance in Canada." *Forum Deutsch* 16 (2008): 1–78.

Prokop, Manfred, and Gerhard Bassler. *German Language Maintenance Across Canada: A Handbook.* Edmonton: Manfred Prokop, 2004.

Proske, Matthias. "'Why Do We Always Have to Say We're Sorry?': A Case Study on Navigating Moral Expectations in Classroom Communication on National Socialism and the Holocaust in Germany." *European Education* 44, no. 3 (2012): 39–66.

Reardon, Terry. *Winston Churchill and Mackenzie King: So Similar, So Different.* Toronto: Dundurn, 2012.

Reitz, Jeffrey G. "Language and Ethnic Community Survival." In *Ethnicity and Ethnic Relations in Canada*, edited by Rita A. Bienvenue and Jay E. Goldstein, 105–23. Toronto: Butterworths, 1985.

Remennick, Larissa. "Russian Jews in the Global City of Toronto: A Pilot Study of Identity and Social Integration." *Espace populations sociétés* 3, no. 1 (2006): 61–81.

Renan, Ernest. "What is a Nation?" Translated by Martin Thorn. In *Nation and Narration*, edited by Homi K. Bhabha, 8–22. London: Routledge, 1990.

Renwick Monroe, Kristen. "Cracking the Code of Genocide: The Moral Psychology of Rescuers, Bystanders, and Nazis During the Holocaust." *Political Psychology* 29, no. 5 (2008): 699–736.

Reynolds, David. "Britain, the Two World Wars, and the Problem of Narrative." *The Historical Journal* 60, no. 1 (2017): 197–231.

Richler, Mordecai. *The Street.* 1969. Reprint, Toronto: McClelland and Stewart, 2002.

Rider, Celeste, ed. *Women Pioneers of Saskatchewan.* Regina: Saskatchewan Genealogical Society, 2009.

Roazen, Paul. *Canada's King: An Essay in Political Psychology.* Oakville, ON: Mosaic Press, 1998.

Rose, Larry D. *Mobilize! Why Canada Was Unprepared for the Second World War.* Toronto: Dundurn, 2013.

Rosenthal, Gabriele, ed. *The Holocaust in Three Generations: Families of Victims and Perpetrators of the Nazi Regime.* New York: Continuum, 1998.

Rosenthal, Gabriele, and Bettina Völter. "Three Generations in Jewish and Non-Jewish German Families After the Unification of Germany." In *International Handbook of Multigenerational Legacies of Trauma*, edited by Yael Danieli, 297–313. New York: Plenum Press, 1998.

Rumbaut, Ruben G. "The Agony of Exile: A study of the Migration and Adaptation of Indochinese Refugee Adults and Children." In *Refugee Children: Theory,*

Research, and Services, edited by Frederick L. Ahearn Jr. and Jean L. Athey, 53–91. Baltimore: Johns Hopkins University Press, 1991.

Rutherdale, Robert. *Hometown Horizons: Local Responses to Canada's Great War.* Vancouver: UBC Press, 2004.

Sarna, Jonathan D. "The Value of Canadian Jewish History to the American Jewish Historian and Vice Versa." *Canadian Jewish Historical Society Journal* 5, no. 1 (1981): 17–22.

Satzewich, Vic. *Points of Entry: How Canada's Immigration Officers Decide Who Gets In.* Vancouver: UBC Press, 2015.

Sauer, Angelika E. "The 'Ideal German Canadian': Politics, Academics and the Historiographical Construction of German-Canadian Identity." In *A Chorus of Different Voices*, edited by Angelika Sauer and Matthias Zimmer, 227–244. New York: Peter Lang, 1998.

Scheibelhofer, Elisabeth. "Understanding European Emigration in the Context of Modernization Processes: Contemporary Migration Biographies and Reflexive Modernity." *Current Sociology* 57, no. 1 (2009): 5–25.

Schild, Erwin. "A Canadian Footnote to the Holocaust. A Review Essay of *Deemed Suspect: A Wartime Blunder*, by Eric Koch." *Canadian Jewish Historical Society Journal* 5, no. 1 (1981): 31–44.

Schmaltz, Eric, and Samuel Sinner. "The Nazi Ethnographic Research of Georg Leibbrandt and Karl Stumpp in Ukraine, and Its North American Legacy." In *German Scholars and Ethnic Cleansing, 1919–1945*, edited by Ingo Haar and Michael Fahlbusch, 51–85. New York: Berghahn Books, 2005.

Schmalz, Roland E. "Former Enemies Come to Canada: Ottawa and the Postwar German Immigration Boom, 1951–57." PhD diss., University of Ottawa, 2000.

Schmidt, Ute. *Bessarabia: German Colonists on the Black Sea.* Translated by J. Gessele. Fargo, ND: Germans from Russia Heritage Collection, 2011.

Schönwälder, Karen. *Historiker und Politik: Geschichtswissenschaft im Nationalsozialismus.* Frankfurt am Main: Campus, 1992.

Schulze, Elizabeth. "Prisoners of War: A German-Canadian Post-war Memory Project." Master's thesis, Simon Fraser University, 2012.

Schulze, Mathias, James M. Skidmore, David G. John, Grit Liebscher, and Sebastian Siebel-Achenbach, eds. *German Diasporic Experiences: Identity, Migration, and Loss.* Waterloo: Wilfrid Laurier University Press, 2008.

Seeberg, Marie Louise, Irene Levin, and Claudia Lenz. *The Holocaust as Active Memory: The Past in the Present.* Abingdon: Routledge, 2013.

Segev, Tom. "Ach, gäbe es doch noch einmal Karpfen wie an der Rehwiese!" In *Die Jeckes. Jüdischer Almanach des Leo Baeck Instituts*, edited by Gisela Dachs, 28–40. Frankfurt: Jüdischer Verlag im Suhrkamp Verlag, 2005.

Sela-Sheffy, Rakefet. "'Europeans in the Levant' Revisited: German Jewish Immigrants in 1930s Palestine and the Question of Culture Retention." *Tel Aviver Jahrbuch für deutsche Geschichte* 41 (2013): 40–59.

———. "Integration through Distinction: German Jewish Immigrants, the Legal Profession and Patterns of Bourgeois Culture in British-Ruled Jewish Palestine." *Journal of Historical Sociology* 19, no. 1 (2006): 34–59.

Shapira, Anita. *Land and Power: The Zionist Resort to Force, 1881–1948*. Stanford: Stanford University Press, 1999.

Sharples, Caroline. *Postwar Germany and the Holocaust*. London: Bloomsbury Academic, 2015.

Shaw, Amy J. *Crisis of Conscience: Conscientious Objection in Canada during the First World War*. Vancouver: UBC Press, 2009.

Sheffi, Na'ama. "Rejecting the Other's Culture: Hebrew and German in Israel 1933–1965." *Tel Aviver Jahrbuch für deutsche Geschichte* 27 (1998): 301–20.

Sheftall, Mark David. *Altered Memories of the Great War: Divergent Narratives of Britain, Australia, New Zealand and Canada*. New York: I.B. Tauris, 2010.

Shifman, Limor, and Elihu Katz. "'Just Call Me Adonai': A Case Study of Ethnic Humor and Immigrant Assimilation." *American Sociological Review* 70, no. 5 (2005): 843–59.

Siegemund, Anja. "Eine Bürgergesellschaft für den Jischuw: Deutsche liberalnationale Zionisten in Palästina." *Tel Aviver Jahrbuch für deutsche Geschichte* 41 (2013): 60–81.

Sinner, Samuel. "New Archival Discoveries on Wannsee Conference Participant Georg Leibbrandt and 'SS-Mann' Karl Stumpp." Paper presented at the German Studies Association Conference, New Orleans, 20 September 2003.

Stadler, Beatrice. *Language Maintenance and Assimilation: The Case of Selected German-Speaking Immigrants in Vancouver, Canada*. Vancouver: Canadian Association of University Teachers of German, 1983.

Steinberg, Michael Stephen. *Sabers and Brown Shirts: The German Students' Path to National Socialism, 1918–1935*. Chicago: University of Chicago Press, 1977.

Stewart, Ian. "Names Written in Water: Canadian National Leaders and Their Reputations among Party Members." *Journal of Canadian Studies/Revue d'études canadiennes* 41, no. 1 (Winter 2007): 31–50.

Storks, Maike. "German Migrants in Montreal: Uses and Meanings of an Ethnic Category." Master's thesis, Concordia University, 2011.

Suleiman, Susan Rubin. "The 1.5 Generation: Thinking about Child Survivors and the Holocaust." *American Imago* 59, no. 3 (2002): 277–95.

Szabo, Franz A.J. "Introduction: The Austrian Immigrant and the Canadian Multiculturalism Spectrum." In *Austrian Immigration to Canada: Selected Essays*, edited by Franz A.J. Szabo, 1–10. Montreal: McGill-Queen's University Press, 1996.

Thompson, John Herd. *The Harvests of War: The Prairie West, 1914–1918*. Toronto: McClelland and Stewart, 1978.

Thompson, John Herd, and Stephen J. Randall. *Canada and the United States: Ambivalent Allies*, 3rd ed. Athens: University of Georgia Press, 2002.

Thompson, Maris. "'It Always Kinda' Frightened Them That They'd Be Sent Back': German American Origin Stories from Southwestern Illinois." *Oral History Forum d'histoire orale* 32 (2012): 1–21.

Toman, Cynthia. *Sister Soldiers of the Great War: The Nurses of the Canadian Army Medical Corps*. Vancouver: UBC Press, 2016.

Trouillot, Michel-Rolph. *Silencing the Past: Power and the Production of History*. Boston, MA: Beacon Press, 1995.

Tumblety, Joan. "Introduction: Working with memory as source and subject." In *Memory and History: Understanding Memory as Source and Subject*, edited by Joan Tumblety, 1–16. New York: Routledge, 2013.

van Alphen, Ernst. "Second-Generation Testimony, Transmission of Trauma, and Postmemory." *Poetics Today* 27, no. 2 (2006): 473–88.

Vance, Jonathan F. *Death So Noble: Memory, Meaning, and the First World War*. Vancouver: UBC Press, 1997.

Vecoli, Rudolph J., and Suzanne M. Sinke, eds. *A Century of European Migrations: 1830–1930*. Urbana-Champaign: University of Illinois Press, 1992.

Vernes, Maurice. *Ernest Renan*. New York: Twayne Publishers, 1968.

Vinitzky-Seroussi, Vered, and Chana Teeger. "Unpacking the Unspoken: Silence in Collective Memory and Forgetting." *Social Forces* 88, no. 3 (2010): 1103–22.

Vogt-Moykopf, Chaim. "Die letzten Jeckes—deutsche Juden in Kanada." *Aufbau: Deutsch-jüdische Zeitung* 9 (1999): 11.

Volkov, Shulamit. "Die Verbürgerlichung der Juden in Deutschland: Eigenart und Paradigma." In *Bürgertum im 19. Jahrhundert: Verbürgerlichung, Recht und Politik*, vol. 3, edited by Jürgen Kocka, 105–33. Göttingen: Vandenhoeck und Ruprecht, 1995.

von Kellenbach, Katharina. "Vanishing Acts: Perpetrators in Postwar Germany." *Holocaust and Genocide Studies* 17, no. 2 (2003): 305–29.

Waddington, Lorna. *Hitler's Crusade: Bolshevism and the Myth of the International Jewish Conspiracy*. London: Tauris Academic Studies, 2007.

Wagner, Jonathan F. *Brothers Beyond the Sea: National Socialism in Canada*. Waterloo: Wilfrid Laurier University Press, 1981.

———. *A History of Migration from Germany to Canada, 1850–1939*. Vancouver: UBC Press, 2006.

———. "Saskatchewan's Sudetendeutsche: The Anti-Nazi Germans of St. Walburg." *Saskatchewan History* 33, no. 3 (1980): 90–101.

Waiser, Bill. *Saskatchewan: A New History*. Calgary: Fifth House, 2005.

Walsh, John C. "Re-thinking Ethnic Boundaries: The Negotiation of German-Canadian Ethnic Identities in Ottawa, 1945–1975." Master's thesis, University of Ottawa, 1996.

Weigel, Sigrid. "'Generation' as a Symbolic Form: On the Genealogical Discourse of Memory since 1945." *The Germanic Review: Literature, Culture, Theory* 77, no. 4 (2002): 264–77.

Weinreich, Max. *Hitler's Professors: The Part of Scholarship in Germany's Crimes Against the Jewish People*. New Haven: Yale University Press, 1946.

Welzer, Harald. "Grandpa Wasn't a Nazi: The Holocaust in German Family Remembrance." American Jewish Committee (2005): 1–33.

Welzer, Harald, Sabine Moller, and Karoline Tschuggnall. *"Opa war kein Nazi": Nationalsozialismus und Holocaust im Familiengedächtnis*. Frankfurt am Main: Fischer Taschenbuch, 2002.

Werner, Hans. *The Constructed Mennonite: History, Memory, and the Second World War.* Winnipeg: University of Manitoba Press, 2013.

———. "'Germans Only in Their Hearts': Making and Breaking the Ethnic German Diaspora in the Twentieth Century." In *Beyond the Nation? Immigrants' Local Lives in Transnational Cultures*, edited by Alexander Freund, 211–26. Toronto: University of Toronto Press, 2012.

———. *Imagined Homes: Soviet German Immigrants in Two Cities.* Winnipeg: University of Manitoba Press, 2007.

White, Clinton. "Education Among German Catholic Settlers in Saskatchewan, 1903–1918: A Reinterpretation." *Canadian Ethnic Studies* 16, no. 1 (1984): 78–95.

Whitehouse, Christine. "'You'll Get Used to It!': The Internment of Jewish Refugees in Canada, 1940–43." PhD diss., Carleton University Ottawa, 2016.

Williams, Robert C. *Culture in Exile: Russian Émigrés in Germany, 1881–1941.* Ithaca: Cornell University Press, 1972.

Wilton, Janis. "Imaging Family Memories: My Mum, Her Photographs, Our Memories." In *Oral History and Photography*, edited by Alexander Freund and Alistair Thomson, 61–76. New York: Palgrave Macmillan, 2012.

Winegard, Timothy C. *For King and Kanata: Canadian Indians and the First World War.* Winnipeg: University of Manitoba Press, 2012.

Winter, Alison. *Memory: Fragments of a Modern History.* Chicago: University of Chicago Press, 2012.

Wormann, Curt D. "German Jews in Israel." *Leo Baeck Institute Year Book* 15 (1970): 73–103.

Zhou, Min. "Changing Generational Dynamics in Chinese America across Time." *Diaspora: A Journal of Transnational Studies* 18, no. 1–2 (2015): 89–116.

Zimmer, Matthias. "Deconstructing German-Canadian Identity." In *A Chorus of Different Voices: German-Canadian Identities*, edited by Angelika E. Sauer and Matthias Zimmer, 21–39. New York: Peter Lang, 1998.

Zimmerman, Ernest Robert. *The Little Third Reich on Lake Superior: A History of Canadian Internment Camp R.* Edited by Michel S. Beaulieu and David K. Ratz. Edmonton: University of Alberta Press, 2015.

Zimmermann, Moshe, and Yotam Hotam, eds. *Zweimal Heimat: Die Jeckes zwischen Mitteleuropa und Nahost.* Frankfurt: beerenverlag, 2005.

CONTRIBUTORS

Karen Brglez received her MA from the Joint Master's Program at the University of Manitoba and the University of Winnipeg for her research on German unification at the end of the Cold War. She currently works as a research assistant for German-Canadian Studies at the University of Winnipeg. Her research interests include migration, settler colonialism, and ethnic relations.

Christine Enßlen is a doctoral student at York University. She has published on the historical conditions of Saskatchewan one-room school teachers. Her work investigates never-married women teachers, social and moral regulation, and Depression-era circumstances of rural teachers.

Patrick Farges is Professor of German and Gender Studies in the Department of History and the Department of Languages and Intercultural Studies at the University of Paris. His research explores migration history, German-Jewish history, gender, and masculinities.

Sara Frankenberger received her Master of Arts in Education from Simon Fraser University in 2017. She now works as the program coordinator at a boarding school in North Vancouver, British Columbia. Her research interests include psychology, immigration, health, education and sustainability.

Alexander Freund is Professor of History at the University of Winnipeg, where he holds the Chair in German-Canadian Studies. His work focuses on oral history and the history of German migrants and refugees.

Roger Frie is Professor of Education at Simon Fraser University, Affiliate Professor of Psychiatry at the University of British Columbia, and Psychoanalytic Faculty and Supervisor at the William Alanson White Institute. He is a historian, philosopher, and psychologist by training and his writings examine memory, social responsibility, and the nature of human interaction.

Anke Patzelt is a PhD candidate in Sociology at the University of Ottawa and a recipient of the Ontario Trillium Scholarship. Her research focuses on German immigrants in Canada, concepts of identity construction, home and belonging, citizenship in Germany and Canada, as well as the vulnerabilities of aging migrants.

Robert Teigrob is a Professor in the Department of History at Ryerson University. His research and teaching concentrates on modern international history, with a particular emphasis on the cultural dimensions of interstate relations.

Elliot Worsfold is a PhD candidate in the Department of History at Western University in London, Ontario. He would like to thank the Social Sciences and Humanities Research Council and the Laurier Archives for their financial support through the Joan Mitchell Travel Award.

INDEX